CANE RIVER'S
Louisiana Living
A Culinary Tour

published by
The Service League of Natchitoches, Inc.
Natchitoches, Louisiana
Founded 1714

Photography by John C. Guillet

Cover Photo:

PRUDHOMME ROUQUIER HOUSE, 446 JEFFERSON STREET: Noted as the largest bousillage house in the United States, this fine home is owned and operated by the Service League of Natchitoches, Inc.. It is listed on the National Register of Historic Places by the U.S. Department of the Interior and is found in the National Historic Landmark District of Natchitoches. The house was built by Francois Rouquier for his wife Marie Louise Prudhomme. It has been dated to the turn of the nineteenth century (late 1700's to 1803). The Service League of Natchitoches Inc., restored, and currently operates, the structure with proceeds from the sale of their first cookbook, *Cane River Cuisine*. It is open for tours by appointment, during the Fall Tour of Historic Homes, and for special events during the month of December. Contact: Service League of Natchitoches, Inc., Group Tours, Post Office Box 2206, Natchitoches, Louisiana, 71457, (318-352-6723).

ISBN 0-9607674-6-0
Copyright 1994

by

The Service League of Natchitoches, Inc.
P.O. Box 2206
Natchitoches, Louisiana 71457

First Printing   October 1994   15,000 copies

Printed in the USA by

The Wimmer Companies, Inc.
Memphis • Dallas

This book is dedicated to the women whose vision and strength resulted in the creation of our first cookbook, *Cane River Cuisine*. Their ambition and willingness to pursue a dream has inspired each of us to make *Louisiana Living* a reality and a lasting tribute to the wonderful town in which we live.

The Service League of Natchitoches, Inc. is an organization of women dedicated to serving the community and helping those in need. Since 1950, the League has worked hard to raise money to fund its many worthwhile projects, including the Marsha Thomas Pendleton Memorial Scholarship and the Shirley Pittman Smiley Memorial Scholarship. The group also receives profits from the sale of the Service League's first cookbook, *Cane River Cuisine*. These profits enabled the group to purchase and restore the historic Prudhomme-Rouquier House.

This cookbook has been a labor of love and is the realization of almost six years of hard work. The group decided to provide not only quality recipes but also a tour of Natchitoches that captures the essence of the wonderful lifestyle offered to its residents. A storyline revolving around the cultural and natural heritages of the Natchtitoches community was chosen as the means to highlight the recipes. Photography was used to enhance the story. And the result is a beautiful book of traditional and modern recipes which accent the flavor of Natchitoches.

Profits derived from the sale of *Louisiana Living* will be used for educational, civic, historical, and cultural improvement of the city of Natchitoches and the general community.

The League wishes to thank each and every person who in any way contributed to the production of this book and regrets that they could not all be listed.

TABLE OF CONTENTS

Whet the appetite .... APPETIZERS 33

Quench your thirst .... BEVERAGES 53

Warm the scene .... SOUPS 59

Do something different .... EGGS & CHEESE 83

Add color, taste, and beauty .... SALADS 89

Add an accent .... CONDIMENTS & SAUCES 109

Bake the best .... BREADS 121

Highlight the menu .... VEGETABLES 137

Prepare a unique addition .... RICE & PASTA 155

Catch the ocean's delight .... SEAFOODS 165

Fashion a memorable entree .... MEATS 195

Compose a special repast .... MAIN DISHES 219

Create a sweet memory .... DESSERTS 241

Eat out at home .... RESTAURANTS 279

Sit back and relax .... GLOSSARY OF PHOTOGRAPHS 286

Find it quick .... INDEX 297

Imagine the peaceful sounds at sunrise as the early morning mist covers Cane River Lake.

Imagine the clatter and spirit as 100,000 people gather to enjoy the Christmas Festival parade and fireworks display.

Imagine the delightful scents of freshly baked Chocolate Pecan Pie and Creole Crayfish Casserole cooked to perfection and teasing your tastebuds.

These images are part of everyday life in Natchitoches, a town whose residents want to preserve its colorful and flavorful history. With brick paved streets, iron-lace balconies, well preserved antebellum homes, colonial structures, and working river plantations, Natchitoches is a beautiful living example of a bygone, simpler age. Here, festivals, food, family, and fellowship share a special kinship that is cherished by visitors and residents alike.

We are proud of our town and want to share it with you. For you we have lovingly prepared a visual and culinary tour. Delight your eyes and tastebuds with the treats that follow! Get a feel for the way we blend yesterday with today to create a lifestyle worth preserving for tomorrow.

NATCHITOCHES MAP
by
Thelma Keyser (1941)

MAP KEY

STRUCTURE	MAP #
Plaque of St. Denis Burial	1
Spiral Staircase	2
Prudhomme-Hughes Building	3
La Coste Building	4
Ducournau Building	5
Roque House	6
Chamber of Commerce	7
Sompayrac Building	8
The Magnolias	9
Walk of Honor	10
Catholic Cemetery	11
Third Train Depot	12
New Courthouse	13
Old Courthouse	14
Lasyone's Old Masonic Temple	15
Williams Building	16
Immaculate Conception Catholic Church	17
Bishop Martin's House and Rectory Buildings	18
Trinity Episcopal Church	19
First Baptist Church	20
Chaplin House	21
First Methodist Church	22
City Hall (Second Train Depot)	23
American Cemetery	24
Site of First Train Depot	25
Gates of Northwestern State University	26
St. Denis Original Homesite	27
Bullard Mansion Columns	28
Old Women's Gym	29
Chaplins Lake	30
Fort St. Jean Baptiste	31
The William and Mary Ackel House	32
Old Bridge	33
Soldini House	34
Country Store (Jeanne's Country Garden)	35
Lemee House	36
Dupleix-Taylor House	37
Rusca-Salim House	38
Bayou Amulet Marker	39
Levy House	40
Metoyer-Brown Townhouse	41
Chamard-Dunahoe House	42
Tante Huppe' House	43
Prudhomme-Rouqier House	44
Kaffie House	45
Buard-Tauzin-Wells Home	46
Rose Lawn House	47

Lemee House

__Autumn___Tours___Color__

History is alive in Natchitoches year-round, and October displays it most vividly during the annual Fall Tour of Homes. Residents welcome you warmly into landmarked homes as history comes alive for you.

Begin at the Lemee House with its unique architecture and interesting history. In 1940 the building was given special recognition by the U. S. Department of the Interior as part of the Historic Homes Survey.

Once the residence of Italian architect Trizzini, and later a branch of the Union Bank of New Orleans, the Lemee House truly contributes to the flavor of our wonderful town.

The Lemee House (left), c. 1843, offers culinary delights of Cheddar Apple Bread and turnovers with Green Pepper Jelly. Pecan Pralines (above) are a special Louisiana temptation.

__The River___Harvest___Thanks__

Many tour homes can be found along Cane River Lake. This lake is our most prized natural treasure. Once part of Red River, Cane River Lake is now a thirty-five mile oxbow which provides a bountiful harvest.

It is on the Cane that Louis Juchereau de St. Denis in 1714 established Natchitoches as the first permanent settlement in the Louisiana Purchase. It is on the Cane that cotton flourished and plantations thrived. It is on the Cane that residents traditionally have gathered to celebrate good living. Hazel's Shrimp Jambalaya and Jalapeño Cornbread are typical of the colorful food we enjoy.

The Lecompte cotton press at Magnolia Plantation (above) predates all other cotton gins. It is slated to become a national landmark. The Lambre-Gwinn House (right), a cypress structure over 150 years old, was originally the home of Odalie Prudhomme Lambre, granddaughter of Antoine Prudhomme of Oakland Plantation.

Lambre-Gwinn House

Magnolia Plantation

__Plantations___Heritage___Cotton__

Residents of plantation homes along Cane River still serve the fare of their forefathers. Hot Tamales and Nanny's Pickled Okra are followed best by Plantation Pie.

Sit on the veranda of a lovely river home and sip iced tea while you savor the scent of Cornish Hen with Herbed Butter and Mandarin Rice — specialties at Magnolia Plantation's Big House. This fascinating structure was built as the plantation's main residence in the 1830's. The home and vast lands still remain in the same family.

South of the old slave cabins, a barn houses the only cotton press in the United States still in its original location. This press predates the present-day cotton gin and is still in working condition (see page 14).

Cotton remains a vital crop in Natchitoches. Jean Baptiste, the builder of Magnolia, and Jean Pierre Prudhomme, the first planter to successfully raise cotton west of the Mississippi River, would be proud that the seeds they planted still flourish.

A plantation supper awaits visitors on the back porch of Magnolia Plantation (left). A portrait of Jean Pierre Prudhomme (above) hangs at Oakland Plantation. Oakland is pictured in the *Cane River Cuisine* cookbook.

Metoyer-Brown Town House

__Holidays___Celebration___Decoration__

Thanksgiving and Christmas celebrations are rooted in the rich traditions of our town. Cornucopias and wreaths, decorated trees and fat red candles bring heightened color and excitement to home and community activities.

The appearance of seasonal foods whets the appetite, already sharpened by the holiday anticipation. How about Crayfish Mousse, Bayou Pecan Brie, and Calico Marinated Veggies followed by Black Forest Cake?

When we prepare for the holiday season, the spirit of family and community pulls us together. Once again we are reminded of special links binding Yesterday and Today.

The Metoyer-Brown Town House (left) traditionally offers Christmas festival guests a delicious buffet. The welcoming doors of a Natchitoches Christmas say "come in and stay awhile." Shown above (upper left) Tante Huppè House; (upper right) The William and Mary Ackel House; (lower left) Rusca-Salim House; and (lower right) Kaffie House.

Cloutier Town House at Ducournau Square

__Christmas___Warmth___Lights__

The excitement and celebration of the holiday season in Natchitoches is not only for us who live here. On the first Saturday of every December, over 100,000 people come to Front Street to be part of the Christmas Festival of Lights. Crowds line the sidewalks to view parades and stroll by the bandstand and booths along the riverbank. Families and friends enjoy conversation and hospitality in historic homes, beautifully decorated and open for the occasion. And, of course, we take the time to savor festival favorites like Natchitoches Meat Pies, Down-and-Dirty Rice Dressing, and Melt-in-Your-Mouth Pecan Pie.

After this mixture of food, family, and fun, the festivities culminate in a dazzling fireworks display, exploding over Cane River. Then, the sudden flash of 170,000 lights brings the historic downtown and riverbank alive with sparkling holiday motifs. In one beautiful and breathtaking moment, Natchitoches becomes the City of Lights, welcoming visitors to the Christmas season.

The Cloutier Town House at Ducournau Square (left) provides a perfect setting to view the Christmas Festival lights (above) as they light the riverbank and reflect in Cane River Lake.

Chaplin House

__Spring___Blossoms___Mardi Gras__

In springtime, Natchitoches dons her colorful dress of floral blossoms as brilliant azaleas, wisteria, dogwoods and forsythia bloom in abundance.

Merry-making revelers enjoy the glittering pageantry of the Crew de St. Denis Mardi Gras Ball, replete with elaborate costumes, ball gowns and the traditional St. Denis King's Cake.

Spring is the time for celebrating our appreciation for life as we renew the family ties that bind us to one another and to our town.

The Chaplin House (left) contains the largest known collection of Clementine Hunter Paintings. The Armadillo Grooms Cake (above) is a wedding reception novelty. It was used in the movie *Steel Magnolias*, a moving storyline and visual portrayal of our town.

__Baskets____Joy____Easter__

The annual Easter Egg Hunt is always held on the spacious grounds of the Gahagan home. This Creole-style structure, with its hand-made bricks and massive oak trees, also played a part in the movie *Steel Magnolias*.

Youngsters eagerly search for the 3,000 eggs lovingly colored and decorated. Filling their baskets brings joy surpassed only by refreshing red punch and Easter cake.

Local churches celebrate the rebirth of Christ with song and sermon. On Easter Sunday, the wonderful symbol of life renewed, we cherish the intertwining of family, food, fun and festivities, continuing today as it has in the past.

Masses of prolific azaleas and dogwoods (above) cover the grounds of the Keegan House on Williams Avenue. A brilliant sunset behind the Tauzin-Gahagan Plantation Home (opposite page) accents the peace and quiet which follow the noise and excitement of the annual Easter egg hunt.

Tauzin-Gahagan Plantation Home

__Gardens___Summer___Lace__

As spring edges into summer, landscaped gardens take shape and bloom, reflecting the pride and respect of their owners. This outward calm hides the bustle of activity inside as the fruits of the season are prepared in so many delicious ways.

Mrs. Williams' Rolls and Blueberry Muffins with Amaretto Peach and Pecan Spread are a few of the tantalizing treats enjoyed with coffee, tea, and spiced whipped cream.

The sprightly sounds of summer. The visual splendor of crepe myrtle blossoms in profusion. The tempting smells of busy kitchens. These combine to remind us of our ties to yesterday and today ... the value of our culture and heritage ... our sense of preservation.

Crepe Myrtle blossoms (above) line the picturesque summer streets of Natchitoches. The tea table in the foreground of the Rose Lawn House (right) seems to invite: "Put on your hat and sit with me; let's have a chat and a cup of tea!"

Rose Lawn House

__Crafts___Cuisine___Culture__

As summer unfolds, preserving the bountiful harvest begins. Amidst the charm of ginger lilies, Melrose Plantation boasts pecans, figs, muscadines, and blackberries - ingredients for delicious foods. Established between 1794 and 1803, Melrose hosts the annual Melrose Arts and Crafts Festival, drawing artists and visitors from many states. A trip to Melrose is a magical experience for anyone.

Three remarkable women are responsible for this local cultural center. A freed slave, Marie Therese Coincoin founded a unique colony of people and an agricultural dynasty. Miss Cammie Henry brought the plantation to its zenith of beauty and made it a mecca for artists, writers, and craftsmen from around the country. Clementine Hunter, a nationally acclaimed artist, used her talent and brush vividly to unfold the history of plantation life and help preserve Melrose's legacy.

The Saint Augustine Church (above), built by Augustine and Louis Metoyer, sons of Marie Therese Coincoin, is a tribute to the fascinating heritage of Melrose Plantation. A quilt made by artist Clementine Hunter (right) accents bountiful fruits proudly displayed on the front lawn of Melrose Plantation's Big House.

Melrose Plantation Big House

__Wilderness___People___Life__

Summer celebrations continue with Northwestern State University's annual Folk Festival, weekly meetings of the Los Adaes Quilting Guild, and reenactments of pioneer life at Fort St. Jean Baptiste.

Nature lovers find an abundance of outdoor activities, from hiking and horseback riding in Kisatchie, Louisiana's only national forest, to the serene beauty of the Caroline Dormon Nature Preserve. And, Cane River Lake offers fishing, boating, water sports and lake-side campsites.

Native irises and a native azalea (*Rhododendrom austrinum*) thrive at Wings Rest Pond in the Caroline Dormon Nature Preserve (above).

Life is good in Natchitoches. We who live here cherish the land, the community and the heritage. Our lifestyle ranges from crayfish boils and fish fries to flamboyant Mardi Gras Balls. We thank you for touring our town through the pages of this book, and we invite you to treat your taste-buds to the delightful and delicious recipes that follow. They have been carefully selected and triple tested for your culinary enjoyment. *Bon appetit!*

Three of the four original columns (above, top left) from Bullard Mansion stand on old Normal Hill at Northwestern State University. The Los Adaes quilters (above, top right) gather at the Old Methodist Church. Pioneer reenactors (above, lower) camp at Fort Saint Jean Baptiste, an exact reconstruction of the original c. 1716 fort.

Cane River Lake

Appetizers

BAYOU BRIE WITH PECAN TOPPING

1 cup finely chopped pecans
¼ cup Kahlúa or other coffee-
  flavored liqueur
3 tablespoons brown sugar
1 (14 ounce) wheel mini Brie
  cheese

Place pecans in shallow microwave-safe dish. Microwave on high setting for 4 to 6 minutes, stirring every 2 minutes until toasted. Add Kahlúa and brown sugar, stirring well. Remove rind from top of Brie and discard. Place Brie on microwave-safe serving dish. Spoon pecan mixture on top of Brie. Microwave, uncovered, on high setting for 1½ to 2 minutes or until Brie softens to desired consistency, rotating dish ½ turn after 1 minute. Serve with Melba toast or green apple wedges. Serves: 12.

Karen Townsend

BAKED BRIE

⅓ (16 ounce) package filo
  dough
2 cups butter, melted
1 (8 inch) wheel Brie cheese
1 to 2 cups peach preserves or
  mayhaw jelly
1 (2 ounce) package slivered
  almonds, toasted

Thaw filo dough in refrigerator for 24 hours. Place 1 (16x10 inch) sheet of filo dough on work surface. Brush with ⅓ cup butter. Repeat 5 times, stacking filo sheets and brushing each with butter. Leaving rind on Brie intact, spread preserves or jelly on top of wheel and sprinkle with almonds. Invert on center of stacked filo sheets. Draw edges of dough over Brie and press to enclose. Invert wrapped Brie, seam sides down, on baking sheet. Bake at 350 degrees for 15 to 20 minutes or until lightly browned. Serves: 30.

Gay Melder

HOT CHILI CHEESE DIP

1 cup mayonnaise
½ cup (2 ounces) grated
  Parmesan cheese
1 cup (4 ounces) shredded
  Monterey Jack cheese
3 (4 ounce) cans chopped green
  chilies, drained
1 (12 ounce) can mexicorn,
  drained
1 (4 ounce) jar chopped
  pimiento, drained
2 tablespoons sliced ripe olives

Combine mayonnaise, Parmesan cheese, Monterey Jack cheese, chilies, mexicorn and pimiento, blending well. Spoon mixture into greased 2-quart casserole. Bake at 325 degrees for 25 to 30 minutes or until thoroughly heated. Garnish with olives. Serve immediately. Makes 4 cups.

Vanessa Robertson

JALAPEÑO CHEESE LOG

1 (16 ounce) package processed
  cheese, softened
1 (8 ounce) package cream
  cheese, softened
hot pepper sauce
¾ cup finely chopped green
  onions
¾ cup finely chopped pecans
¾ cup finely chopped jalapeño
  peppers

Place cheese on buttered wax paper and roll to ½-inch thickness. Spread cream cheese on cheese spread. Sprinkle with hot pepper sauce and spread evenly on cream cheese. Sprinkle green onions, pecans and jalapeño peppers on cream cheese layer. Lifting 1 end of wax paper, roll cheese to form log. Serve as a spread with crackers. Serves: 10.

Aimee Wright

CHEESE AND STRAWBERRIES

4 cups (16 ounces) grated mild
  Cheddar cheese
1 pound bacon, cooked and
  crumbled
1 bunch green onions, minced
1 (1½ ounce) package sliced
  almonds
mayonnaise
strawberry preserves

Combine cheese, bacon, green onions and almonds, mixing well. Add mayonnaise to bind ingredients. Spoon mixture into mold prepared with vegetable cooking spray. Chill for several hours. Invert on serving dish. Top with strawberry preserves. Serve with round buttery crackers. Serves: 20.

Betty Ledet

PIMIENTO CHEESE

1 (16 ounce) package mild
  colby cheese, finely grated
1 (4 ounce) jar pimiento with
  liquid, chopped
3 or 4 green onions, minced
dash of Worcestershire sauce
mayonnaise
salt to taste
black pepper to taste
red pepper to taste
pecans, finely chopped
  (optional)

Combine cheese, pimiento, green onions and Worcestershire sauce. Add mayonnaise until desired consistency for spreading. Season with salt, black pepper and red pepper. Stir in pecans. Recipe may be doubled. Serves: 10 to 15 as dip, makes approximately 50 finger sandwiches.

Marteel Henry

BLACKEYED PEA DIP

1 (16 ounce) can blackeyed
  peas with jalapeño peppers,
  drained
½ cup margarine
5 green onions, finely chopped
6 slices bacon, cooked and
  crumbled
1 (8 ounce) package low-fat
  processed cheese, cubed
1 teaspoon garlic powder

Mash peas in large bowl until smooth. Add margarine and blend well. Stir in green onions, bacon, cheese spread and garlic powder, mixing well. Pour mixture into 1-quart microwave-safe dish. Microwave at high setting for 3 to 4 minutes or until cheese is melted. Stir well. Serve with tortilla chips or raw vegetables. Makes 1½ cups.

Joanne Yankowski

RAW RADISH DIP

1 (8 ounce) package cream
  cheese, softened
1 tablespoon lemon juice
1 clove garlic, pressed
1 teaspoon salt
¼ teaspoon dillweed
1 cup grated radishes

Combine cream cheese, lemon juice, garlic, salt and dill weed, blending well. Stir in radishes. Chill, covered, for at least 2 hours. Makes 1 cup.

Cathy Walker

ITALIAN HEARTS OF PALM DIP

1 cup mayonnaise
1 cup sour cream
1 packet dry garlic and herb
   salad dressing mix
1 (14 ounce) can hearts of palm,
   drained and chopped
1 (8 ounce) can mushrooms,
   drained and chopped
1 cup (4 ounces) grated
   mozzarella cheese
¾ cup (3 ounces) freshly grated
   Parmesan cheese

Combine mayonnaise, sour cream and salad dressing mix, blending well. Stir in hearts of palm, mushrooms, mozzarella cheese and Parmesan cheese. Spread mixture in a 9-inch pie or quiche pan prepared lightly with vegetable cooking spray. Bake at 350 degrees for 20 to 30 minutes or until bubbly and lightly browned. Serve with wheat biscuit or other snack crackers. Serves: 10 to 12.

Shirley Walker

TERRY'S SALSA DIP

2 (16 ounce) cans chunky
   stewed tomatoes
2 (10 ounce) cans diced
   tomatoes with chilies
1 tablespoon Worcestershire
   sauce
1 tablespoon olive oil
1 teaspoon dried cilantro
1 tablespoon dried or chopped
   fresh parsley
½ to 1 teaspoon hot pepper
   sauce
2 green bell peppers
1 large onion
2 bunches green onions

Combine stewed tomatoes, tomatoes with chilies, Worcestershire sauce, oil, cilantro, parsley and hot pepper sauce. Chill, covered, for several hours. Chop bell pepper, onion and green onions by hand (do not use food processor) and chill. Just before serving, add fresh vegetables to tomato mixture. Serve with tortilla chips. Makes 2 cups.

Lana Scott

SPINACH VEGETABLE DIP

1 cup frozen chopped spinach, thawed and pressed dry
½ cup chopped parsley
½ cup chopped green onions
2 cups mayonnaise
1 teaspoon salt
1 teaspoon black pepper
1 teaspoon dill weed

Combine spinach, parsley, green onions, mayonnaise, salt, black pepper and dill weed, mixing well. Chill for at least 24 hours. Serve with chips or crackers. Serves: 10.

Evie Posey

BARNEY'S CRAB MOUSSE

1 tablespoon gelatin
3 tablespoons cold water
hot water
¼ cup mayonnaise
2 tablespoons lime juice
2 tablespoons lemon juice
1 tablespoon chopped parsley
1 tablespoon chopped chives
2 teaspoons prepared mustard
salt and black pepper to taste
2 cups lump crabmeat, chilled
¾ cup whipping cream, whipped
guacamole (optional)

Add gelatin to cold water in small bowl, then place small bowl in larger bowl of hot water, being careful to avoid adding extra water to gelatin. Combine dissolved gelatin, mayonnaise, lime juice, lemon juice, parsley, chives, mustard, salt and black pepper. Fold crabmeat and whipped cream into gelatin mixture. Pour into buttered 5-cup ring mold. Chill until firm. Unmold on chilled platter. Fill center of mold with guacamole. Serve with buttered crackers. Serves: 25 or more.

Pam DeBlieux

CHEESY CRAB DIP

6 green onions, chopped
2 teaspoons minced garlic
½ cup butter
2 (6 ounce) cans white lump
    crabmeat, rinsed and drained
2 cups mayonnaise
1 packet dry ranch-style party
    dip mix
1½ cups (6 ounces) grated
    Cheddar cheese
1 loaf French or other crusty
    bread

Sauté green onions and garlic in butter in 10-inch skillet until vegetables are tender. Add crabmeat and cook for 2 to 3 minutes, stirring to coat crabmeat with butter. Combine mayonnaise and dip mix in large bowl, mixing thoroughly. Add crabmeat mixture and cheese, mixing well. Cut slice from top of bread loaf and remove bread, forming a shell from loaf. Spoon crabmeat mixture into bread shell. Bake at 350 degrees for 20 minutes or until cheese is melted. Serve with crackers or tortilla chips. Serves: 12.

Lana Scott
Shirley Walker

CRAB CANOE

2 (6 ounce) cans crabmeat,
    drained
5 green onions, minced
3 cups (12 ounces) grated
    Cheddar cheese
1 cup mayonnaise
1 small loaf French bread

Combine crabmeat, green onions, cheese and mayonnaise. Chill, covered tightly, overnight. Cut slice from top of bread loaf and remove bread in bite-sized cubes, forming a shell from loaf. Reserve bread cubes. Spoon crabmeat mixture into bread shell and place on baking sheet. Bake at 350 degrees for 25 to 30 minutes. Serve with bread cubes or crackers. Serves: 10.

Lana Scott

CRAB MORNAY

4 green onions, chopped
½ cup butter or margarine, melted
1 (8 ounce) package cream cheese, softened
1 pound fresh lump crabmeat
¼ teaspoon salt
¼ teaspoon black pepper
¼ cup chopped parsley

Sauté green onions in butter or margarine until tender. Add cream cheese and stir until melted. Add crabmeat, salt, black pepper and parsley, blending well and heating thoroughly. Serve hot in chafing dish with plain buttered crackers. Serves: 6.

Jeanne McGlathery

CRAWFISH MOUSSE

1½ envelopes unflavored gelatin
½ cup water
½ (8 ounce) package cream cheese
½ cup homemade mayonnaise
½ cup chopped onion
½ cup chopped celery
½ cup chopped parsley
½ cup chopped green bell pepper
2 tablespoons butter
1 (12 ounce) package crawfish tails
1 teaspoon Creole seasoning
1 teaspoon garlic powder
1 cup whipping cream, whipped

Dissolve gelatin in water in saucepan over low heat. Set aside to cool to lukewarm. Beat cream cheese, add mayonnaise and blend until smooth. Sauté onion, celery, parsley and bell pepper in butter until vegetables are tender. Add crawfish tails and sauté. Stir in Creole seasoning and garlic powder. Add lukewarm gelatin liquid to cream cheese mixture. Stir in crawfish tails and vegetables. Fold whipped cream into crawfish mixture. Pour into 3-cup mold. Makes 3 cups.

Sara Nell Williams

FEE FEE'S CHICKEN MOUSSE

4 envelopes unflavored gelatin
½ cup cold water
1 (10¾ ounce) can cream of
  mushroom soup, undiluted
2½ cups chicken broth
1½ cups diced celery
5 cups diced cooked chicken
  breast
1½ teaspoons minced onion
1 cup mayonnaise
2 teaspoons lemon juice
1 teaspoon Worcestershire
  sauce
2 teaspoons salt
¼ teaspoon white pepper
2 teaspoons parsley
1 cup frozen whipped topping,
  thawed

Soften gelatin in cold water, stirring to dissolve, and set aside. Combine soup and broth in saucepan. Bring to a boil, then remove from heat. Stir in gelatin mixture. Combine celery, chicken, onion, mayonnaise, lemon juice, Worcestershire sauce, salt, white pepper and parsley. Stir chicken mixture into soup mixture. Add whipped topping and stir until blended and smooth. Spoon mixture into molds or miniature muffin pans prepared with vegetable cooking spray. Chill, covered with plastic wrap, overnight. Unmold just before serving; if unmolded too far in advance, mousse will soften and begin to liquefy. Mousse can be garnished with piping of colored cream cheese. Serve with round buttery crackers. Makes 8 to 10 dozen small muffin cups.

Tanya Conlay

SALMON PÂTÉ

1 (7¾ ounce) can salmon,
  drained
1 packet Italian salad dressing
  mix
1 (8 ounce) package cream
  cheese, softened
⅓ cup chopped cucumber

Combine salmon and salad dressing mix. Add cream cheese and cucumber to salmon, mixing well. Press mixture into 2-cup mold or 7x4x2-inch loaf pan lined with plastic wrap. Chill overnight. Unmold on serving plate and garnish with lemon pepper and parsley. Serves: 10.

Melissa Cloutier

MEXICAN SHRIMP DIP

1 (10 ounce) can tomatoes with chilies
2 packets ranch-style party dip mix
1 packet guacamole dip mix
4 cups sour cream
1 (4 ounce) can chopped ripe olives
2 (4 ounce) cans green chilies, drained
1 cup (4 ounces) grated Cheddar cheese, divided
2 (6 ounce) cans shrimp, rinsed and drained
chili powder

Drain tomatoes in colander for several minutes. Combine ranch-style dip mix, guacamole dip mix and sour cream, mixing well. Add tomatoes, olives, chilies, ¾ cup cheese and shrimp, stirring to blend thoroughly. Spoon dip into serving bowl and garnish with ¼ cup cheese and chili powder. Chill for several hours. Makes 5 cups.

Shirley Walker

HOT SEAFOOD DIP

1 pound small shrimp, peeled and deveined
2 tablespoons butter
1 bunch green onions, chopped
3 jalapeño peppers, chopped
2 cups mayonnaise
2 tablespoons lemon juice
1 cup (4 ounces) grated Parmesan cheese
hot pepper sauce to taste
1 pound crabmeat
2 (14 ounce) cans artichoke hearts, drained and finely chopped
salt to taste
⅓ cup sliced almonds

Lightly sauté shrimp in butter for 2 minutes. Combine green onions, jalapeño peppers, mayonnaise, lemon juice, Parmesan cheese and hot pepper sauce in large bowl. Add shrimp, crabmeat and artichokes. Season with salt. Spread mixture in buttered 13x9x2-inch baking dish. Sprinkle with almonds. Bake at 375 degrees for 25 to 30 minutes or until mixture is bubbly. Serve with Melba rounds. Serves: 15 to 20.

Cathy Seymour

SHRIMP BUTTER

1 (8 ounce) package cream
  cheese, softened
¼ cup mayonnaise
¾ cup margarine, softened
juice of 1 lemon
2 (6 ounce) cans shrimp,
  drained
1½ tablespoons minced onion

Using electric mixer, combine cream cheese, mayonnaise, margarine, lemon juice, shrimp and onion, blending well. Serve with crackers. Makes 2 cups.

Shirley Smiley

AMARETTO PEACH AND PECAN SPREAD

1 (16 ounce) jar peach
  preserves
3 tablespoons amaretto liqueur
1 cup chopped pecans
1 (8 ounce) package cream
  cheese

Combine preserves, amaretto and pecans in non-metallic bowl. To serve, spoon 4 to 5 tablespoons of preserve mixture on cream cheese block. Variation: Soften cream cheese, add ¼ cup preserve mixture, mix and shape into a ball. Chill, wrapped in wax paper, until firm. Top with more preserve mixture and serve with crackers. Serves: 18 to 20.

Kathryn Smith

CINNAMON FRUIT DIP

1 (8 ounce) package cream
  cheese, softened
1 (8 ounce) jar honey
1 teaspoon vanilla
1 teaspoon cinnamon

Combine cream cheese, honey, vanilla and cinnamon, blending until smooth. Chill for 2 hours. Serve with fresh strawberries, melon, bananas, pineapple and other fresh fruit. Makes 1 cup.

Vanessa Robertson

TOASTED BREAD SQUARES

1 large loaf thin sliced or
sandwich bread

Using electric knife, trim crusts from bread slices and cut each slice into 4 squares. Press bottom of ¾-inch pill bottle firmly in center of each bread square to make indention; do not tear. Place in single layer on baking sheet. Bake at 350 degrees until lightly browned. Let stand until cool. Store in air-tight container. For garlic buttered squares, brush slices with melted butter and garlic before cutting into squares. Makes 80.

Shirley Scott
Lana Scott

ASPARAGUS CANAPÉS

2 small loaves sliced bread,
crusts trimmed
1 (4 ounce) package blue
cheese, crumbled
1 (8 ounce) package cream
cheese, softened
1 tablespoon mayonnaise
1 egg, beaten
1 tablespoon grated onion
½ teaspoon Worcestershire
sauce
2 (14½ ounce) cans asparagus
spears, drained
melted butter

Using rolling pin, flatten bread slices. Combine blue cheese, cream cheese, mayonnaise, egg, onion and Worcestershire sauce, mixing well. Spread mixture on bread slices. Top each with asparagus spear, roll up and cut in 1-inch pieces. Dip each in melted butter and place on ungreased baking sheet. Freeze until firm. Bake at 350 degrees for 15 minutes. Frozen canapés can be removed from baking sheets, placed in zipper-lock plastic bags and frozen until ready to use. Serves: 50.

Pam DeBlieux

JO ANN'S CRUSTLESS QUICHE

4 cups (16 ounces) grated
  Monterey Jack cheese
4 cups (16 ounces) grated sharp
  Cheddar cheese
9 eggs
1 (5 ounce) can evaporated
  milk
2 or 3 jalapeño peppers,
  chopped
1 (4 ounce) can green chilies,
  chopped

Combine Monterey Jack and Cheddar cheeses, eggs, milk, jalapeño peppers and chilies, mixing well with wooden spoon. Pour mixture into 13x9x2-inch baking dish. Bake at 350 degrees for 40 minutes. Let stand until cool. Cut into 1-inch squares. Serves approximately 36.

Pam DeBlieux

MUSHROOM CUPS

1 small bunch green onions,
  chopped
½ cup butter
1 pound fresh mushrooms,
  finely chopped
2 tablespoons all-purpose flour
1 cup whipping cream
½ teaspoon salt
¼ teaspoon cayenne pepper
2 teaspoons lemon juice
1 tablespoon chopped parsley
  (optional)
2 tablespoons chopped chives
  (optional)

Crust Cups:
2 loaves (48 slices) bread
½ cup butter, melted

Prepare crust cups. Using round cookie cutter, cut bread slices into circles. Dip each piece in melted butter and press into cup of miniature muffin pan. Bake at 350 degrees for 15 minutes or until lightly browned. While cups are toasting, prepare filling. Sauté green onions in butter for about 4 minutes or until softened. Add mushrooms and sauté for 10 to 15 minutes or until softened. Remove vegetables from heat. Sprinkle with flour and stir until smooth. Gradually add cream, stirring until smooth. Add salt, cayenne pepper, lemon juice, parsley and chives. Heat, stirring often, until mixture is thickened. Spoon into toasted cups, filling each. Bake at 350 degrees for 10 to 15 minutes. Makes 48.

Jeanne McGlathery
Toni Gwinn

MARINATED CRAB FINGERS

1 (8 ounce) bottle Italian salad
  dressing
½ cup olive oil
½ cup red wine vinegar
½ cup water
1 tablespoon Worcestershire
  sauce
juice of ½ lemon
1 cup chopped green onions
2 stalks celery, minced
lemon pepper to taste
garlic powder to taste
extra spicy salt-free herb blend
  seasoning to taste
1 (12 ounce) carton crab fingers

Combine salad dressing, oil, vinegar, water, Worcestershire sauce, lemon juice, green onions, celery, lemon pepper, garlic powder and herb blend seasoning in large bowl. Add crab fingers and toss gently. Chill for 8 hours or overnight. Drain before serving, reserving some of dressing for dipping. Serves: 6.

Sara Nell Williams

CUCUMBER PARTY SANDWICHES

2 cucumbers
1 (8 ounce) package cream
  cheese, softened
1 teaspoon pureed white onion
2 teaspoons Worcestershire
  sauce
2 tablespoons parsley flakes
2 loaves sandwich bread, crusts
  trimmed

Peel and quarter cucumbers lengthwise, remove seeds and discard. Using food processor, chop to minced consistency. Drain on paper towel. Beat cream cheese until smooth. Add onion, Worcestershire sauce and parsley, mixing well. Add cucumber to cream cheese mixture, mixing gently. Spread on bread slices. Cut for party-size appetizers. Makes 60 to 80 finger sandwiches.

Jan Frederick

SPICY SPINACH SQUARES

2 eggs, beaten
1 cup milk
½ cup margarine, melted
1 (10 ounce) package frozen chopped spinach, thawed and well drained
1 (8 ounce) package jalapeño pepper processed cheese spread
½ cup chopped onion
1 cup all-purpose flour
1 teaspoon baking powder
1 teaspoon salt
½ teaspoon hot pepper sauce

Combine eggs, milk and margarine, mixing well. Add spinach, cheese spread, onion, flour, baking powder, salt and hot pepper sauce, mixing thoroughly. Pour mixture into 13x9x2-inch baking pan. Bake at 350 degrees for 30 minutes. Cool before cutting into 1-inch squares. Serves: 30

Marian Keator

ZUCCHINI SQUARES

3 eggs, beaten
½ cup vegetable oil
1 cup buttermilk biscuit baking mix
⅔ cup (2½ ounces) grated Parmesan cheese
½ cup chopped green onions
3 cups thinly-sliced peeled zucchini
2 tablespoons chopped parsley
½ teaspoon salt
½ teaspoon seasoned pepper
½ teaspoon Italian seasoning
¼ teaspoon garlic powder
dash of hot pepper sauce

Combine eggs, oil and biscuit mix. Add cheese, green onions, zucchini, parsley, salt, seasoned pepper, Italian seasoning, garlic powder and hot pepper sauce, mixing well. Spread batter in greased 13x9x2-inch baking dish. Bake at 350 degrees for 25 to 30 minutes or until golden brown. Let stand until cool enough to touch. Cut into small squares. Serve hot or at room temperature. Serves: 15 to 20.

Annette Hill

ORIENTAL CHICKEN WINGS

3 pounds chicken wings
1 cup water
1 cup soy sauce
¼ to ½ cup pineapple juice
¼ cup vegetable oil
¼ cup sugar
1 teaspoon garlic powder
1 teaspoon ginger

Cut tips from chicken wings and discard. Cut wings at joint. Combine water, soy sauce, pineapple juice, oil, sugar, garlic powder and ginger for marinade. Marinate wings overnight. Remove wings from marinade, place in shallow baking pan and add small amount of marinade to pan. Bake at 350 degrees for 1 hour. Serves: 12.

Debbie Murphy

CLIFF'S COCKTAIL CHICKEN

½ cup margarine
½ cup soy sauce
½ cup red wine
¼ cup fresh lemon juice
1 cup firmly-packed brown
  sugar
2 teaspoons dry mustard
minced garlic to taste
black pepper to taste
35 to 50 chicken wings, cut at
  joints

Combine margarine, soy sauce, wine, lemon juice, brown sugar, mustard, garlic and black pepper in saucepan. Heat until brown sugar is dissolved. Place chicken in large shallow baking dish. Pour warm sauce over chicken and let stand for one hour. Preheat oven at 350 degrees, then reduce temperature to 250 degrees. Bake for 4 to 5 hours, turning wings 2 or 3 times. If all of sauce mixture is not absorbed, drain excess and return wings to oven, baking to dry slightly. Serves: 8 to 10 as main course or 25 to 35 as appetizer.

Cliff Conine

OYSTERS EN BROCHETTE WITH GARLIC BUTTER SAUCE

**1 pound sliced bacon, cut in
  3-inch pieces**
boiling water
**5½ dozen medium or large
  shucked oysters
  (approximately 3 pounds)**
1¼ tablespoons salt
1 teaspoon black pepper
½ teaspoon ground red pepper
¾ teaspoon white pepper
1½ tablespoons garlic powder
1½ tablespoons paprika
¾ teaspoon dried oregano
¾ teaspoon onion powder
½ teaspoon dried thyme
¼ teaspoon dried basil
¾ cup all-purpose flour
vegetable oil for frying
¾ cup unsalted butter
2½ teaspoons minced garlic
1½ tablespoons minced parsley

Blanch bacon pieces in boiling water for 5 minutes. Pour into colander, rinse with cold water and drain. Beginning and ending with bacon, alternate bacon pieces and oysters on wooden skewers, filling each. Combine salt, black pepper, red pepper, white pepper, garlic powder, paprika, oregano, onion powder, thyme and basil, mixing well. Combine 2 teaspoons of seasoning mixture with flour. Pour oil into skillet to 1-inch depth and heat to 350 degrees. Sprinkle 1 teaspoon seasoning mixture on each assembled skewer and dredge in seasoned flour, shaking to remove excess. Fry skewers in oil for about 3 minutes on each side or until golden brown. Drain on paper towel. Prepare garlic butter by melting butter in saucepan over high heat until half melted, stirring constantly. Add garlic and cook for about 3 minutes or until butter is melted, foaming at surface and is lightly browned. Stir in parsley and cook for about 2 minutes or until sauce is lightly browned and foamy. Immediately pour garlic butter over fried oysters and bacon. Serves: 6 entree portions or 12 appetizer portions.

Edwina Friedman

MARINATED CAULIFLOWER

1 large head cauliflower
¾ cup sour cream
¼ cup mayonnaise
2 teaspoons vinegar
3 green onions, chopped
1 packet dry Italian salad
   dressing mix
1 teaspoon sugar
½ teaspoon red pepper or
   paprika

Separate cauliflower into flowerets. Crisp by placing in ice water, draining well before assembling salad. Combine sour cream, mayonnaise, vinegar, green onions, salad dressing mix and sugar, mixing well. Pour dressing over cauliflower, tossing gently. Chill, covered, for several hours or overnight. Sprinkle with red pepper or paprika before serving. Serves 8 to 10.

Lynn Pierson

CALICO MARINATED VEGGIES

1 small bunch green onions, cut
   in 1-inch pieces
1 pound large fresh mushrooms
1 (6 ounce) can large pitted ripe
   olives, drained
1 (14 ounce) can artichoke
   hearts, drained and quartered
1 cup olive oil
½ cup vinegar
2 cloves garlic, crushed
3 tablespoons chopped parsley
⅛ teaspoon salt
⅛ teaspoon white pepper
dash of black pepper
dash of celery salt

Combine green onions, mushrooms, olives and artichokes in large bowl. Combine oil, vinegar, garlic, parsley, salt, white pepper, black pepper and celery salt, mixing well. Pour dressing over vegetables, mixing gently. Marinate, covered, in refrigerator. Vegetables can be used as appetizers or on a salad with marinade for dressing. Serves: 6 to 8.

Betty Carnahan

WHITE CHOCOLATE PARTY MIX

1 (16 ounce) package white
  chocolate
3 cups rice cereal squares
3 cups corn cereal squares
3 cup O-shaped oat cereal
3 cups stick pretzels
2 cups dry roasted peanuts
1 (12 ounce) package candy-
  coated plain chocolate
  candies

Melt white chocolate in top of double boiler over simmering water. Combine rice, corn and oat cereal, pretzels, peanuts and candies in large bowl. Slowly pour melted chocolate over cereal mixture, stirring to coat evenly. Spread mixture on wax paper and let stand until cool. Break into bite-sized pieces. Store in air-tight container in refrigerator to keep fresh. Serves: 12 to 14.

Edwina Friedman

Beverages

ALMOND TEA

1½ quarts water
1¼ cups sugar (optional)
juice of 1 lemon
grated peel of 1 lemon
1 (6 ounce) can frozen
  lemonade concentrate,
  undiluted
2 cups strong tea or 1 family
  size tea bag plus 2 cups water
1 tablespoon vanilla
1 tablespoon almond extract

Combine water and sugar in saucepan. Bring to a boil. Add lemon juice and peel. Simmer for 3 to 5 minutes. Add lemonade concentrate and tea or tea bag and water. Bring to a boil, then remove from heat. Remove tea bag if used. Stir in vanilla and almond flavorings. Serve tea warm or cold. Sweeten with sugar substitute if sugar is omitted. Serves: 16.

Vanessa Robertson
Cathy Sutton

BEST MINTED ICED TEA

1 quart boiling water
1 cup sugar
½ cup instant tea granules
2 to 4 tablespoons slightly
  crushed mint leaves
2 quarts cold water
1 (6 ounce) can frozen
  lemonade concentrate,
  thawed, undiluted

Combine boiling water, sugar, tea granules and mint in 4-quart non-metal container. Let stand for 15 minutes. Stir in cold water and lemonade. Serve tea over ice. Serves: 12.

Vanessa Robertson

FRIENDSHIP TEA

1 (18 ounce) jar instant orange
  drink granules
½ cup pre-sweetened lemonade
  mix
1 (3 ounce) package apricot
  gelatin
1 cup sugar
2½ teaspoons ground cinnamon
1 teaspoon ground cloves

Combine orange drink granules, lemonade mix, gelatin, sugar, cinnamon and cloves, mixing well. Store in air-tight container. For 1 serving, mix 1½ tablespoons tea mix with 1 cup boiling water. Serves: 50.

Cathy Sutton

BANANA PUNCH

¾ cup sugar
¼ cup water
5 ripe bananas, mashed
1 cup lemon juice
2 cups orange juice
1 (46 ounce) can pineapple
  juice
2 quarts ginger ale

Dissolve sugar in water. Combine sugar water, bananas, lemon juice, orange juice and pineapple juice. Pour into freezer-safe container. Freeze for 24 hours. Remove from freezer 30 minutes before serving. Add ginger ale. Serves: 12.

Marion Salter

"B" AND MADELINE'S BUBBLY PUNCH

3 (14 ounce) jars instant orange
  drink granules
8 quarts cold water
4 quarts chilled cranberry juice
4 quarts chilled ginger ale

Combine orange drink granules and cold water in large container, stirring to dissolve granules. Add cranberry juice. Just before serving, add ginger ale and ice. Makes 5 gallons or 100 (¾ cup) servings, 125 (⅔ cup) servings or 150 (½ cup) servings.

Pam DeBlieux

MOCHA PUNCH

¼ cup sugar
⅓ cup instant coffee granules
½ cup hot water
1 teaspoon vanilla
5 cups milk
½ gallon vanilla ice cream
1 cup frozen whipped topping, thawed
nutmeg (optional)

Dissolve sugar and coffee granules in hot water. Add vanilla and milk, mixing well. Chill overnight or longer. Fill punch bowl with scoops of ice cream. Pour chilled milk liquid over ice cream. Serve in cups, topping each with dollop of whipped topping and sprinkle of nutmeg. Serves: 12.

Marion Hawkins Salter
Marion Hawkins Doss

COFFEE PUNCH FOR 100

1 (4 ounce) jar instant coffee granules
1 quart boiling water
4 cups sugar
3 gallons milk
1 gallon dark chocolate or fudge ripple ice cream
1 gallon vanilla ice cream
4 cups whipping cream, whipped

Combine coffee granules, boiling water and sugar in saucepan. Bring to a boil and cook for 5 minutes. Let stand until lukewarm, then store in refrigerator until ready to use. To prepare punch, combine milk, ice cream and coffee syrup, stirring to blend. Pour whipped cream on surface of punch. Serves: 100.

Bobbye Nell Ellis
Marion Hawkins Salter
Marion Hawkins Doss

MILK PUNCH

1 gallon milk
1 (16 ounce) package powdered sugar
1⅓ cups rum
1⅓ cups bourbon
1⅓ cups brandy
¼ cup vanilla
grated nutmeg

Combine milk, powdered sugar, rum, bourbon, brandy and vanilla, stirring to dissolve sugar. Serve in individual glasses, garnishing each with nutmeg. Serves: 20.

Susan Pierson Burndt

CHAMPAGNE ROSÉ PUNCH

**2 (¾ liter) bottles rosé wine,
   chilled**
**2 (16 ounce) packages frozen
   strawberries, thawed**
**1 (1 liter) bottle champagne,
   chilled**
**1 (6 ounce) can frozen
   lemonade concentrate,
   thawed and undiluted**

Let 1 bottle rosé wine stand at room temperature for 1 hour. Pour into 6-quart container. Press strawberries through sieve and add to wine. Add remaining bottle of wine, champagne and lemonade, mixing well. Pour punch over ice in punch bowl. Serves: 20 to 25.

Gail Varner
Kay Foshee
Vanessa Robertson
Cathy Sutton

KAY'S AMARETTO

2 cups water
3 cups sugar
peel of 1 lemon
2 tablespoons almond extract
2 teaspoons vanilla
1 teaspoon chocolate extract
2¾ cups vodka

Combine water, sugar and lemon peel in 2-quart saucepan. Bring to a boil, reduce heat and simmer for 20 minutes. Remove from heat and let stand for about 30 minutes. Combine almond, vanilla and chocolate flavorings with vodka. Add to lemon syrup, stirring to blend. Remove lemon peel. Serves: 8 to 10.

Elizabeth Post
Marion Hawkins Salter
Marion Hawkins Doss

BLOODY MARY MIX

1 (46 ounce) can tomato or
   vegetable juice
1 (10½ ounce) can beef bouillon
   (not consommé)
juice and pulp of 2 lemons
¼ cup Worcestershire sauce
12 dashes hot pepper sauce
celery seed (not celery salt) to
   taste
salt and black pepper to taste
vodka
lemon or lime slices for garnish
celery strips for garnish

Combine tomato or vegetable juice, bouillon, lemon juice and pulp, Worcestershire sauce, hot pepper sauce, celery seed, salt and black pepper in 2-quart container with tight-fitting lid. Shake well. To prepare a Bloody Mary, pour 1 jigger vodka into glass, add ice and fill glass with juice mixture. Stir and garnish with lemon or lime and celery. Serves: 8 to 10.

David Walker

FROZEN MARGARITAS

lime wedge
salt
1 (6 ounce) can frozen limeade
   concentrate, thawed,
   undiluted
¾ cup tequila
¼ cup Triple Sec liqueur
crushed ice

Rub rim of 4 cocktail glasses with lime. Place salt in saucer and spin rim of each glass in salt to coat. Combine limeade, tequila and Triple Sec in blender container; blend well. Add crushed ice and blend until crushed and thickened. Pour into prepared glasses. Serves: 4.

Pam Smith
Elaine Sandifer

Soups

MARY'S HEARTY BEEF STEW

2 pounds stewing beef, cubed
3 or 4 large white potatoes,
  peeled and cubed
2 large onions, chopped
1 cup sliced fresh carrots
1 (16 ounce) can cut green
  beans, undrained
1 (10½ ounce) can tomato soup,
  undiluted
½ soup can water
1 bay leaf
salt and black pepper to taste

Combine beef, potatoes, onion, carrots, green beans, soup, water, bay leaf, salt and black pepper in 4-quart casserole or oven-safe Dutch oven. Bake at 275 degrees for at least 5 hours and up to 7 hours. Remove bay leaf. Stew can be frozen. Serve with French bread or cornbread. This is very tasty and unusually easy to prepare. Serves: 6.

Mary Keyser

MEXICAN TORTILLA CHIP SOUP

1 small onion, chopped
1 small jalapeño pepper,
  seeded, peeled and chopped
2 large cloves garlic, minced
2 pounds stewing beef,
  tenderized and cubed
2 tablespoons olive oil
1 (16 ounce) can stewed
  tomatoes
1 (10 ounce) tomatoes with
  green chilies
1 (10½ ounce) can beef bouillon
1 (14½ ounce) can chicken
  broth
1 (10½ ounce) can tomato soup
1 cup water
1½ teaspoons chili powder
3 cups slightly broken corn
  tortilla chips
1 cup (4 ounces) grated
  Cheddar cheese

Sauté onion, jalapeño pepper, garlic and beef in oil in large heavy saucepan or Dutch oven, cooking until beef is browned. Add tomatoes, tomatoes with chilies, beef bouillon, chicken broth, tomato soup, water and chili powder. Simmer, covered, for 1 hour. Place ½ to ¾ cup chips in each individual serving bowl, ladle soup on chips and top with grated cheese. Soup can be prepared in advance and stored in refrigerator or frozen. Serves: 6 to 8.

Tanya Conlay

HOMEMADE CHILI

2 pounds ground chuck
2 medium-sized onions, minced
1 large green bell pepper, finely chopped
4 cloves garlic, minced
5 beef bouillon cubes
1 cup hot water
1 (16 ounce) can tomatoes, chopped, undrained
1 (15 ounce) can tomato sauce
1 (12 ounce) can tomato paste
1 teaspoon salt
¼ cup plus 1 tablespoon chili powder
2 teaspoons coarsely ground red pepper
dash of hot pepper sauce or to taste
water
1 (16 ounce) can chili beans (optional)

Brown beef in heavy saucepan or Dutch oven, stirring to crumble. Drain excess fat. Add onion, bell pepper and garlic. Sauté until vegetables are softened. Dissolve bouillon in hot water. Add bouillon liquid, tomatoes, tomato sauce, tomato paste, salt, chili powder, red pepper and hot pepper sauce, stirring until well blended. Add water to desired consistency. Check seasonings and add additional red pepper and hot pepper sauce if desired. Add chili beans. Simmer on medium-low heat for 3 hours. Serve with grated Cheddar cheese and crackers. Chili can be prepared in advance and frozen. Serves: 6.

Kay Aaron

HEARTY VEGETABLE SOUP

1½ pounds stewing beef
soup bone with meat
6 cups water
2 cups tomato juice
2 teaspoons Worcestershire
  sauce
1 tablespoon salt
dash of black pepper
½ cup coarsely chopped onion
1 cup diced celery and leaves
1 cup sliced carrots
1 cup diced red potatoes
1 cup chopped cabbage
1 cup canned corn, drained
1 cup canned green beans,
  drained
1 (16 ounce) can tomatoes,
  undrained, coarsely chopped
1½ tablespoons sugar

Combine beef, bone, water, tomato juice, Worcestershire sauce, salt and black pepper in stock pot. Simmer, covered, for about 3 hours. Remove beef and bone and tear beef into bite-sized pieces. If desired, broth can be chilled to solidify fat for easy removal. Add beef, onion, celery, carrots, potatoes, cabbage, corn, green beans, tomatoes and sugar to broth. Simmer, covered, for 1 to 1½ hours. Soup can be frozen. Serves: 8.

Pam Smith

BUSY DAY VEGETABLE SOUP

2 pounds ground chuck
1 small yellow onion, chopped
1 clove garlic, minced
2 tablespoons olive oil
1 (28 ounce) can tomato puree
1 (16 ounce) can whole kernel
   corn, undrained
1 (16 ounce) can sliced carrots,
   undrained
1 (16 ounce) can lima beans,
   undrained
1 (8 ounce) can sliced
   mushrooms, undrained
salt and black pepper to taste
2 teaspoons dried thyme
2 teaspoons parsley flakes
water

Brown beef in stock pot, stirring to crumble. Drain excess fat and set beef aside. Sauté onion and garlic in oil until onion is transparent. Add beef to onion, stirring to mix. Add tomato puree, corn, carrots, lima beans and mushrooms. Season with salt, black pepper, thyme and parsley. Simmer for 20 to 30 minutes, adding water if necessary for desired consistency. Soup can be made in advance and reheated or can be frozen. This is an easy dish to do on a busy day, made from items found in almost everyone's kitchen. Serves: 8 to 10.

Tanya Conlay

CREAM OF CRAB SOUP

1 vegetable bouillon cube
1 cup boiling water
¼ cup chopped onion
¼ cup vegetable oil or
   shortening
2 tablespoons all-purpose flour
1 teaspoon salt
¼ teaspoon celery salt
dash of black pepper
4 drops hot pepper sauce
4 cups milk
1 pound blue crabmeat
chopped parsley for garnish

Dissolve bouillon in boiling water. Sauté onion in oil or shortening in large saucepan until softened. Blend in flour, salt, celery salt, black pepper and hot pepper sauce. Gradually add milk and bouillon, stirring constantly, and cook until thickened. Add crabmeat and heat thoroughly; do not boil. Sprinkle parsley on individual servings. Soup can be prepared 1 day in advance and stored in refrigerator. It should not be frozen. Serves: 6.

Evie Posey

LOUISIANA CRAB BISQUE

2 cups fresh lump crabmeat
   (do not use canned)
2 (10¾ ounce) cans cream of
   mushroom soup, undiluted
2 (10¾ ounce) cans cream of
   asparagus soup, undiluted
2 cups whipping cream
2½ cups milk
1 teaspoon Worcestershire
   sauce
¾ teaspoon hot pepper sauce
⅔ cup dry sherry
white pepper to taste
¼ cup chopped chives

Combine crabmeat, mushroom soup and asparagus soup in blender or food processor. Blend well. Pour soup mixture into heavy saucepan. Add whipping cream, milk, Worcestershire sauce, hot pepper sauce and sherry. Heat thoroughly, stirring occasionally; do not boil. Season with white pepper. Sprinkle chives on individual servings in soup bowls or demitasse cups. Soup can be prepared 1 day in advance and stored in refrigerator but should not be frozen. Serves: 10 to 12 soup bowl portions or 20 to 22 demitasse portions.

Sharon Gahagan

CRAB AND BROCCOLI SOUP

1 (10 ounce) package frozen
   chopped broccoli
½ cup chopped onion
3 tablespoons butter
2 tablespoons all-purpose flour
2 cups milk
2 cups half and half
2 chicken bouillon cubes
½ teaspoon thyme
½ teaspoon salt
¼ teaspoon black pepper
1 (6 to 8 ounce) package frozen
   Alaskan King crab, thawed
   and sliced, or 1 (7½ ounce)
   can crabmeat, drained

Prepare broccoli according to package directions, drain and set aside. Sauté onion in butter until softened. Blend in flour. Add milk and half and half, stirring and cooking until thickened and smooth. Add bouillon and stir until dissolved. Add thyme, salt, black pepper, crabmeat and broccoli. Simmer until thoroughly heated; do not boil. Soup can be prepared a day in advance of serving. Serves: 4 to 6.

Camille Bolinger

OYSTER AND ARTICHOKE SOUP

1 bunch shallots, chopped
pinch of thyme
pinch of cayenne pepper
3 bay leaves
2 tablespoons butter or
    margarine
2 tablespoons all-purpose flour
1 (14½ ounce) can chicken
    broth
2 cups oyster liquid or canned
    clam juice
1 pint small oysters
1 (14 ounce) can artichoke
    hearts, quartered
3 sprigs parsley, chopped
½ cup whipping cream
salt to taste

Sauté shallots, thyme, cayenne pepper and bay leaves in butter or margarine in heavy saucepan until shallots are softened. Whisk in flour. Add broth and oyster liquid or clam juice. Simmer for 15 minutes. Add oysters, artichoke hearts and parsley. Simmer for 20 minutes. Remove bay leaves. Stir in whipping cream, season with salt and heat thoroughly; do not boil. Serve immediately. Serves: 6.

Gayle Henry

OYSTER AND SPINACH SOUP

1 (10 ounce) package frozen
    chopped spinach, cooked and
    well drained
1 (10¾ ounce) can cream of
    mushroom soup, undiluted
1 cup sour cream
2 bunches green onions with
    tops, chopped
2 cups milk
1 quart oysters, drained
1 teaspoon salt
1 teaspoon black pepper
¼ teaspoon red pepper
1 tablespoon Worcestershire
    sauce
1½ teaspoons hot pepper sauce

Combine spinach, soup and sour cream in 4-quart saucepan. Cook over low heat for 10 minutes; do not boil. Add onions, reduce heat and simmer for 15 minutes or until onions are softened; do not boil. Stir in milk, oysters, salt, black pepper, red pepper, Worcestershire sauce and hot pepper sauce. Simmer until oysters curl on edges; do not boil. Serve immediately. Serves: 8 appetizer portions or 4 main dish portions.

Mary Jean Thomas

SPICY SHRIMP AND CORN CHOWDER

2 cups minced onion
1 cup finely chopped celery
½ cup finely chopped green bell
  pepper
½ cup grated carrots
¼ cup margarine
½ bay leaf, crumbled
2 cups diced potatoes
¼ cup water
2 tablespoons all-purpose flour
4 cups shrimp stock
1 or 2 (16 ounce) cans cream-
  style corn
1 (14 ounce) can low-fat
  evaporated milk
2 pounds shrimp, peeled and
  cooked
1 tablespoon salt
½ teaspoon black pepper
½ teaspoon cayenne pepper
hot pepper sauce to taste
½ pound bacon, cooked and
  crumbled

Sauté onion, celery, bell pepper and carrots in margarine in stock pot until vegetables are softened. Add bay leaf, potatoes and water. Cook for 5 to 10 minutes. Sprinkle flour on vegetables, mixing well. Add shrimp stock. Bring to a boil. Stir in corn, milk, shrimp, salt, black pepper, cayenne pepper and hot pepper sauce. Simmer for about 30 minutes. Sprinkle bacon on individual servings. Soup can be prepared 1 day in advance and stored in refrigerator. Serves: 6 to 8.

Cindy Smith

GULF BOUNTY SOUP

1 large onion, chopped
1 tablespoon minced garlic
½ cup chopped green bell
   pepper
¼ cup olive or vegetable oil
¼ cup margarine
1 (29 ounce) can tomatoes
1 (6 ounce) can tomato paste
1 bay leaf
⅓ cup chopped parsley
2 teaspoons salt
½ teaspoon black pepper
2 teaspoons oregano
2 teaspoons basil
1 (10½ ounce) can cream of
   shrimp soup, undiluted
¼ soup can water
1½ to 2 pounds speckled trout
   or any white fish fillets
1 pound shrimp, peeled and
   deveined, or ½ pound shrimp
   and ½ pound scallops
½ pound crabmeat
chopped parsley or chives

Sauté onion, garlic and bell pepper in oil and margarine in heavy stock pot until vegetables are tender. Add tomatoes, tomato paste, bay leaf, parsley, salt, black pepper, oregano and basil. Bring to a boil, reduce heat and simmer for 2 hours, stirring occasionally. Discard bay leaf. Stir in soup and water. Add fish, shrimp or shrimp and scallops. Simmer for 10 minutes. Add crabmeat and simmer, covered, for 5 minutes. Sprinkle parsley or chives on individual servings. Soup can be prepared 1 to 2 days in advance and stored in refrigerator. Serves: 6 to 8.

Rhonda Guidroz

CREOLE GUMBO

3 tablespoons bacon drippings
2 envelopes brown gravy mix
1 large onion, chopped
½ green bell pepper, finely
  chopped
1 (16 ounce) package hot-
  flavored smoked sausage,
  sliced
10 cups water
18 chicken bouillon cubes
garlic powder to taste
1 tablespoon filé
1 (16 ounce) package frozen cut
  okra
8 chicken breast halves
black pepper to taste
2 pounds large shrimp, peeled
1 pound lump crabmeat
1 bunch green onions with tops,
  chopped
cooked rice

Cook bacon drippings with gravy mix in stock pot to form roux. Sauté onion and bell pepper in roux. In separate skillet, sauté sausage for several minutes. Drain on paper towel and set aside. Add water and bouillon cubes to roux mixture. Stir in garlic powder. Remove 1 cup liquid from gumbo, add filé and stir to dissolve. Add filé liquid to gumbo. Stir in okra, chicken, sausage and black pepper. Simmer for 2 hours. Remove chicken, discard bones and return chicken to gumbo. Add shrimp, crabmeat and green onions. Simmer for 30 minutes. Remove from heat and let stand to cool to room temperature. Chill, then skim fat from surface. Reheat to serve hot over rice. Gumbo can be prepared a day in advance. It can be frozen but is better if served fresh. Serves: 12.

Sara Nell Williams

CHICKEN AND SAUSAGE GUMBO WITH OKRA

½ cup vegetable oil
1 cup all-purpose flour
4 quarts water
2 or 3 large onions, chopped
2 cloves garlic, chopped
¼ cup finely chopped parsley
½ cup chopped celery
salt and black pepper to taste
1 or 2 (10 ounce) packages
   frozen okra
1 chicken, skin removed, boned
   and cut in chunks
1 (16 ounce) package smoked
   pork sausage, sliced
cooked rice
filé

Heat oil in heavy stock pot over medium heat. Stir in flour and cook, stirring constantly, to form roux. Mixture should be dark caramel color; avoid burning roux. Remove from heat and add water, onion, garlic, parsley, celery, salt, black pepper, okra, chicken and sausage. Simmer for 2 hours or until chicken is tender and gumbo is thickened. Ladle gumbo over hot rice and sprinkle with filé. Serve with large slice of baked sweet potato. Gumbo can be frozen. Serves: 6 to 8.

Tamara Ford

CREAM OF ARTICHOKE SOUP

1 medium carrot, finely
   chopped
1 stalk celery, finely chopped
½ cup chopped green onions
3 tablespoons butter or
   margarine
4 cups chicken broth
1 bay leaf
pinch of dried whole thyme
1 (14 ounce) can artichoke
   hearts, drained and sliced
2 egg yolks
1 cup whipping cream

Sauté carrot, celery and green onions in butter or margarine in heavy saucepan until onion is tender. Add chicken broth, bay leaf and thyme. Simmer, covered, for 15 minutes, stirring often. Add artichoke hearts and cook for 10 minutes, stirring frequently. Beat egg yolks until thickened and lemon colored. Gradually stir ¼ hot broth into yolks, then add yolks to artichoke mixture, stirring constantly. Add whipping cream and simmer, stirring constantly, until thoroughly heated. Remove bay leaf. Serve immediately. Serves: 4 to 6.

Pam Hetherwick

BLACK BEAN SOUP

2 cups dried black beans
water
2 cups chopped onion
1 cup chopped celery
6 sprigs parsley
2 sprigs thyme or ¼ teaspoon
   crumbled dried thyme
1 bay leaf
3 tablespoons unsalted butter
½ to ¾ pound ham, diced
6 cups beef broth
4 cups water
salt and black pepper to taste
lemon juice to taste
chopped hard-cooked eggs for
   garnish
chopped onion for garnish
lemon slices for garnish

Soak beans, covered in water, overnight. Drain. Sauté onion, celery, parsley, thyme and bay leaf in butter in 4-quart saucepan or stock pot for 10 minutes. Add ham, beans, broth and 4 cups water. Season with salt and black pepper. Bring to a boil, reduce heat and simmer, uncovered, for 3 hours, adding more water as needed to cover beans. Check seasoning. Remove bay leaf. Soup can be thinned by adding hot water. Serve with egg, onion and lemon slices as garnish on side. Can be prepared in advance and stored in refrigerator for several days or frozen. Serves: 6 to 8.

Karen Townsend

LIMA AND HAM SOUP

1 (16 ounce) package dried lima
   beans
water
2 quarts water
½ pound ham, cubed
1 large onion, chopped
1 (29 ounce) can tomatoes,
   undrained
2 tablespoons chopped parsley
1 cup chopped celery
1 tablespoon lemon juice
2 tablespoons Creole seasoning
salt and black pepper to taste

Place beans in stock pot and add water to cover. Let stand overnight. Drain water from beans. Add 2 quarts fresh water and ham. Bring to a boil, reduce heat and simmer for 2½ hours, stirring occasionally. Add onion, tomatoes, parsley, celery, lemon juice and Creole seasoning. Season with salt and black pepper. Soup can be frozen. Serves: 10 to 12.

Mary Louise Bryan

FRENCH MARKET SOUP

2½ cups dried bean mixture
   (¼ cup each of black beans,
   garbanzo beans, barley,
   lentils, navy beans, pinto
   beans, blackeyed peas, red
   beans, split peas and baby
   lima beans)
water
1 tablespoon salt
3 quarts water
4 cups canned tomatoes
6 stalks celery, chopped
1 or 2 ham hocks
2 medium-sized onions,
   chopped
1 large green bell pepper,
   chopped
1 bay leaf
½ teaspoon thyme
2 cloves garlic, pressed
red pepper to taste
1 pound link sausage, sliced
½ chicken, cooked, skin and
   bone removed, cubed
chopped fresh parsley
salt to taste

Pour beans into stock pot. Add water to cover and add salt. Let stand, covered, overnight. Drain beans and return to stock pot. Add 3 quarts water, tomatoes, celery, ham hocks, onion, bell pepper, bay leaf, thyme, garlic, red pepper, sausage and chicken. Simmer, covered, for 3 hours. Add parsley and salt. Simmer for 15 minutes. Remove bay leaf. Soup can be prepared in advance and stored in refrigerator or frozen in small quantities for quick meals. Bean mixture can be packaged in 2½ cup amounts for later use or given as gifts with recipe. Serves: 16.

Cathy Seymour

BROCCOLI SOUP

1 (10 ounce) package frozen
  chopped broccoli
milk
1 cup half and half
1 (10¾ ounce) can cream of
  chicken soup, undiluted
1 teaspoon chicken bouillon
  granules
½ teaspoon seasoning salt
¼ teaspoon white pepper
½ teaspoon dry mustard
½ teaspoon onion powder
1 tablespoon butter
paprika for garnish
grated Parmesan cheese for
  garnish

Prepare broccoli according to package directions; do not overcook. Drain broccoli, reserving cooking liquid. Rinse broccoli with cold water and drain well. Using food processor, chop broccoli to fine consistency. Set aside. Add milk to reserved cooking liquid to measure 1 cup. Combine milk mixture, half and half, soup, bouillon, seasoning salt, white pepper, mustard, onion powder and butter in large saucepan. Heat until soup is blended. Stir in broccoli and heat until steamy; do not boil. Sprinkle paprika and Parmesan cheese on individual servings. Soup can be prepared in advance and stored in refrigerator for 3 to 4 days or frozen. Serves: 4 or 5.

Mary Ellen Boozman

CREAM OF BROCCOLI SOUP

¼ cup butter
1½ cups peeled, cubed potatoes
1 large onion, coarsely chopped
1 medium to large bunch
  broccoli
5 cups chicken broth or 3 (14½
  ounce) cans chicken broth
salt and black pepper to taste
1 cup half and half
1 tablespoon fresh lemon juice
nutmeg for garnish

Melt butter in large heavy saucepan. Add potatoes and onion to butter. Cook, covered, over low to medium heat, stirring occasionally, for 15 to 20 minutes or until potatoes are tender. While vegetables are cooking, cut broccoli into flowerets and discard woody stems. Cook in boiling water or by microwave method. Drain well. Cut broccoli into small pieces and puree in blender or food processor. Add puree and broth to potatoes. Simmer for 30 minutes. Season with salt and black pepper. Blend in half and half and lemon juice. Simmer until thoroughly heated. Sprinkle nutmeg on individual servings. Soup can be prepared in advance; reheat on low heat just prior to serving. Soup can be frozen. Serves: 4.

Christina Smith

CARROT BISQUE

3 to 5 slices bacon, chopped
4 cups coarsely chopped
  carrots
1 cup coarsely chopped
  mushrooms
½ cup coarsely chopped
  scallions with tops
1 cup coarsely chopped celery
  with leaves
5½ cups chicken broth
¼ teaspoon thyme
1 small bay leaf
1¼ cups half and half
salt and black pepper to taste
chopped scallion tops for
  garnish

Fry bacon in large heavy saucepan or Dutch oven over medium heat until crisp. Add carrots, mushrooms, scallions and celery, stirring to thoroughly coat with bacon drippings. Sauté, stirring frequently, for about 5 minutes or until scallions and celery are wilted. Reduce heat and simmer, covered, for 10 minutes. Stir in broth, thyme and bay leaf. Bring to a boil, reduce heat and simmer, covered, for 50 minutes. Remove from heat and let stand to cool slightly. Discard bay leaf. Using blender or food processor, puree vegetable mixture. Pour into saucepan and add half and half. Cook over medium heat, stirring frequently, just until thoroughly heated; do not boil. Season with salt and black pepper. Sprinkle individual servings with chopped scallions. Soup can be prepared in advance and stored in refrigerator for up to 4 days or frozen. Serves: 6 to 8.

Patricia Boozman Arceneaux

CHEESE SOUP WITH GARLIC CROUTONS

1 medium to large onion,
  chopped
1 clove garlic, minced
3 tablespoons butter
⅓ cup all-purpose flour
black pepper to taste
4 cups milk, warmed
2 cups (8 ounces) grated
  Cheddar or Colby-Jack cheese
2 tablespoons tomato sauce
1 tablespoon Worcestershire
  sauce

Croutons:
4 slices French bread, cut in
  ½-inch cubes
2 tablespoons olive oil
3 tablespoons butter
2 cloves garlic, minced
1 tablespoon parsley flakes

Prepare croutons by combining bread cubes, oil, butter, garlic and parsley in microwave-safe bowl, stirring well. Microwave at high setting for 2 minutes, remove, stir, and continue to microwave for 1 minute periods, stirring well, until crisp. Set aside. Sauté onion and garlic in butter in large saucepan until onion is transparent. Stir in flour and black pepper. Cook for 2 minutes. Gradually add warmed milk, stirring constantly with whisk. Add cheese and stir until melted. Add tomato sauce and Worcestershire sauce. Simmer for 15 minutes, stirring occasionally. Serve immediately with croutons sprinkled on individual portions. Croutons can also be served as an appetizer or with salad.

Tanya Conlay

CANE RIVER CORN SOUP

8 chicken bouillon cubes
1 cup boiling water
1 (16 ounce) package smoked
    sausage, cut in ¼-inch slices
¼ cup vegetable oil
½ cup all-purpose flour
1 medium-sized onion, chopped
⅓ cup chopped green onions
1 (10¾ ounce) can cream of
    chicken soup, undiluted
3 cups water
4 (16 ounce) cans corn or 8
    cups fresh corn
1 (29 ounce) can Italian style
    tomatoes, cut up
1 pound shrimp, peeled and
    deveined
salt and black pepper to taste
hot pepper sauce to taste

Dissolve bouillon cubes in boiling water and set aside. Fry sausage slices to reduce fat, drain on paper towel and set aside. Heat oil in heavy stock pot. Add flour and stir until smooth. Cook over medium high heat, stirring constantly, for 5 minutes. Reduce heat to medium low and cook, stirring frequently, until mixture is dark reddish-brown. Add onion and green onions. Cook until onion is softened. Add bouillon liquid, sausage, soup, water, corn and tomatoes. Bring to a boil, reduce heat and simmer for 20 minutes. Add shrimp and simmer for 10 to 15 minutes or until shrimp are done. Season with salt, black pepper and hot pepper sauce. Soup can be prepared in advance and stored in refrigerator or frozen. Serves: 12.

Rhonda Guidroz

VELVET CORN SOUP

¼ cup minced onion
¼ cup butter
3 cups fresh or frozen corn
4 cups half and half
1 egg, beaten
1¼ teaspoons salt
½ teaspoon white pepper

Sauté onion in butter until softened but not browned. Add corn, half and half and egg. Bring to a boil, stirring constantly, cooking for about 3 minutes. Add salt and black pepper. Let stand to cool slightly. Puree in blender or food processor until creamy. Reheat to serve or serve cold. Serves: 8 to 12.

Judy Diefendorf

NEW ENGLAND CORN CHOWDER

½ **pound bacon**
1 large onion, chopped
6 medium potatoes, peeled and
  cubed
water
2 (16 ounce) cans cream-style
  corn
1 (12 ounce) can evaporated
  milk
salt and black pepper to taste
milk (not evaporated)

Fry bacon until crisp, remove from skillet, drain on paper towels and crumble. Sauté onion in bacon drippings until tender. Combine potatoes with just enough water to cover in large saucepan and cook for 10 minutes; do not drain. Reduce heat. Add ½ of bacon, corn and evaporated milk. Season with salt and black pepper. Add regular milk if thinner consistency is desired. Simmer until thoroughly heated; do not boil. Sprinkle remaining bacon on individual servings. Soup can be frozen. Serves: 10 to 12.

Mary Ellen Boozman

CREAMY CORN SOUP

2 slices bacon, chopped
2 tablespoons chopped onion
2 cups frozen corn, thawed
2 tablespoons butter or
  margarine
2 tablespoons all-purpose flour
2 cups milk
1 teaspoon salt
½ **teaspoon black pepper**
2 cups half and half

Fry bacon in large saucepan until crisp. Add onion and sauté until onion is softened. Using blender or food processor, puree corn. Add corn to onion mixture and simmer for 5 minutes, stirring often. Blend in butter and flour. Simmer for 3 minutes. If desired, corn mixture can be frozen for later use. Add milk, salt and black pepper. Cook until thickened. Add half and half and simmer, stirring often, for about 20 minutes or until slightly thickened. This is a lighter corn soup and good as a first course. Serves: 4.

Kay Aaron

SPICY ONION SOUP

2 or 3 medium to large onions,
  thinly sliced
1 or 2 cloves garlic, chopped
1 small jalapeño pepper,
  chopped (optional)
2 tablespoons vegetable oil
1 (16 ounce) can Cajun or
  Italian seasoned stewed
  tomatoes
1 (10¾ ounce) can beef bouillon
  soup
1 (10¾ ounce) can chicken
  broth
1½ cups water
1 or 2 packets instant beef broth
  or beef bouillon cubes
6 to 8 slices French bread
grated Monterey Jack, Swiss or
  mozzarella cheese

Sauté onion, garlic and jalapeño pepper in oil in stock pot until vegetables are tender. Add tomatoes, beef bouillon soup, chicken broth, water and beef broth granules or cubes. Bring to a boil, reduce heat and simmer, covered, for 30 minutes to 1 hour. To serve, ladle soup into oven-safe bowls. Place French bread slice on soup and sprinkle with cheese. Broil until cheese is lightly browned. Serve immediately. Soup can be frozen. Serves: 6 to 8.

Toni Gwinn

ONION-TOMATO-RICE SOUP

6 large onions, coarsely
  chopped
3 cloves garlic, minced
1 cup chopped ham
¼ cup chopped parsley
1 bay leaf
¼ teaspoon thyme
2 tablespoons olive oil
6 cups beef broth
1 (16 ounce) can stewed
  tomatoes
1 cup uncooked regular rice
salt and black pepper to taste
⅛ teaspoon or more hot pepper
  sauce

Sauté onion, garlic, ham, parsley, bay leaf and thyme in oil in stock pot until onion is transparent. Add broth and tomatoes. Bring to a boil, reduce heat and simmer for 30 minutes. Prepare rice according to package directions. Add rice to soup and season with salt, black pepper and hot pepper sauce. Remove bay leaf. Serve with crusty French bread and cheese. Soup can be frozen. Serves: 8.

Pat Thomas
Toni Gwinn

CHEESY POTATO SOUP

2 large potatoes, peeled and
  diced
1 large onion, minced
½ cup finely chopped carrot
½ cup finely chopped celery
3 cups water
1 tablespoon chicken bouillon
  granules
2 cups (8 ounces) shredded
  extra sharp New York
  Cheddar cheese
dash of hot pepper sauce
1 cup half and half
⅓ cup snipped parsley

Combine potatoes, onion, carrot, celery and water in 3-quart saucepan. Bring to a boil, reduce heat and simmer, covered, for about 20 minutes or until vegetables are tender. Stir in cheese and hot pepper sauce. Add half and half and heat thoroughly; do not boil. Sprinkle individual servings with parsley. Soup can be partially prepared 1 day in advance, storing in refrigerator after cheese and hot pepper sauce have been added to vegetables. Soup should not be frozen. Makes 8 to 10 cups.

Juanita Murphy

POTATO BACON SOUP

8 slices bacon
1 cup chopped onion
2 cups peeled, diced red
  potatoes
1 cup water
½ teaspoon salt
dash of black pepper
1 (10¾ ounce) can cream of
  chicken soup, undiluted
1 cup sour cream
1¾ cups milk
2 tablespoons chopped parsley

Fry bacon in large heavy saucepan until crisp. Remove bacon and place on paper towel to drain. Cook onion in bacon drippings over medium heat for about 3 minutes or until tender. Remove onion, discard bacon drippings and return onion and bacon to pan. Add potatoes, water, salt and black pepper. Bring to a boil, reduce heat and simmer, covered, for 10 to 15 minutes or until potatoes are tender. Blend soup, sour cream and milk together. Gradually add to potato mixture and simmer until thoroughly heated; do not boil. Sprinkle parsley on individual servings. Soup can be prepared 1 day in advance and stored in refrigerator. Serves: 6 to 8.

Ellen Rae Aaron

GAZPACHO

1 (14 ounce) can seasoned
  stewed tomatoes
1 (14½ ounce) can beef broth
1 cup peeled, minced
  cucumbers
½ cup minced green bell pepper
¼ cup minced green onions
1 tablespoon olive oil
1 tablespoon sugar
1 tablespoon red wine vinegar
1 teaspoon salt
¼ teaspoon black pepper
½ teaspoon garlic powder
¼ teaspoon hot pepper sauce
avocado wedges for garnish
  (optional)

Mash tomatoes or use food processor to lightly puree. Combine tomatoes, beef broth, cucumbers, bell pepper, green onions, oil, sugar, vinegar, salt, black pepper, garlic powder and hot pepper sauce in large bowl. Chill, covered, for at least 2 hours or overnight. Garnish individual servings with avocado. By using food processor to prepare tomatoes, cucumbers, bell pepper and onions, this is a quick and easy recipe for gazpacho without sacrificing intensity of flavor. Serves: 6 to 8.

Cathy Seymour

DILLED ZUCCHINI SOUP

4 medium zucchini squash,
  sliced
1 (14½ ounce) can chicken
  broth
2 cups half and half
¼ teaspoon garlic salt
½ teaspoon black pepper
1 tablespoon fresh dillweed

Combine zucchini and broth in large saucepan. Bring to a boil, reduce heat and simmer, covered, for 12 to 15 minutes or until zucchini is tender. Remove from heat. Using blender or food processor, puree zucchini with broth. Combine puree, half and half, garlic salt, black pepper and dillweed in saucepan. Simmer, stirring constantly, until thoroughly heated; do not boil. Soup can be prepared 1 to 2 days in advance and stored in refrigerator. It should not be frozen. Serve as a first course. Serves: 6.

Vanessa Robertson

ZUCCHINI SOUP

½ cup margarine
3 medium zucchini squash,
  sliced
2 medium potatoes, peeled,
  quartered and sliced
1 medium-sized onion, coarsely
  chopped
1 (14½ ounce) can chicken
  broth
1 (12 ounce) can evaporated
  milk
1 rounded teaspoon Creole
  seasoning

Melt margarine in heavy saucepan over medium heat. Add vegetables. Cook, covered, stirring frequently, until vegetables are tender. Place vegetable mixture, broth, evaporated milk and Creole seasoning in blender or food processor. Blend until smooth. Check seasoning. Pour into saucepan and cook over low to medium heat until thoroughly heated. Soup can be frozen. Serves: 8 to 10.

Shirley Smiley

CHEESY VEGETABLE SOUP

2 tablespoons chopped onion
1 clove garlic, minced
1 tablespoon butter or
  margarine
1 cup frozen loose-pack corn
½ cup chopped broccoli
¼ cup shredded carrots
¼ cup water
3 tablespoons chopped green
  onion tops
1 (10¾ ounce) can cream of
  potato soup, undiluted
1 cup milk
¼ cup (1 ounce) shredded
  Cheddar cheese
1 ounce Provolone cheese,
  diced
dash of black pepper or to taste

Sauté onion and garlic in butter or margarine in medium saucepan until tender but not browned. Add corn, broccoli, carrots and water. Bring to a boil, reduce heat and simmer, covered, for 10 minutes or until vegetables are tender. Stir in green onions, soup, milk, Cheddar cheese, Provolone cheese and black pepper. Cook over medium heat, stirring often, until cheese is melted and soup is thoroughly heated; do not boil. Serves: 4.

Karen Townsend

Eggs and Cheese

SAUSAGE AND EGG CASSEROLE

1½ pounds bulk pork sausage,
  cooked, drained and
  crumbled
3 cups (12 ounces) pasteurized
  process cheese spread, grated
3 cups (12 ounces) sharp
  Cheddar cheese, grated
6 eggs
2½ cups milk
8 slices bread, buttered, crusts
  trimmed and cubed
1 small onion, minced
1 clove garlic, minced
½ teaspoon salt
½ teaspoon black pepper
½ teaspoon dry mustard
½ teaspoon Worcestershire
  sauce
½ teaspoon Beau Monde
  seasoning
1 cup chopped parsley or ½ cup
  parsley flakes

Assemble casserole the day before serving. Combine sausage, cheese spread, Cheddar cheese, eggs, milk, bread cubes, onion, garlic, salt, black pepper, mustard, Worcestershire sauce, seasoning and parsley, stirring with wire whisk. Pour mixture into 3-quart casserole. Chill at least 24 hours. Bake, uncovered, at 325 degrees for 1 hour. Unbaked casserole can be frozen; thaw before baking. Serves: 8 to 10.

Karen Townsend

BREAKFAST TORTILLAS

12 flour tortillas
butter
12 eggs, lightly beaten
½ cup (2 ounces) grated
  Cheddar cheese
½ cup sliced pepperoni
½ cup chopped green onions
sour cream for garnish
salsa for garnish

Place tortillas on microwave-safe dinner plate and invert second plate over tortillas. Microwave at high setting for 50 seconds. Spread tortillas with butter. Combine eggs, Cheddar cheese, pepperoni and green onions in skillet, cooking and stirring to scramble. Spoon egg mixture on center of each tortilla and roll up. Garnish with sour cream and salsa. Recipe may be halved or doubled. Serves: 12.

Patti Wingo

COMPANY BREAKFAST CASSEROLE

¼ cup chopped green onions
1 cup cubed ham
1 tablespoon butter
12 eggs
1 (4½ ounce) jar jalapeño
 flavored cheese
½ cup butter, melted
1 cup breadcrumbs

Assemble casserole the day before serving. Sauté green onions and ham in 1 tablespoon butter in large skillet until onions are softened. Add eggs and stir to scramble. Remove from heat and stir in cheese. Pour mixture into buttered 1½-quart casserole. Mix melted butter and breadcrumbs. Sprinkle on egg mixture. Chill, covered, overnight. Bake at 350 degrees for 30 minutes. Recipe may be halved or doubled. Serves: 6.

Aimee Wright

CHEESE, BACON AND TOMATO PIE

1 medium-sized onion, chopped
2 tablespoons all-purpose flour
1 unbaked 9-inch pastry shell
8 slices bacon, cooked and
 crumbled
1 medium tomato, thinly sliced
2 cups (8 ounces) shredded
 mozzarella cheese
2 cups shredded lettuce

Combine onion and flour. Sprinkle mixture in pastry shell. Add bacon, layer tomatoes on bacon and top with mozzarella cheese. Bake at 400 degrees for about 25 minutes. Sprinkle lettuce on pie. For crispier crust, pastry shell can be pre-baked for a few minutes before filling. Unbaked pie can be stored in refrigerator for up to 24 hours. Serves: 8.

Anne Giering

JO'S MUSHROOM SOUFFLÉ

8 slices light wheat bread
butter, softened
5 eggs, beaten
1 cup evaporated milk plus 1
 cup water or 2 cups milk
1 (8 ounce) can sliced
 mushrooms, drained
4 cups (16 ounces) grated old
 English sharp Cheddar cheese

The day before serving, assemble soufflé. Spread both sides of bread slices with butter and cut into large cubes. Combine eggs, milk, mushrooms and Cheddar cheese. Layer bread and milk mixture in soufflé dish. Chill overnight. Bake at 325 degrees for 1 hour or until lightly browned. Serve immediately. Serves: 8.

Jo Breedlove

SPECIAL OCCASION EGG CASSEROLE

2 cups plain croutons
1 cup (4 ounces) shredded mild
  Cheddar cheese
1 (4 ounce) can mushrooms,
  drained
4 eggs
2 cups milk
dash of black pepper
¼ teaspoon onion powder
¼ teaspoon prepared mustard
1 (16 ounce) package bacon,
  cooked and crumbled in bite-
  sized pieces

Combine croutons, Cheddar cheese and mushrooms. Spread mixture in greased 13x9x2-inch baking dish. Combine eggs, milk, black pepper, onion powder and mustard, beating slightly. Pour egg liquid over crouton mixture. Sprinkle with bacon pieces. Bake at 350 degrees for 1 hour. Let stand for 10 minutes before cutting or serving. Recipe may be halved or doubled. Baked casserole can be frozen. Serves: 6.

Claudia Rees

BREAKFAST FAJITAS

1 pound bulk pork sausage
8 eggs
10 flour tortillas
4 cups (16 ounces) grated
  Cheddar cheese
4 cups (16 ounces) grated
  Monterey Jack cheese
sour cream

Picante Sauce:
1 tablespoon vegetable oil
1 tablespoon vinegar
1 tablespoon garlic powder
2 or 3 jalapeño peppers,
  chopped
1 (29 ounce) can whole
  tomatoes

Prepare picante sauce by combining oil, vinegar, garlic powder and jalapeño peppers in blender. Add juice from tomatoes and blend to puree consistency. Add tomatoes and pulse blender 2 or 3 times; salsa should be chunky. Set aside. Cook sausage, stirring to crumble, until browned. Drain well. Scramble eggs until just cooked. Add sausage to eggs. Serve buffet style, allowing diners to assemble fajitas from egg mixture, flour tortillas, Cheddar cheese, Monterey Jack cheese, picante sauce and sour cream. Recipe may be halved or doubled. Serves: 10.

Kim Johnson

CRAB QUICHE

4 eggs, well beaten
2 cups half and half
⅓ cup minced onion
salt to taste
⅛ teaspoon cayenne pepper
1 (7½ ounce) can crabmeat,
  drained and blotted dry
1 cup (4 ounces) shredded
  Swiss or mozzarella cheese
1 unbaked 9-inch pastry shell
chopped parsley

Combine eggs, half and half, onion, salt and cayenne pepper. Sprinkle crabmeat and Swiss or mozzarella cheese in pastry shell. Pour egg liquid over crabmeat mixture. Sprinkle with parsley. Bake at 425 degrees for 15 minutes, reduce oven temperature to 300 degrees and bake for additional 30 minutes or until knife tip inserted 1 inch from edge comes out clean. Let stand for 10 minutes before cutting into wedges. Serves: 8.

Lydia Lee

CRAWFISH QUICHE

1½ teaspoons onion flakes
water
1 cup (4 ounces) grated Swiss
  cheese
1 unbaked 10-inch pastry shell
½ pound crawfish, coarsely
  chopped
4 eggs, lightly beaten
1 cup whipping cream
½ teaspoon salt
⅛ teaspoon red pepper

Soak onion in water to soften. Drain well. Sprinkle cheese in pastry shell, add crawfish and top with onion. Combine eggs, whipping cream, salt and red pepper, mixing well. Pour seasoned cream over crawfish. Bake at 375 degrees for 35 to 40 minutes. Serves: 6 to 8.

Cecilia Dalme

LES AMIES 25TH ANNIVERSARY SEAFOOD QUICHE

⅓ cup mayonnaise
2 tablespoons all-purpose flour
3 eggs, beaten
¾ cup milk
1 (4¼ ounce) can crabmeat, drained
1 (4¼ ounce) can cocktail shrimp, drained
2 cups (8 ounces) grated Swiss cheese
5 green onions, chopped
¼ teaspoon salt
black pepper to taste
1 unbaked 9-inch pastry shell
grated Parmesan cheese
1 tablespoon butter

Combine mayonnaise, flour, eggs and milk, mixing well. Stir in crabmeat, shrimp, Swiss cheese and onions. Season with salt and black pepper. Pour seafood mixture into pastry shell. Sprinkle with Parmesan cheese and dot with butter. Bake at 350 degrees for 40 to 45 minutes. Serves: 7 or 8.

Juanita Murphy

SPINACH QUICHE

1 cup biscuit baking mix
¼ cup cold water
1 cup chopped fresh spinach
1 cup (4 ounces) shredded Swiss cheese
½ cup French fried onion rings
1 (4 ounce) can mushroom stems and pieces, drained
1 cup whipping cream
4 eggs
¼ teaspoon sugar
⅛ teaspoon cayenne pepper

Combine baking mix and cold water, mixing to form soft dough. Beat vigorously for 20 strokes. Spread on lightly-floured work surface and knead 5 times. Roll dough to 11x11-inch square. Fit dough loosely in 9x9x2-inch baking pan. Sprinkle spinach, Swiss cheese, onion rings and mushrooms on dough. Using electric mixer, beat whipping cream, eggs, sugar and cayenne pepper together. Pour over cheese and vegetables. Bake at 425 degrees for 15 minutes, reduce oven temperature to 300 degrees and bake for additional 35 minutes. Let stand 10 minutes before cutting. Egg substitute can be used. Serves: 4 to 6.

Dawn Celles

Salads

GARY'S PASTA SALAD

1 (12 ounce) package vermicelli
   pasta
olive oil
1 cup chopped green onions
   with tops
1 cup sliced black olives
1 cup sliced fresh mushrooms
1 cup sliced cherry tomatoes
¾ cup (3 ounces) shredded
   Parmesan cheese, divided
1 (4 ounce) jar diced pimiento,
   drained

Dressing:
⅔ cup olive oil
¼ cup white vinegar
1 packet zesty Italian salad
   dressing mix

Prepare pasta according to package directions. Rinse with cold water and drain well. Toss pasta with oil until well coated. Set aside to cool. Combine green onions, olives, mushrooms, tomatoes, ½ cup Parmesan cheese and pimiento in large bowl. Prepare dressing by combining oil, vinegar and salad dressing mix, whisking until smooth. Pour dressing over vegetable mixture, tossing to coat. Add pasta to vegetables and toss well. Sprinkle ¼ cup cheese on salad. Chill for at least 2 hours. Serves: 6 to 8.

Tanya Conlay

CASHEW CHICKEN SALAD

4 chicken breast halves, skin
   removed, boned and cut in
   bite-sized pieces
1 tablespoon vegetable oil
½ cup diced pineapple, drained
1 cup chopped celery
1 cup bean sprouts
½ cup diced water chestnuts
½ cup thinly sliced green
   onions, divided
½ cup sliced black olives,
   divided
½ cup cashews
½ cup sour cream
⅓ cup mayonnaise
¼ teaspoon curry powder

Stir-fry chicken in oil for about 4 minutes. Add pineapple and continue to stir-fry for 5 minutes. Transfer chicken and pineapple to bowl. Chill thoroughly. About 10 minutes before serving, add celery, bean sprouts, water chestnuts, ⅓ cup green onions, ⅓ cup olives, cashews, sour cream, mayonnaise and curry powder to chicken and pineapple, stirring well. Garnish with remaining green onions and olives. Serves: 6 to 8.

Beverly Harrell

HAWAIIAN CHICKEN SALAD

1 whole chicken, cooked, skin
   removed, boned and cut in
   bite-sized pieces
1 (16 ounce) can pineapple
   chunks, drained
1 (4 ounce) can water chestnuts,
   drained and chopped
1 cup green seedless grapes
1 cup golden raisins
1 (3½ ounce) package slivered
   almonds

Dressing:
3 to 4 tablespoons mayonnaise
1 teaspoon soy sauce
2 teaspoons curry powder

Combine chicken, pineapple, water chestnuts, grapes, raisins and almonds. Prepare dressing by combining mayonnaise, soy sauce and curry powder. Add dressing to chicken mixture and mix well. Chill thoroughly. Serve on lettuce or spinach leaf. Serves: 8.

Debbie Murphy

SUPERB HOT CRABMEAT-AVOCADO SALAD

1 (7½ ounce) can crabmeat,
  drained
⅓ cup chopped celery
3 hard-cooked eggs, finely
  chopped
1 tablespoon chopped pimiento
1 tablespoon chopped green
  onions
½ cup mayonnaise
¼ teaspoon salt
3 large or 4 small ripe avocados
lemon juice
salt
3 tablespoons dry breadcrumbs
1 teaspoon butter, melted
2 tablespoons slivered almonds

Combine crabmeat, celery, eggs, pimiento, green onions, mayonnaise and salt. Set aside. Cut unpeeled avocados in halves lengthwise and remove pits. Brush cut surfaces with lemon juice and sprinkle lightly with salt. Spoon crabmeat mixture into avocado halves and place in ungreased shallow baking dish. Toss bread crumbs in butter and sprinkle on crabmeat mixture. Bake, uncovered at 400 degrees for 10 minutes. Sprinkle almonds on crumb topping and bake for additional 5 minutes or until bubbly. Serves: 6 to 8.

Lydia Lee

SHRIMP SALAD

2 to 3 pounds boiled shrimp,
  peeled and chopped
½ cup chopped celery
½ cup chopped onion
2 hard-cooked eggs, chopped
¼ cup chopped dill pickle
1 tablespoon sweet pickle relish

Dressing:
½ cup mayonnaise
¼ cup ketchup
1 tablespoon horseradish
1 tablespoon lemon juice
1 teaspoon salt
¼ teaspoon black pepper
¼ teaspoon red pepper

Combine shrimp, celery, onion, egg, pickle and pickle relish. Prepare dressing by combining mayonnaise, ketchup, horseradish, lemon juice, salt, black pepper and red pepper. Add dressing to shrimp mixture, stirring to mix thoroughly. Serves: 6.

Lynn Pierson

SHRIMP AND PASTA SALAD

⅔ (6 ounce) package frozen
  snow peas
1 (8 ounce) package rotini pasta
¼ pound fresh mushrooms,
  sliced
1 carrot, sliced
½ pound small shrimp, peeled
  and cooked

Dressing:
⅓ cup olive oil
⅓ cup lemon juice
3 tablespoons soy sauce
1 tablespoon plus 1 teaspoon
  sugar
1 teaspoon dry mustard
1 teaspoon sesame seed, toasted

Thaw snow peas at room temperature for 30 minutes. Prepare pasta according to package directions. Rinse with cold water and drain well. Prepare dressing by combining oil, lemon juice, soy sauce, sugar, mustard and sesame seed in jar with tight-fitting lid, shaking well. Combine snow peas, pasta, mushrooms and carrots. Add dressing and mix. Chill thoroughly. Add shrimp just before serving. Serves: 8.

Pauline Ackel

MARINATED SHRIMP AND VEGETABLES

4 to 5 pounds medium to large shrimp, peeled and deveined
boiling water
1 tablespoon plus 1 teaspoon salt
1 bag crab boil seasoning
½ pound fresh mushrooms
1 head cauliflower, separated in flowerets

Marinade:
6 onions, thinly sliced in rings
8 bay leaves
1 cup olive oil
1 cup vegetable oil
1 cup white vinegar
juice of 1 lemon
1 (3½ ounce) jar capers, undrained
few dashes hot pepper sauce
few dashes Worcestershire sauce
1½ teaspoons salt
1 tablespoon plus 1 teaspoon celery seed

Prepare 48 hours in advance of serving. Place shrimp in large stock pot. Add boiling water to cover, salt and crab boil bag. Cook over high heat for 15 minutes. Drain and rinse shrimp with cold water to cool. Combine shrimp, mushrooms and cauliflower. Prepare marinade by combining onion, bay leaves, olive oil, vegetable oil, vinegar, lemon juice, capers, hot pepper sauce, Worcestershire sauce, salt and celery seed. Pour marinade over shrimp mixture. Chill for 48 hours, stirring occasionally. Serves: 10 to 12.

Sarah Luster

BROCCOLI SALAD

1 bunch broccoli, cut in
 flowerets
¼ cup chopped onion
1 (7 ounce) jar pimiento stuffed
 green olives, drained
1 cup chopped celery

Dressing:
1 cup mayonnaise
1 teaspoon lemon juice
1 teaspoon seasoned salt
1½ teaspoons dill weed

Combine broccoli, onion, olives and celery. Prepare dressing by combining mayonnaise, lemon juice, seasoned salt and dill weed, mixing well. Stir dressing into vegetable mixture. Chill, tightly covered, overnight. Carrot slices and cauliflower can be added to salad. Serves: 6 to 8.

Vanessa Robertson

BROCCOLI-GRAPE SALAD

4 cups chopped broccoli
 flowerets
ice water
½ cup thinly sliced purple
 onion, cut in half-moon
 slivers
½ cup green grape halves
1 cup diagonally sliced water
 chestnuts
12 slices bacon, cooked and
 crumbled

Dressing:
1 cup mayonnaise
2 tablespoons cider vinegar
¼ to ⅓ cup sugar

Prepare salad 12 to 24 hours in advance of serving. Crisp broccoli in ice water. Drain well. Combine broccoli, onion, grapes, water chestnuts and bacon. Prepare dressing by combining mayonnaise, vinegar and sugar, blending well. Pour dressing over vegetable mixture, tossing to coat. Serves: 8.

Jo Ann Ford

24 HOUR SLAW

1 large head cabbage, grated
2 large onions, chopped
1 green bell pepper, chopped
1 cup sugar

Dressing:
2 tablespoons all-purpose flour
2 tablespoons sugar (optional)
1 tablespoon salt
1 teaspoon celery seed
1 teaspoon dry mustard
  (optional)
¾ cup vegetable oil
1 cup vinegar

Combine cabbage, onion and bell pepper. Sprinkle sugar on vegetables. Prepare dressing by combining flour, sugar, salt, celery seed, mustard, oil and vinegar in saucepan. Bring to a boil. Remove from heat and let stand until cool. Pour cooled dressing over vegetables. Chill, covered, for 24 hours. Serves: 8 to 10.

Dorothy Barnette

NUTTY COLE SLAW

4 cups chopped cabbage
1 cup chopped celery
½ cup sour cream
½ cup mayonnaise
¼ cup chopped green onions
¼ cup chopped green bell
  pepper
½ cup chopped cucumber
½ cup salted peanuts
1 tablespoon butter
2 tablespoons Parmesan cheese

Toss cabbage and celery together. Chill. Combine sour cream, mayonnaise, green onions, bell pepper and cucumber. Add to cabbage mixture. Sauté peanuts in butter for a few minutes. Add cheese and remove from heat. Add peanuts with cheese to salad just before serving. Serves: 6 to 8.

Kay Aaron

ENGLISH PEA SALAD

1 (16 ounce) can white corn,
  drained
1 (16 ounce) can English peas,
  drained
1 cup chopped celery
1 green bell pepper, finely
  chopped
2 bunches green onions,
  chopped

Marinade:
½ cup oil
½ cup vinegar
1 tablespoon water
½ cup sugar
1 tablespoon salt
2 tablespoons black pepper

Combine corn, peas, celery, bell pepper and green onions. Set aside. Prepare marinade by mixing oil, vinegar, water, sugar, salt and black pepper, stirring to dissolve sugar and salt. Pour marinade over vegetables. Chill for at least 6 hours before serving. Serves: 8 to 10.

Debbie Maynard

MARINATED TOMATOES

8 medium-sized tomatoes
¼ cup chopped parsley

Marinade:
¼ cup olive oil
2 tablespoons tarragon vinegar
2 teaspoons prepared mustard
1 clove garlic, crushed
1 teaspoon sugar
1 teaspoon salt
¼ teaspoon black pepper

Peel tomatoes and remove cores. Place in dish. Prepare marinade by combining oil, vinegar, mustard, garlic, sugar, salt and black pepper, mixing well. Pour marinade into center of each tomato. Chill, covered, for several hours. Sprinkle parsley on tomatoes when serving. Serves: 8.

Martha Taylor

SUMMER MARINATED TOMATOES

2 or 3 large firm ripe tomatoes
boiling water
parsley sprigs for garnish

Marinade:
1 cup olive oil
½ cup tarragon vinegar
1 tablespoon plus 1 teaspoon
   Creole mustard
1 cup finely chopped fresh
   parsley
4 cloves garlic, crushed
1 tablespoon plus 1 teaspoon
   salt
1 tablespoon plus 1 teaspoon
   sugar
1½ to 2 teaspoons black pepper

Prepare marinade by combining oil, vinegar, mustard, parsley, garlic, salt, sugar and black pepper. Set aside. Peel tomatoes, dipping first in boiling water to loosen skin. Cut tomatoes into thick slices and place in shallow dish. Pour dressing over tomatoes, completely covering. Chill for 24 hours. Drain tomatoes, reserving dressing, and place on serving platter. Garnish with parsley. Reserved dressing can be drizzled over tomatoes when served. Recipe can be doubled. Serves: 2 or 3.

Sharon Gahagan

LIGHT AND EASY TOMATO ASPIC

1 cup tomato juice
1 (3 ounce) package lemon
   gelatin
1 cup spicy cocktail vegetable
   juice

Pour tomato juice into saucepan. Bring to a boil. Pour hot juice over gelatin and stir until dissolved. Add juice and mix. Pour into individual molds. Chill for several hours or until firm. Serves: 6.

Mary Louise Bryan

MAXWELL'S CAESAR SALAD

1 large head Romaine lettuce
4 slices white sandwich bread
2 tablespoons olive oil
1 clove garlic, minced or
   crushed

Dressing:
1 egg white
hot water
4 anchovy fillets
1 large clove garlic
¼ cup olive oil
2 tablespoons red wine vinegar
¼ teaspoon salt
freshly ground black pepper to
   taste
1 tablespoon lemon juice
¼ cup (1 ounce) grated
   Parmesan cheese

Tear lettuce into bite-sized pieces. Chill until ready to use. Prepare croutons by lightly toasting bread in toaster. Trim crusts and cut toast into small cubes. Sauté in oil with garlic for a few minutes. Set aside. Prepare dressing by coddling egg, submersing in hot water for about 5 minutes or just until white begins to solidify. Place anchovies, garlic and egg white in large wooden bowl. Using back of large spoon and a fork, mash to paste consistency. Add oil, vinegar, salt and black pepper. If dressing is too thick, add small amount of oil. Add lettuce to dressing and toss well. Add lemon juice, then Parmesan cheese, tossing after each addition. Sprinkle black pepper and croutons on individual servings of salad. Serves: 4.

Pat Thomas

COMPANY CAESAR SALAD

20 to 30 cubes French bread
olive oil
garlic
2 eggs, coddled
hot water
1 head Romaine lettuce, chilled
1 head leaf lettuce, chilled
¼ teaspoon dry mustard
¼ teaspoon coarsely ground
   black pepper
1½ cups (6 ounces) freshly
   grated Parmesan cheese
¼ cup plus 2 tablespoons olive
   oil
¼ cup tarragon vinegar
1 (2 ounce) can anchovies
2 teaspoons capers, drained

Place bread cubes in baking pan. Bake at 200 degrees until lightly browned. Toss cubes in olive oil lightly flavored with garlic. Drain and set aside. Coddle eggs by submersing in hot water for about 5 minutes or just until white begins to solidify. Tear Romaine and leaf lettuce into bite-sized pieces. Sprinkle with dry mustard and black pepper. Add Parmesan cheese, oil and vinegar, tossing to mix. Break eggs into lettuce mixture, add anchovies and capers and toss gently to mix. Drain excess liquid from bowl. Add croutons just before serving and toss gently. Serves: 6 to 8.

Tamara Ford

Salads

MANDARIN-WALNUT SALAD

½ head red leaf lettuce
½ head iceberg lettuce
1 (11 ounce) can mandarin oranges, drained and chilled
1 medium-sized purple onion, thinly sliced in rings
1 green bell pepper, sliced in rings
1 cup walnut halves
½ pound fresh mushrooms, sliced
1 avocado, sliced
walnut halves for garnish

Dressing:
⅓ cup vegetable oil
⅓ cup apple cider vinegar
2 tablespoons sugar
1 teaspoon black pepper
½ teaspoon basil
½ teaspoon garlic salt
1 teaspoon poppy seed

Tear red leaf and iceberg lettuce into bite-sized pieces and place in salad bowl. Add oranges, onion, bell pepper, walnuts, mushrooms and avocado. Prepare dressing by combining oil, vinegar, sugar, black pepper, basil, garlic salt and poppy seed in jar with tight-fitting lid. Shake to blend and dissolve sugar and salt. Add dressing to salad just before serving, tossing to mix. Top with additional walnuts. Serves: 8.

Kim Johnson

101

SPINACH SALAD

½ head iceberg lettuce,
  shredded
1 (10 ounce) package spinach,
  torn in bite-sized pieces
10 slices bacon, cooked and
  crumbled
1 onion, sliced
2 cups cottage cheese
1 pound fresh mushrooms,
  sliced
4 hard-cooked eggs, slivered or
  grated

Dressing:
⅓ cup cider vinegar
2 teaspoons chopped onion
¼ cup sugar
1 teaspoon salt
1 teaspoon dry mustard
1 cup vegetable oil

Toss lettuce, spinach, bacon, onion, cottage cheese, mushrooms and eggs together. Prepare dressing by combining vinegar, onion, sugar, salt and mustard in food processor bowl. Gradually add oil, processing until well blended. Pour dressing over vegetable mixture. Serves: 10 to 12.

Rosemary Baker

SPINACH SALAD DRESSING

1 cup vegetable oil
¼ cup plus 1 tablespoon red
  wine vinegar
¼ cup sour cream
2 tablespoons chopped parsley
2 cloves garlic, minced
1 teaspoon salt
freshly ground black pepper
  to taste
½ teaspoon dry mustard

Combine oil, vinegar, sour cream, parsley, garlic, salt, black pepper and mustard in jar with tight-fitting lid. Shake to blend. Chill overnight before using. Dressing can be stored in refrigerator for about 1 week. Makes about 2 cups.

Melissa Cloutier

SUNFLOWER DRESSING

2½ cups vegetable oil
½ cup plus 1 teaspoon honey
2½ teaspoons white pepper
1¼ cups sugar
1 cup vinegar
1 rounded tablespoon salt
1 (⅛ ounce) jar freeze-dried
   chives
3 tablespoons minced garlic
¼ cup plus 1 tablespoon
   roasted sunflower seeds

Pour oil into mixing bowl. Using electric mixer at medium speed, beat in ingredients in order listed: honey, white pepper, sugar, vinegar, salt, chives and garlic. Stir in sunflower seeds. Dressing can be stored in refrigerator for up to 1 week. Makes 5 cups.

Marion Salter

SALAD DRESSING PARMESAN

¼ cup plus 1 tablespoon red
   wine vinegar
1 teaspoon sugar
1 teaspoon salt
1 tablespoon dry mustard
1 cup extra virgin olive oil
¼ cup (1 ounce) freshly grated
   Parmesan cheese
¼ cup plus 1 tablespoon
   mayonnaise
1 clove garlic, crushed

Using food processor or blender, combine vinegar, sugar, salt and mustard. Gradually add oil, Parmesan cheese and mayonnaise, blending constantly. Place garlic in jar and add dressing. Chill. Shake well before using. Makes 2 cups.

Edwina Friedman

CITRUS GREEN

¾ cup vegetable oil
½ cup orange juice
1 tablespoon plus 1 teaspoon
  lemon juice
3 tablespoons vinegar
2 tablespoons grated orange
  peel
2 teaspoons sugar
¼ teaspoon salt
1½ teaspoons dry mustard

Combine oil, orange juice, lemon juice, vinegar, orange peel, sugar, salt and mustard in jar with tight-fitting lid. Shake well. Serve on Romaine lettuce with sliced purple onion, avocados and mandarin orange slices. Makes 1½ cups.

Jo Ann Ford

FRUIT WITH SWEET AND SOUR DRESSING

2 pints fresh strawberries
3 kiwi, sliced
3 bananas, sliced
1 cup blueberries
1 cup seedless grapes

Dressing:
½ cup vegetable oil
¾ cup vinegar
½ to ¾ cup sugar
½ teaspoon salt
1 teaspoon black pepper
½ teaspoon dry mustard

Combine strawberries, kiwi, bananas, blueberries and grapes. Prepare dressing by combining oil, vinegar, sugar, salt, black pepper and mustard, stirring until sugar is dissolved. Pour dressing over fruit mixture, stirring to coat. Chill, covered, for at least 8 hours. Drain fruit before serving. Serves: 4 to 6.

Cathy Seymour

SPICY MELON BOAT

1 large watermelon, carved to
   form shell
2 cantaloupes
2 (15 ounce) cans pineapple
   chunks, drained
grapes, cherries, blueberries or
   other fruit in season

Sauce:
1 cup tequila
½ cup orange juice
¼ cup grenadine
½ cup powdered sugar

Cut watermelon and cantaloupe into cubes, balls or slices. Place in large mixing bowl with remaining fruits. Prepare sauce by combining tequila, orange juice, grenadine and powdered sugar, blending thoroughly. Pour sauce over fruit, stirring to mix. Place fruit mixture in watermelon shell. Serves: 20.

Karen Townsend

MINT FRUIT DRESSING FOR MELONS

1 cup orange juice (fresh or
   made from frozen
   concentrate)
3 tablespoons fresh lemon juice
½ cup sugar
¼ cup crushed mint leaves
1 tablespoon grated lemon peel
2 cups watermelon wedges
2 cups honeydew melon wedges
2 cups cantaloupe wedges

Combine orange juice, lemon juice, sugar, mint and lemon peel in heavy saucepan. Cook over low heat, stirring frequently, until sugar is dissolved. Bring to a boil and cook for 1 minute. Remove from heat and let stand until cool. Combine watermelon, honeydew and cantaloupe in large bowl. Strain cooled syrup over fruit. Chill overnight. Serves: 8.

Janell DeVargas

PINEAPPLE FRUIT DRESSING

½ cup plus 2 teaspoons sugar, divided
2 tablespoons all-purpose flour
1 egg, lightly beaten
1 cup pineapple juice
2 tablespoons butter
1 cup whipping cream

Combine ½ cup sugar, flour and egg in heavy saucepan, mixing well. Add pineapple juice and butter. Cook over medium heat, stirring occasionally, for about 20 minutes or until thickened. Remove from heat and let stand until cool. Whip cream with 2 teaspoons sugar until thickened. Fold whipped cream into cooled pineapple mixture. Serve as dip for fruit or fold into mixed fruit salad. Makes 3½ cups.

Janell DeVargas

AUNT PARALEE'S SALAD

2 (3 ounce) packages orange gelatin
1 cup boiling water
2 cups miniature marshmallows
1 (6 ounce) can frozen orange juice concentrate, thawed, undiluted
½ cup sugar
1 (11 ounce) can mandarin oranges
1 (8 ounce) package cream cheese, softened
1 (8 ounce) can crushed pineapple
2 bananas, mashed
1 cup whipping cream, whipped

Dissolve gelatin in boiling water. Add marshmallows and stir until dissolved. Add orange juice and sugar, mixing until sugar is dissolved. Add mandarin oranges, cream cheese, pineapple and bananas. Fold whipped cream into fruit mixture. Chill for 3 hours. Serves: 8.

Paralee Williams

BAKED APRICOTS

1 (16 ounce) package round
   buttery crackers
4 (16 ounce) cans apricot
   halves, drained
2 (16 ounce) packages light
   brown sugar
1 cup butter, cut in pats

Using food processor, grind crackers to crumb consistency. In greased 13x9x2-inch baking dish, layer ½ of ingredients in order listed: apricots, brown sugar, cracker crumbs and butter; repeat layers. Bake at 350 degrees until hot and bubbly. This is a great dish for Thanksgiving or Christmas meals. Because of sweetness, servings can be small. Serves: 12.

Sarah Katherine Ahrens

STUFFED ORANGES

8 navel oranges
¼ cup grenadine syrup
3 egg whites
½ cup sugar
1 pint very firm ice cream

Cut slice from top of oranges and scoop out pulp, reserving shells. Cut pulp into small pieces and mix with grenadine syrup. Chill. Beat egg whites with sugar until stiff peaks form. Spoon orange mixture into orange shells, fill with ice cream and top with meringue, being sure to seal at edge of shell. Bake at 400 degrees for 3 to 5 minutes or until meringue is lightly browned. Serves: 8.

Nita Caspari Sutton

Condiments and Sauces

BOBBY'S BARBECUE SAUCE

¼ cup margarine
¾ cup sugar
1 cup firmly-packed brown
  sugar
¼ cup plus 1 tablespoon maple
  syrup
1 (32 ounce) bottle ketchup
1 cup vinegar
juice of 1 lemon
2 tablespoons mustard
2 tablespoons oil
2 tablespoons Worcestershire
  sauce
1 tablespoon salt
1½ tablespoons black pepper

Combine margarine, sugar, brown sugar and syrup in heavy saucepan, cooking until sugars are dissolved. Stir in ketchup, vinegar, lemon juice, mustard, oil, Worcestershire sauce, salt and black pepper. Simmer for 1 hour. Sauce can be stored in refrigerator for weeks. Makes 7 cups.

Lynn Pierson

OUR FAVORITE BARBECUE SAUCE

2 (12 ounce) bottles chili sauce
½ cup lemon juice
¼ cup olive oil
½ cup water
2 tablespoons tarragon vinegar
2 cups chopped onion
3 cloves garlic, minced
1 tablespoon brown sugar
1 teaspoon salt
1 teaspoon dry mustard
1 bay leaf, crumbled
hot pepper sauce to taste

Combine chili sauce, lemon juice, oil, water, vinegar, onion, garlic, brown sugar, salt, mustard, bay leaf and hot pepper sauce in 2-quart saucepan. Bring to a boil, stirring frequently to prevent scorching. Reduce heat and simmer for 20 minutes, stirring occasionally. Sauce is good accompaniment to poultry, lamb or ground beef. It can be stored in refrigerator for 1 week. Makes 5½ cups.

Pat Thomas

EASY BÉARNAISE SAUCE

1 cup butter
4 egg yolks, at room
    temperature
1½ teaspoons Worcestershire
    sauce
2 tablespoons dry vermouth
juice of medium-sized lemon
pinch of red pepper
2 teaspoons tarragon

Melt butter in small saucepan over medium heat; do not burn. Using blender at low speed, blend yolks. Gradually add butter in steady stream to egg yolks, blending at low speed. Add Worcestershire sauce, vermouth, lemon juice, red pepper and tarragon. Blend for 30 seconds. Let stand at room temperature until ready to serve. Serves: 6.

Shelley West

GIBLET GRAVY

giblets and neck from 1 turkey
2 cups chicken broth
1 medium-sized onion, chopped
1 cup chopped celery
½ teaspoon poultry seasoning
½ cup cornbread dressing
salt and black pepper to taste
2 hard-cooked eggs, sliced

Cook turkey giblets and neck in broth for about 2 hours or until tender. Remove giblets and neck from broth, discarding neck. Chop giblets and add to broth. Stir in onion, celery, poultry seasoning and cornbread dressing. Cook until vegetables are tender. Season with salt and black pepper. Add egg slices to gravy. For thicker gravy, add additional dressing. Makes about 2 cups.

Marteel Henry

SNAPPY HORSERADISH SAUCE

½ cup sour cream
¼ cup mayonnaise
1½ teaspoons prepared
  horseradish
¼ teaspoon onion salt
¼ teaspoon garlic salt

Combine sour cream, mayonnaise, horse-radish, onion salt and garlic salt, mixing thoroughly. Chill, covered, for at least 1 hour to blend flavors. Serve with cold, sliced lean beef. For special dinner, fill large mushroom caps with sauce, garnish with minced chives or green onions and bake at 325 degrees for 10 to 15 minutes. Serve with prime rib, steak or roast beef. Makes ¾ cup.

Linda Burke

ORANGE RAISIN SAUCE

⅔ cup orange juice
1 cup water
2 tablespoons cornstarch
⅛ teaspoon ground allspice
½ cup marmalade
1 cup raisins

Combine orange juice, water, cornstarch and allspice in small saucepan. Cook, stir-ring constantly, until mixture is thickened. Stir in marmalade and raisins and heat thoroughly. Serve sauce over ham or pork. Makes 2 cups.

Linda Burke

BING CHERRY-PORT WINE SAUCE

3 cups ruby port wine
1½ teaspoons grated orange
  peel
3 cloves
1 teaspoon nutmeg
1 teaspoon allspice
1 teaspoon thyme
¾ cup chicken broth
1½ cups red currant jelly
¼ cup butter, divided
⅔ cup orange juice
1 tablespoon plus 1 teaspoon
  cornstarch
3 (16 ounce) cans pitted dark
  sweet Bing cherries, drained
  and ½ cup juice reserved

Combine wine, peel, cloves, nutmeg, all-spice and thyme in saucepan. Simmer until ½ of liquid is evaporated. Add broth, jelly and 1 tablespoon butter. Stir until jelly and butter is melted. Add orange juice and 3 tablespoons butter. Bring to a boil. Dissolve cornstarch in reserved cherry juice and add to wine mixture. Reduce heat to medium and cook, stirring constantly, until thickened. Remove from heat. Add cherries. Sauce can be stored in refrigerator for 2 days or frozen. Colorful and delicious, sauce can be served over Rock Cornish game hens, chicken breasts or duck. Makes 10 cups.

Mildred Bailey

BORDELAISE SAUCE

3 tablespoons butter
3 tablespoons all-purpose flour
1½ cups beef broth
1 cup dry red wine
¼ cup minced onion
1 teaspoon thyme
1 tablespoon brandy
1 tablespoon lemon juice
salt and black pepper to taste
1 tablespoon chopped parsley

Melt butter in heavy 1-quart saucepan over low heat. Stir in flour and cook for several minutes until well blended. Gradually add broth, cooking and stirring until sauce is thickened. Remove from heat and set aside. In separate 1-quart saucepan, combine wine, onion and thyme. Cook over medium heat until liquid is evaporated to ⅓ cup. Strain wine liquid into broth liquid. Add brandy, lemon juice, salt and black pepper. Simmer for 4 to 5 minutes. Stir in parsley. Sauce can be stored in refrigerator for 2 to 3 days. It is good over broiled steak.

Evie Posey

DELIGHTFUL WHITE RÉMOULADE SAUCE

1 cup chopped celery
1 cup chopped parsley
5 cloves minced garlic
4 cups mayonnaise
4 cups Creole mustard
4 cups horseradish

Chop vegetables with knife; do not use food processor. Combine vegetables with mayonnaise, mustard and horseradish. Chill for at least 24 hours, stirring 3 or 4 times. Serve with boiled shrimp or crawfish tails or fried shrimp or crawfish tails. Makes 3½ quarts.

Sharon Gahagan

LEMON-CHABLIS FISH SAUCE

2 lemons
1 tablespoon cornstarch
½ teaspoon salt
1 cup Chablis wine
1½ tablespoons butter

Remove peel from 1 lemon; thinly slice lemon. Squeeze juice from second lemon and set aside. Combine cornstarch and salt. Gradually add wine, stirring to form smooth paste. Melt butter in small saucepan over low heat. Add wine paste and cook, stirring constantly, until mixture is clear and slightly thickened. Add lemon juice and slices. Heat for 2½ to 3 minutes. Remove from heat. Serve on baked, broiled or poached fish. Makes 1¼ cups.

Susan Cloutier

LAURA'S MEAT MARINADE

⅓ cup wine vinegar
⅓ cup red wine
⅓ cup Worcestershire sauce
¼ cup vegetable oil
3 tablespoons soy sauce
1 onion, chopped
garlic salt to taste
black pepper to taste

Combine vinegar, wine, Worcestershire sauce, oil, soy sauce, onion, garlic salt and black pepper, mixing well. Pour marinade over pork tenderloin, beef tenderloin or any roast or steak. Let stand for 24 hours. Drain marinade before cooking meat on grill or roasting in oven. Makes 1½ cups.

Laura Gresham

SOUR CREAM HOLLANDAISE SAUCE

2 egg yolks
3 tablespoons lemon juice
½ cup butter, divided
1 cup sour cream

Combine egg yolks and lemon juice in small saucepan. Stir briskly with wooden spoon. Add ¼ cup butter. Heat, stirring frequently, over low heat until butter is melted. Add remaining butter, stirring briskly until butter is melted and sauce is thickened. Butter should be melted slowly to allow egg yolks adequate time to cook without curdling. Remove from heat. Gradually add sour cream, stirring constantly. Sauce can be stored in refrigerator for several days. It can be served hot or at room temperature. Makes about 2 cups.

Linda Burke

MUSHROOM SAUCE FOR BILL

½ pound fresh mushrooms,
** sliced**
½ cup butter
½ cup chopped green onions
2 cloves garlic, minced
3 tablespoons all-purpose flour
1 cup half and half
1 tablespoon tarragon
salt and black pepper to taste

Sauté mushrooms in butter in 1-quart saucepan over low heat for 10 minutes. Stir in green onions, garlic and flour. Gradually add half and half and continue to cook. Season with tarragon, salt and black pepper. Cook until sauce is thickened. Makes 2 to 2¼ cups.

Shelley West

BOURBONNAISE SAUCE

2 cups sugar
¼ cup butter
½ cup whipping cream
½ to 1 cup bourbon

Place heavy 1-quart skillet over medium heat. When palm of hand held over skillet can sense heat through skillet bottom, pour sugar into skillet and stir with wooden spoon. Continue stirring as sugar melts, becoming a golden syrup. Remove from heat and place on heatproof surface. Stir butter into melted sugar. When butter is completely melted, gradually add whipping cream, stirring constantly. Stir bourbon into sauce. Let stand until cool, pour into 1-quart jar, cover and chill to consistency of caramel sauce. Sauce is good over fresh and canned fruits and is especially good over strawberries and ice cream. Makes 3 cups.

Susan Cloutier

CREAMY ORANGE FRUIT SAUCE

1 (8 ounce) package cream
  cheese, softened
⅓ cup sugar
1 teaspoon vanilla
2 tablespoons grated orange
  peel
¼ cup orange juice

Combine cream cheese and sugar, beating until smooth. Add vanilla and orange peel, beating well. Gradually add orange juice, beating until smooth; add additional orange juice if sauce is too thick. Serve over fresh fruit. Makes about 1½ cups.

Sharon Gahagan

FRESH HERB FLAVORED BUTTER

1 cup butter, softened
2 tablespoons finely chopped
  basil
2 tablespoons finely chopped
  chives
2 tablespoons finely chopped
  parsley
garlic powder to taste
white pepper to taste

Whip butter with fork. Mixing after each herb is added, blend in basil, chives and parsley. Season with garlic powder and white pepper, mixing well. Chill for at least 24 hours to blend flavors. Lemon basil can be substituted for basil. Makes 1 cup.

Sharon Gahagan

TOMATO SALSA

4 ripe tomatoes, diced
1 medium-sized onion, minced
4 or fewer small jalapeño
  peppers, finely chopped
¼ cup vinegar
½ teaspoon salt

Combine tomatoes, onion, jalapeño peppers, vinegar and salt, mixing well. Chill before serving. Salsa can be stored in refrigerator for several days. Makes about 1½ cups.

Elouise DeBlieux

NANNY'S PICKLED OKRA

3 quarts okra
6 cloves garlic
6 hot peppers
2 tablespoons dill seed
4 cups vinegar
1 cup water
½ cup salt

Prepare okra by trimming part of stem, leaving part of stem in place. Place 1 clove garlic and 1 hot pepper in each of 6 hot sterilized pint canning jars. Pack whole okra firmly in jars and add 1 teaspoon dill seed to each jar. Combine vinegar, water and salt in saucepan. Bring to a boil, reduce heat and simmer for 5 minutes. Pour solution over okra in jars and seal according to jar manufacturer's directions. Turn jars upside down overnight. Let stand 10 days before using. Makes 6 pints.

Imogene Kelly

CINNAMON CUCUMBER PICKLES

6 quarts large cucumbers,
  peeled, seeds removed and
  sliced
1 cup pickling lime
1 gallon water
3 cups vinegar, divided
1 tablespoon alum
1 (1 ounce) bottle red food
  coloring
7½ cups sugar
1 (1 ounce) package cinnamon
  sticks
½ cup red hot cinnamon candy

Preparation occurs over a 4-day period. First Day: Place cucumber slices in 8-quart container. Combine pickling lime and 1 gallon water. Pour over cucumbers, covering all slices; if insufficient, mix and add additional lime and water solution. Soak for at least 12 hours, stirring occasionally. Second Day: Drain lime solution and thoroughly rinse cucumber slices to remove lime. Place in 8-quart stock pot. Add water to cover and stir in 1 cup vinegar, alum and food coloring. Bring to a boil, reduce heat and simmer, uncovered, for 2 hours. Let stand until cool, cover and set aside. Third Day: Drain water solution. Combine 2 cups vinegar, 3 cups water, sugar, cinnamon sticks and cinnamon candy. Pour over cucumber slices. Bring to a boil. Remove from heat and set aside. Fourth Day: Bring to a boil. Pack pickles and juice in hot sterilized canning jars and seal according to jar manufacturer's directions.

Imogene Kelly

SQUASH PICKLES

8 cups sliced squash
2 cups chopped onion
1 cup chopped green bell
  pepper
1 tablespoon salt
2 cups cider vinegar
3½ cups sugar
1 teaspoon mustard seed
1 teaspoon celery seed

Combine squash, onion and bell pepper. Sprinkle salt over vegetables. Let stand for 1 hour. Combine vinegar, sugar, mustard seed and celery seed in 4-quart saucepan. Bring to a boil. Add vegetables, bring to a boil and cook for 1 minute. Remove from heat. Spoon vegetables and pickling solution into hot sterilized canning jars and seal according to jar manufacturer's directions. Let stand to cool to room temperature. Makes 6 pints.

Kathryn Smith

PICKLED BOILED EGGS

12 hard-cooked eggs, peeled
2 cups malt vinegar
2 tablespoons sugar
1 teaspoon salt
2 teaspoons ginger
2 teaspoons pickling spice
12 peppercorns
water
2 medium-sized onions, sliced
3 cloves garlic, crushed
½ teaspoon dillweed

Place eggs in 1-gallon crock or jar and set aside. Combine vinegar, sugar, salt, ginger, pickling spice and peppercorns in saucepan. Bring to a boil, reduce heat and simmer for 5 minutes. Add hot liquid and enough water to completely cover eggs. Add onion, garlic and dillweed. Seal with air-tight lid. Chill for several days before serving. Eggs can be stored in refrigerator for up to 1 month. Makes 12.

Frances Conine

GREEN PEPPER JELLY

Microwave:
¼ cup finely chopped seeded
  jalapeño peppers
¾ cup finely chopped green bell
  pepper
6½ cups sugar
1½ cups cider vinegar
¾ cup liquid fruit pectin
2 or 3 drops green food coloring

Combine jalapeño pepper and bell pepper with own juices, sugar, vinegar, pectin and food coloring in microwave-safe 5-quart casserole; peppers and vinegar can be pureed. Cook, covered, at high setting (100 percent) for 10 to 12 minutes, stirring twice during cooking time. Stir well. Pour into hot sterilized jars. Seal with paraffin and lids. Serve with cream cheese and crackers or as accompaniment to lamb, fowl, pork or wild game. Makes 3 pints.

Ursula Williams

CRANAPPLE COMPOTE

Slow Cooker:
3 medium-sized cooking apples,
  peeled, cored and quartered
1 (16 ounce) can whole
  cranberry sauce
⅓ cup light corn syrup
⅛ teaspoon salt
1 (2 inch) cinnamon stick

Place apples in slow cooker. Combine cranberry sauce, syrup, salt and cinnamon stick, mixing well. Pour sauce over apples. Cook, covered, at low setting for 2½ hours or until apples are tender, stirring after 1 hour. Serve as accompaniment to meat or as dessert topping. Makes 3 cups.

Rhonda Guidroz

Breads

BREAD MAKERS' HONEY BUTTERMILK BREAD

1½ teaspoons dry active yeast
2 cups bread flour
1 teaspoon salt
2 tablespoons honey
½ cup buttermilk, at room
    temperature
2 teaspoons butter, at room
    temperature
⅓ cup warm water

In order listed, place ingredients in bread machine: yeast, flour, salt, honey, buttermilk, butter and water. Select breadmaking mode on machine and start. Serves: 6 to 8.

Juanita Murphy

BUTTERMILK ROLLS

1 cup buttermilk
1 package dry active yeast
3 tablespoons vegetable oil
1 tablespoon sugar
½ teaspoon soda
1 teaspoon salt
2 to 2½ cups all-purpose flour
butter, melted

Heat buttermilk to lukewarm (105 to 115 degrees). Add yeast, oil, sugar, soda and salt, stirring until yeast is dissolved. Add enough flour to form soft dough. Stir well, place on lightly floured surface and cut or pinch dough into rolls. Place in greased pan and brush with melted butter. Let rise for about 1 hour. Bake at 375 degrees for 12 to 15 minutes. Makes 16 to 20.

Elouise DeBlieux

POTATO REFRIGERATOR ROLLS

1 cup mashed potatoes
1 cup milk, scalded
¼ cup sugar
½ cup vegetable shortening
2 eggs, lightly beaten
1½ tablespoons salt
1 package dry active yeast
½ cup lukewarm (105 to 115
  degrees) water
5 to 6 cups all-purpose flour
butter, melted

Combine potatoes and milk, mixing well. Add sugar, shortening, eggs and salt. Let stand until lukewarm. Dissolve yeast in lukewarm water. Add yeast liquid to potato mixture. Add flour to form soft dough. Let rise until doubled in bulk, punch down and place in greased bowl, turning to coat. Chill until ready to use. Shape pieces of dough into rolls, dip in melted butter and place on baking sheet or in muffin pans. Let rise for about 2 hours. Bake at 400 degrees for about 20 minutes. Makes 20.

Rosemary Baker

SAVORY PULL-APART ROLLS

¼ cup (1 ounce) grated
  Parmesan cheese
3 tablespoons sesame seed
½ teaspoon dried basil
1 (30 ounce) package frozen
  unbaked yeast rolls
¼ cup margarine, melted
2 tablespoons bacon bits
  (optional)

Combine Parmesan cheese, sesame seed and basil. Add ⅓ of mixture to greased 10-inch fluted tube pan, turning to coat sides and bottom. Place ½ of rolls in pan, drizzle with ½ of melted margarine and sprinkle with ½ of remaining cheese mixture; repeat layers. Chill, covered with aluminum foil, for 12 to 24 hours. Let stand at room temperature 30 minutes before baking. Bake, uncovered, at 350 degrees for 20 minutes. Cover with foil and bake additional 10 to 15 minutes or until golden brown. Invert on platter and serve warm. Serves: 12.

Karen Townsend

MRS. WILLIAMS' ROLLS

2 cakes active yeast
½ cup lukewarm (105 to 115
  degrees) water
½ cup sugar
1½ teaspoons salt
1 egg, lightly beaten
¼ cup plus 1 tablespoon
  vegetable shortening
1½ cups warm water
7 cups all-purpose flour

Dissolve yeast in lukewarm water in mixing bowl. Add sugar and blend well. Stir in salt, egg and shortening, blending until smooth. Add water. Gradually add flour. Let rise until doubled in bulk. Punch down, shape rolls and place in baking pan. Let rise until doubled in bulk. Bake at 425 degrees for 10 to 12 minutes. Makes 36.

Elaine Sandifer

WHOLE WHEAT ROLLS

1 cup milk
1 tablespoon honey
2 tablespoons brown sugar
1 teaspoon salt
¼ cup margarine, softened
2 tablespoons or 4 envelopes
  dry active yeast
½ cup lukewarm (105 to 115
  degrees) water
2¼ cups all-purpose flour
2¼ cups whole wheat flour
margarine, melted

Scald milk. Stir in honey, brown sugar, salt and softened margarine. Dissolve yeast in lukewarm water, then add to milk liquid. Add 1 cup all-purpose flour and 1 cup whole wheat flour, beating to blend. Add remaining flour and knead for 8 to 10 minutes. Let rise until doubled in bulk. Punch down, shape into rolls, brush with melted margarine and place in baking pan. Let rise until doubled in bulk. Bake at 400 degrees for 15 minutes. Makes 24.

Roberta Cassagne
Ronnell Whitehead

BEIGNETS

Creole Doughnuts:
2 tablespoons shortening
¼ cup sugar
½ teaspoon salt
½ cup boiling water
½ cup evaporated milk
½ package dry active yeast
¼ cup lukewarm (105 to 115 degrees) water
1 egg, beaten
3¾ cups cake flour
vegetable oil for deep-frying
powdered sugar

Combine shortening, sugar and salt. Pour boiling water over mixture and stir until shortening is melted. Add milk and let stand to cool to warm. Dissolve yeast in lukewarm water in mixing bowl. Add milk liquid and egg to yeast. Stir in 2 cups flour and beat until smooth. Transfer batter to greased bowl, grease top of soft dough, cover with wax paper and a cloth and chill until ready to use. Sprinkle 1¾ cups cake flour on work surface, knead dough, then roll dough to ¼-inch thickness. Do not let dough rise before frying. Cut into squares and deep-fry, a few at a time, in oil heated to 360 degrees, browning on 1 side, then turning to brown on second side. Drain on paper towel. Sprinkle with powdered sugar. Makes 30.

Rhonda Guidroz

CHEDDAR-APPLE BREAD

2½ cups all-purpose flour
¾ cup sugar
2 teaspoons baking powder
½ teaspoon salt
½ teaspoon cinnamon
2 eggs, beaten
¾ cup milk
⅓ cup margarine, melted
2 cups (8 ounces) shredded sharp Cheddar cheese
1½ cups chopped peeled apples

Combine flour, sugar, baking powder, salt and cinnamon. Combine eggs, milk and margarine. Add liquid mixture to dry ingredients, mixing well. Stir in Cheddar cheese and apples. Spoon batter into well greased and floured 9x5x3-inch loaf pan. Bake at 350 degrees for 65 to 70 minutes or until wooden pick inserted in center of loaf comes out clean. Cool in pan for 5 minutes, then invert on wire rack to cool. Makes 1 loaf.

Sheila Cooper

MR. G'S CINNAMON-SWIRL BREAD

1 cup raisins
water
1 cup milk
½ cup sugar
1 egg
½ cup margarine, melted
4 cups self-rising flour
½ cup margarine, softened
cinnamon to taste
1 cup firmly-packed brown
   sugar
1 cup powdered sugar
2 tablespoons water
sliced almonds (optional)

Soak raisins in water until plump. Drain well. Combine milk, sugar, egg and melted margarine in large bowl, mixing well. Gradually add flour to form soft dough. Place on lightly floured surface and knead until smooth and elastic. Place on lightly floured surface and roll to 14x12-inch rectangle. Spread softened margarine on dough. Sprinkle with cinnamon, brown sugar and raisins. Roll up, jelly roll fashion. Using sharp knife, cut roll into 1-inch slices. Place slices on foil-covered pizza pan, arranging to slightly overlap in ring shape. Bake at 375 degrees for 15 to 20 minutes or until top is browned. Blend powdered sugar and water. Spread on top of bread and garnish with almonds. Serves: 8 to 12.

Fred Gianforte

BREAKFAST PASTRY

2 (8 ounce) packages
   refrigerated crescent roll
   dough
2 (8 ounce) packages cream
   cheese, softened
½ cup sugar
1 teaspoon vanilla
2 eggs, separated

Unroll 1 package dough and place rectangles to fit bottom of 13x9x2-inch baking pan. Combine cream cheese, sugar, vanilla and 2 eggs yolks, blending well. Spread mixture on dough in pan. Unroll second package of dough and place rectangles on filling layer. Lightly beat egg whites and brush top of dough with egg white. Bake at 350 degrees for 25 to 30 minutes. Recipe can be halved. Serves: 6 to 8.

Marion Salter

SAUSAGE BREAD

1 (3 loaf) package frozen bread
  dough
2 pounds bulk pork sausage
1 short stick pepperoni, thinly
  sliced
1 small onion, chopped
½ medium-sized green bell
  pepper, chopped
2 to 3 cups (8 to 12 ounces)
  grated Cheddar cheese
2 to 3 cups (8 to 12 ounces)
  grated mozzarella cheese
2 to 3 cups (8 to 12 ounces)
  grated Monterey Jack cheese
black olives, sliced (optional)

Thaw bread; do not let rise. Cook sausage, stirring to crumble, until well done. Drain excess grease and set aside. Heat pepperoni in skillet and add to sausage. Sauté onion and bell pepper in meat drippings until softened. Add to meat mixture. On lightly floured surface, roll each loaf of dough to 18x15-inch oval. Divide meat mixture and cheeses into 3 portions. On 1 side of each dough oval, sprinkle meat, then cheese. Top with olives. Fold dough over filling and press to seal edges. Place on baking sheet. Bake at 350 degrees until golden brown. Loaves can be frozen. Makes 3 large loaves, each serving 4 to 6.

Debbie Hardy

CRANBERRY BREAD

1 orange
water
2 cups all-purpose flour
1 cup sugar
½ teaspoon baking powder
2 tablespoons vegetable
  shortening
1 egg, well beaten
1 cup chopped English walnuts
  or pecans
1 cup chopped cranberries

Squeeze juice from orange, add water to measure ¾ cup and pour into saucepan. Bring to a boil. Grate orange peel and add to juice. Combine flour, sugar and baking powder. Cut shortening into dry ingredients. Using electric mixer, blend in juice mixture. Add egg and mix well. Stir in walnuts or pecans and cranberries. Pour batter into greased 9x5x3-inch loaf pan. Bake at 350 degrees for 1 hour. Doubled recipe will make 7 (6x3x2-inch) loaves; bake small loaves for 50 minutes. Makes 1 loaf.

Glennelle Brown

STRAWBERRY BREAD AND GLAZE

3 cups all-purpose flour
2 cups sugar
1 teaspoon baking soda
1 teaspoon salt
1 teaspoon cinnamon
4 eggs, beaten
1¼ cups vegetable oil
1¼ cups chopped pecans
2 (10 ounce) packages frozen
   strawberries, thawed, drained
   and juice reserved

Glaze:
1 cup powdered sugar
1 tablespoon lemon juice

Combine flour, sugar, baking soda, salt and cinnamon. Make a well in center of dry ingredients. Add egg and oil, mixing thoroughly. Stir in pecans, strawberries and 1 tablespoon strawberry juice. Pour batter into 2 greased and floured 9x5x3-inch loaf pans. Bake at 350 degrees or 1 hour or until wooden pick inserted in center of loaves comes out clean; if using smaller pans, bake for 40 minutes. Prepare glazing by mixing powdered sugar, lemon juice and remaining strawberry juice. Pour glaze over hot loaves. Makes 2 loaves.

Marion Salter

ZUCCHINI BREAD

3 eggs, beaten
2 cups sugar
1 cup vegetable oil
2 teaspoons vanilla
2 cups peeled, grated zucchini
   squash
3 cups all-purpose flour
1 teaspoon baking powder
1 teaspoon salt
1 teaspoon cinnamon
1 cup chopped nuts (optional)

Combine eggs, sugar, oil and vanilla, beating until blended. Stir in zucchini. Sift flour, baking powder, salt and cinnamon together. Add dry ingredients to zucchini mixture, mixing well. Stir in nuts. Spread batter in 2 greased and floured 9x5x3-inch loaf pans. Bake at 350 degrees for 1 hour or until wooden pick inserted at center of loaves comes out clean. Makes 2 loaves.

Debbie Murphy

MAMA'S FRENCH TOAST

2 eggs, well beaten
¼ cup whipping cream or milk
½ cup sugar
1 teaspoon vanilla
6 to 8 slices bread
¼ cup margarine, divided
cinnamon to taste

Combine eggs, cream or milk, sugar and vanilla, blending to dissolve sugar. Dip bread slices in egg mixture. Melt 2 tablespoons margarine in skillet. Fry bread slices in margarine until lightly browned. Fry 1 side, then turn. While frying second side, sprinkle upper side generously with cinnamon. Turn and while frying first side again for 30 seconds or until cinnamon gets crusty, sprinkle upper side generously with cinnamon. Turn again and fry second side for 30 seconds. Serves: 4.

Lynn Pierson

RANCH DRESSING CHEESE PUFFS

2 cups (8 ounces) shredded
** sharp Cheddar cheese**
¾ cup mayonnaise
1 tablespoon ranch style salad
** dressing**
10 (1-inch) slices French bread

Combine Cheddar cheese, mayonnaise and salad dressing, blending well. Spread mixture on bread slices and place on baking sheet. Broil for 3 to 4 minutes or until golden brown and puffed. Serves: 4 or 5.

Bridget Bella
Patti Wingo

QUICK BISCUITS

2 cups self-rising flour
¼ cup mayonnaise
1 cup milk

Combine flour, mayonnaise and milk, blending well. Drop dough by tablespoonful into ungreased 9-inch round baking pan. Bake at 450 degrees for 18 to 20 minutes. Makes 12.

Charlotte Cross

CHEESE BISCUITS

3 cups buttermilk biscuit
  baking mix
½ teaspoon baking powder
dash of salt
¾ cup plus 2 tablespoons milk
2 tablespoons vegetable oil
1½ cups (6 ounces) grated
  sharp Cheddar cheese
½ teaspoon red pepper

Combine baking mix, baking powder and salt. Add milk and oil, stirring just until dry ingredients are moistened. Fold Cheddar cheese and red pepper into dough. On lightly floured surface, roll dough to ½-inch thickness. Cut with biscuit cutter and place on ungreased baking sheet. Bake at 425 degrees for 6 to 7 minutes. Serves: 6.

Jo Ann Gardner
Annette Hill

BUTTERMILK HUSH PUPPIES

2 cups cornmeal
1 tablespoon all-purpose flour
1 teaspoon baking soda
1 teaspoon salt
1 egg
1½ cups buttermilk
¼ cup plus 2 tablespoons
  chopped onion
¼ cup plus 2 tablespoons
  chopped green bell pepper
2 cups (8 ounces) grated sharp
  Cheddar cheese
vegetable oil for deep-frying

Combine cornmeal, flour, baking soda and salt. Add egg, buttermilk, onion, bell pepper and cheese, mixing well. Drop batter by teaspoonful into oil and deep-fry until golden brown. Makes 24.

Lisa Bostick

DOWN SOUTH HUSH PUPPIES

1 cup yellow cornmeal
1 cup all-purpose flour
1½ teaspoons baking powder
½ to 1 tablespoon sugar
salt to taste
garlic powder to taste
1 bunch chopped green onions
2 small jalapeño peppers,
  chopped
1 (8 ounce) can cream-style
  corn
½ cup milk
vegetable oil for deep-frying

Combine cornmeal, flour, baking powder, sugar, salt and garlic powder. Add green onions, jalapeño peppers and corn, mixing well. Add milk, a small amount at a time, until batter is thick consistency. Drop batter by teaspoonful into oil and deep-fry until golden brown. Serves: 8 to 10.

Debbie Maynard

BROCCOLI CORNBREAD

2 (8½ ounce) packages
  cornbread mix
4 eggs
1 (12 ounce) carton cottage
  cheese
1 (10 ounce) package frozen
  chopped broccoli, cooked and
  drained, or 2 cups chopped
  cooked fresh broccoli
1 cup margarine, melted

Combine cornbread mix, eggs, cottage cheese, broccoli and margarine, stirring until blended. Pour batter into greased 13x9x2-inch baking pan. Bake at 350 degrees for 30 minutes or until golden brown. Serves: 12 to 16.

Cindy Smith

JALAPEÑO CORNBREAD

1½ cups cornmeal
2 eggs
1 tablespoon baking powder
1 (8 ounce) can cream-style
  corn
1 teaspoon salt
1 cup buttermilk
2 jalapeño peppers, chopped
½ cup vegetable oil
1¼ cups (5 ounces) grated
  sharp cheese

Combine ingredients in order listed: cornmeal, eggs, baking powder, corn, salt, buttermilk, peppers, oil and cheese, mixing well. Pour batter into hot greased skillet or muffin pan. Bake at 350 degrees for 35 to 40 minutes. Serves: 9 to 12.

Debbie Maynard

CARLISLE CORN MUFFINS

1 cup sifted all-purpose flour
¼ cup sugar
1 tablespoon salt
¾ cup cornmeal
1 cup milk
¼ cup vegetable oil
1 egg, well beaten
¾ cup (3 ounces) shredded
  sharp cheese
2 tablespoons pepper jelly

Sift flour, sugar and salt together. Stir in cornmeal. Add milk, oil, egg and cheese, mixing just until dry ingredients are moistened. Spoon batter into well greased muffin pans, filling cups ½ full. Place about ½ teaspoon jelly on top of batter in each cup and add batter. Bake at 425 degrees for 10 to 15 minutes. Makes 12.

Sarah Katherine Ahrens

APPLESAUCE-BRAN MUFFINS

1 (15 ounce) package raisin
  bran cereal
5 cups flour
3 cups sugar
2 teaspoons salt
1 tablespoon plus 2 teaspoons
  cinnamon
4 eggs, beaten
1 cup vegetable oil
4 cups buttermilk
1 (15 ounce) can regular
  applesauce

Combine cereal, flour, sugar, salt and cinnamon in very large bowl. Add eggs, oil and buttermilk, mixing well. Fold applesauce into batter. Store in refrigerator overnight before using. Do not stir; spoon batter into greased muffin pans. Bake at 400 degrees for 15 to 20 minutes. Batter can be stored in refrigerator for 1 week. Baked muffins can be frozen. Makes 48 to 60.

Marian Keator

BRAN MUFFINS

2 cups all-purpose flour
1½ cups bran cereal
2 tablespoons sugar
1¼ teaspoons baking powder
¼ teaspoon salt
2 cups buttermilk
1 egg, beaten
½ cup molasses or cane syrup
2 to 4 tablespoons butter,
  melted
½ cup pecans
½ cup raisins

Combine flour, cereal, sugar, baking powder and salt. Combine buttermilk, egg, molasses or syrup and melted butter; beating well. Add liquid mixture to dry ingredients, mixing with few strokes just until flour is moistened. Fold pecans and raisins into batter. Spoon batter into greased muffin pans. Bake at 350 degrees for about 25 minutes. Makes 20.

Marion Salter

BLUEBERRY MUFFINS

1 cup butter, softened
1½ cups sugar
3 eggs
3 cups all-purpose flour
1 tablespoon baking powder
1 teaspoon salt
1 cup milk
1½ cups fresh or canned
    blueberries or wild
    huckleberries

Cream butter and sugar together until smooth. Add eggs, 1 at a time, beating well after each addition. Sift flour, baking powder and salt together. Alternately add dry ingredients and milk to creamed mixture, beating after each addition. Fold blueberries or huckleberries into batter. Spoon batter into greased muffin pans. Bake at 375 degrees for 15 minutes or until golden brown. Makes 9 to 12.

Rosemary Baker

JALAPEÑO CHEESE MUFFINS

2 cups all-purpose flour
1 teaspoon sugar
1 tablespoon baking powder
½ teaspoon salt
½ cup unsalted butter, very
    cold
¾ cup half and half
1 cup (4 ounces) grated
    Monterey Jack cheese with
    jalapeño peppers

Sift flour, sugar, baking powder and salt together. Cut butter into small pieces. Using pastry blender, cut butter into dry ingredients until consistency of coarse crumbs. Add half and half, stirring well. Add cheese and mix well. Dust hands with flour, then shape dough into small rolls to fit in miniature muffin pans. Prepare pans with butter flavored vegetable cooking spray. Place rolls in pans. Bake at 400 degrees for 8 to 10 minutes or until puffed and golden. Cool on wire rack. Makes 24.

Tanya Conlay

OAT MUFFINS

2 cups oat flake cereal, divided
1 cup all-purpose flour
¼ cup whole wheat flour
¼ cup firmly-packed brown
  sugar
1 tablespoon baking powder
dash of salt
¼ teaspoon cinnamon
2 egg whites, lightly beaten
1 cup skim milk
3 tablespoons vegetable oil
cinnamon

Combine 1¾ cups cereal, flour, wheat flour, brown sugar, baking powder, salt and cinnamon. In separate bowl, blend egg whites, milk and oil. Add liquid mixture to dry ingredients, mixing just to moisten flour; do not overmix. Spoon batter into greased muffin pans, filling cups about ⅔ full. Combine ¼ cup cereal and cinnamon to taste. Sprinkle on batter in cups. Bake at 400 degrees for 15 minutes. Muffins can be frozen. Makes 12.

Gayle Henry

STRAWBERRY MUFFINS WITH ORANGE BUTTER GLAZE

1½ cups frozen strawberries,
  thawed
1 egg, lightly beaten
⅓ cup milk
2 tablespoons vegetable oil
2 cups biscuit baking mix
⅓ cup sugar
¼ teaspoon grated orange peel

Glaze:
¼ cup butter, melted
grated peel of 1 orange
2 to 3 teaspoons sugar

Drain strawberries, reserving juice. Mash berries and set aside. Combine egg, milk, oil, ⅓ cup strawberry juice, baking mix, sugar and peel, mixing well. Stir in strawberries. Spoon batter into greased muffin pans, filling cups ⅔ full. Bake at 350 degrees for 13 to 15 minutes. Prepare glaze by combining melted butter, peel and sugar blending until smooth. Spoon glaze on hot muffins. Makes 12.

Juanita Murphy

Vegetables

COWPOKE BEANS

1 pound ground beef
2 medium-sized onions,
  chopped
1 tablespoon minced garlic
¼ cup butter
2 (16 ounce) cans pork and
  beans
3 (15 ounce) cans ranch style
  beans
½ cup firmly-packed brown
  sugar
¼ cup maple syrup
¼ cup prepared mustard
1 cup ketchup

Cook beef, stirring to crumble, until browned. Drain excess grease and set aside. Sauté onion and garlic in butter until softened. Add beef, pork and beans, ranch style beans, brown sugar, syrup, mustard and ketchup, mixing well. Pour mixture into 3-quart casserole. Chill overnight. Bake, uncovered, at 300 degrees for 1½ hours. Serves: 10 to 12.

Susan Cloutier

HERBED LIMA AND GREEN BEANS

1½ pounds green beans,
  trimmed
water
salt
2 (10 ounce) packages frozen
  lima beans
½ cup butter or margarine
3 tablespoons minced parsley
4 scallions, minced
½ teaspoon dillweed
4 stalks celery with leaves,
  finely chopped
1 clove garlic, minced

Cook green beans in boiling salted water for 5 minutes, drain and rinse with cold water. Cook lima beans in boiling salted water until tender, drain and rinse with cold water. Melt butter in large skillet. Add beans, stirring to coat thoroughly with butter. Add parsley, scallions, dillweed, celery and garlic. Heat for 2 to 3 minutes. Serves: 12.

Joyce Romine

GREEN BEANS PIQUANT

8 slices bacon
¼ cup red wine vinegar
2 tablespoons Worcestershire
  sauce
½ teaspoon sugar
½ teaspoon dry mustard
¼ teaspoon hot pepper sauce
¼ cup diced pimiento
2 (16 ounce) cans green beans,
  drained

Fry bacon until crisp, drain on paper towel, crumble and set aside. Retain 2 tablespoons bacon drippings in pan. Add vinegar, Worcestershire sauce, sugar, mustard, hot pepper sauce and pimiento. Stirring to blend, bring to a boil. Add green beans, mix to coat with sauce and heat thoroughly. Stir in bacon pieces. Serves: 6 to 8.

Pat Thomas

KING CABBAGE CASSEROLE

1 large head cabbage, quartered
water
1 large onion, chopped
1½ cups chopped celery
¼ cup butter
1 large green bell pepper,
  chopped
2 cloves garlic, minced
6 slices bread, crusts trimmed
½ cup milk
2 cups (8 ounces) grated
  American cheese
½ cup half and half
salt and black pepper to taste
1 cup breadcrumbs
½ cup chopped pecans
  (optional)

Parboil cabbage in water, drain and chop to fine consistency. Sauté onion and celery in butter in large skillet over medium heat until vegetables are softened. Add cabbage and cook until wilted. Stir in bell pepper and garlic. Mix bread with milk, then add to cabbage. Add American cheese and half and half, stirring until cheese is melted. Season with salt and black pepper. Pour mixture into buttered 2-quart casserole. Sprinkle with breadcrumbs and pecans. Bake at 350 degrees for 30 minutes. Serves: 6 to 8.

Shelley West

CARROTS MARSALA

1 pound carrots, sliced
  diagonally
¼ cup butter
⅔ cup dry Marsala wine
2 tablespoons chicken broth or
  water
chopped parsley for garnish

Sauté carrots in butter in large skillet for about 2 minutes or until coated with butter. Stir in wine. Cook, tightly covered, over medium low heat until liquid is reduced, adding extra broth or water if needed, and carrots are tender. Sprinkle with parsley. Serves: 6 to 8.

Pam DeBlieux

CARROT SOUFFLÉ

1 (16 ounce) can carrots,
  drained
½ cup plus 2 tablespoons
  margarine, melted
3 tablespoons all-purpose flour
1 cup sugar
1 teaspoon baking powder
¼ teaspoon salt
3 eggs
1 teaspoon vanilla extract

Using food processor, blend carrots with margarine. Combine flour, sugar, baking powder, salt, eggs and vanilla. Add to carrots and mix well. Spread carrot mixture in buttered 8x8x2-inch baking dish. Bake, uncovered, at 350 degrees for about 45 minutes. Serves: 6.

Marian Keator

CAULIFLOWER ITALIANA

1 head cauliflower, cut in
  flowerets and pieces
½ cup margarine, melted
½ cup Italian seasoned or plain
  breadcrumbs
⅓ cup (1⅓ ounces) grated
  Parmesan cheese
½ teaspoon Italian seasoning
¼ teaspoon garlic powder
parsley sprigs for garnish
paprika for garnish
chopped chives for garnish

Place cauliflower in large bowl, add margarine and toss until well coated. Combine breadcrumbs, Parmesan cheese, Italian seasoning and garlic powder in plastic bag and shake well. Add cauliflower pieces and shake to coat with breadcrumb mixture. Place cauliflower on baking sheet. Bake at 350 degrees for 20 minutes. Garnish with parsley, paprika and chives. Serves: 4 to 6.

Libby Swafford

CAULIFLOWER WITH RED PEPPER SAUCE

1 tablespoon vinegar
1 tablespoon plus 2 teaspoons
   salt, divided
4 cups water
1 (3 pound) head cauliflower,
   leaves trimmed
⅓ cup minced onion
2 large cloves garlic, crushed
¼ cup butter or margarine
1 tablespoon all-purpose flour
½ cup half and half
⅛ teaspoon ground red pepper
2 (7 ounce) jars roasted sweet
   red peppers
shredded lettuce for garnish
red pepper strips for garnish

Combine vinegar, 1 tablespoon salt and water in 5-quart Dutch oven and bring to a boil. Place cauliflower, stem down, in water. Bring to a boil, reduce, heat and simmer, covered, for 15 minutes or until cauliflower is tender. Drain in colander and keep warm. Sauté onion and garlic in butter in skillet over medium-high heat for about 3 minutes or until golden. Remove from heat. Stir in flour, blending well, and cook for 1 minute or until bubbly. Gradually add half and half. Season with salt and ground red pepper. Bring to a boil, reduce heat and simmer for 1 minute. Using food processor, puree roasted red peppers and onion mixture. Pour into skillet and bring to a boil. Place cauliflower on large platter. Spoon part of sauce over cauliflower. Garnish with lettuce and red peppers and pour remaining sauce in bowl to pass. Consider serving at Christmas dinner as the color is spectacular. Serves: 6 to 8.

Marti Vienne

LENA LEIGH'S CHILI CORN

1 (16 ounce) can cream-style
   corn
1 cup milk
2 eggs, beaten
1 cup (4 ounces) grated sharp
   Cheddar cheese
½ cup cornmeal
2 tablespoons vegetable oil
1 (4 ounce) can green chilies,
   mashed or minced
salt and black pepper to taste

Combine corn, milk, eggs, Cheddar cheese, cornmeal, oil, chilies, salt and black pepper. Pour into 2-quart casserole. Bake at 350 degrees for 45 minutes to 1 hour or until firm and browned. Serves: 8.

Sarah Luster

EGGPLANT CASSEROLE

1 (7 ounce) package Mexican
  cornbread mix
1 large or 2 small eggplants,
  peeled and cubed
water
1 large onion, chopped
1 green bell pepper, chopped
¼ cup plus 2 tablespoons
  margarine
1 (10 ounce) can tomatoes with
  green chilies
1½ cups (6 ounces) grated
  cheese
2 eggs, beaten

Prepare cornbread according to package directions. Let stand until cool, then crumble. Reserve ½ cup crumbs for topping. Parboil eggplant in small amount of water until tender. Drain and set aside. Sauté onion and bell pepper in margarine in large skillet. Stir in tomatoes, eggplant, cornbread crumbs, 1 cup cheese and eggs. Pour mixture into greased 2-quart casserole. Sprinkle with reserved cornbread and ½ cup cheese. Bake at 350 degrees for 30 to 35 minutes or until hot and bubbly. Serves: 8 to 10.

Karen Townsend

BAKED EGGPLANT

1 large eggplant, peeled and cut
  in ½-inch slices
vegetable oil
¾ cup chopped onion
2 cloves garlic, minced
1 (14½ ounce) can whole
  tomatoes, drained and
  crushed
¾ cup whipped cream
⅓ cup ricotta cheese
1 egg, beaten
⅛ teaspoon salt
⅛ teaspoon black pepper
2 tablespoons basil
¼ cup (1 ounce) grated
  Parmesan cheese

Sauté eggplant, a few slices at a time, in 3 tablespoons oil in large skillet until each begins to soften. Add oil as needed to cover bottom of skillet. Drain slices on paper towel. Sauté onion and garlic in 1 tablespoon oil until softened. Add tomatoes and simmer for 5 minutes or until liquid is evaporated. Remove from heat. Combine cream, ricotta cheese, egg, salt, black pepper, basil and 2 tablespoons Parmesan cheese, mixing well. In 8x8x2-inch baking dish, layer ½ of eggplant, ½ of tomato sauce and repeat layers. Spoon cheese mixture on layer of sauce and sprinkle with 2 tablespoons Parmesan cheese. Bake at 375 degrees for 30 to 40 minutes. Serves: 6 to 8.

Cathy Seymour

MUSHROOM CASSEROLE

1½ pounds fresh mushrooms,
sliced
½ cup margarine or butter
1 onion, minced
2 tablespoons all-purpose flour
1 cup sour cream
¼ teaspoon chopped parsley
salt and black pepper to taste
¼ cup seasoned breadcrumbs

Sauté mushrooms in margarine or butter in skillet over medium heat until lightly browned. Add onion and sauté until onion is translucent. Stir in flour and cook over low heat, stirring constantly, until blended. Add sour cream, parsley, salt and black pepper. Cook until thickened. Pour mixture into buttered 1½-quart casserole. Sprinkle breadcrumbs over mushroom mixture and dot with butter. Bake at 350 degrees for about 35 minutes or until firm and lightly browned. Serves: 6.

Marilyn Williams

SCALLOPED MUSHROOM ALMONDINE

3 pounds small fresh
mushrooms
⅓ cup butter or margarine
2 cups half and half
¼ cup all-purpose flour
2 tablespoons water
⅓ cup sliced almonds, toasted
salt and black pepper to taste
3 tablespoons chopped parsley
paprika for garnish

Cook mushrooms in butter or margarine for about 5 minutes; do not brown. Add half and half and bring to a boil. Blend flour with water and add to mushroom mixture. Simmer for a few minutes. Stir in almonds and season with salt and black pepper. Pour mixture into 2-quart casserole. Bake at 350 degrees for 15 to 20 minutes. Sprinkle with parsley and paprika before serving. Serves: 8.

Betty Ledet

ONION SURPRISE CASSEROLE

3 medium 1015 Texas or
   Vidalia onions, chopped
¼ cup plus 2 tablespoons
   butter, divided
2 cups (8 ounces) grated Swiss
   cheese, divided
1 cup crushed saltine crackers,
   divided
2 eggs
¾ cup half and half
½ to ¾ teaspoon salt
½ teaspoon black pepper

Sauté onion in ¼ cup butter in large skillet until onions are softened but not brown. Place ½ of onions in 9x9x2-inch baking dish or deep dish 10-inch pie pan. Sprinkle 1 cup Swiss cheese and ½ cup cracker crumbs over onions. Repeat layers. Combine eggs, half and half, salt and black pepper, beating to blend thoroughly. Pour over layered ingredients. Melt 2 tablespoons butter in skillet and stir in ½ cup cracker crumbs; sauté until lightly browned. Sprinkle crumbs over onions. Bake at 350 degrees for about 25 minutes. Serves: 6 to 8.

Dot Townsend

BAKED ONIONS

4 large yellow onions
½ cup butter or margarine
Tony Chachere's unsalted
   Creole seasoning to taste

Slice top and bottom from each onion, then cut top in criss-cross pattern, leaving bottom ¼ intact. Stuff each onion with 2 tablespoons butter and sprinkle with seasoning to taste. Place onions in casserole prepared with vegetable cooking spray. Bake, covered with aluminum foil, at 325 degrees for 1 to 1¼ hours or until onion is translucent. Serves: 4.

Tanya Conlay

LAEL'S POTATOES

1 cup margarine, divided
2 tablespoons garlic powder, divided
2 or 3 large baking potatoes, peeled and cut in ¼-inch slices
2 large onions, thinly sliced
¼ cup (1 ounce) grated Parmesan cheese

Melt ½ cup margarine in 12x7x2-inch baking dish. Blend in 1 tablespoon garlic powder. Alternate layers of potatoes and onion in baking dish, beginning and ending with layer of potatoes. Melt ½ cup margarine, add 1 tablespoon garlic powder and pour over layered vegetables. Sprinkle with Parmesan cheese. Bake at 350 degrees for 1 hour or until potatoes are tender. Serves: 6 to 8.

Karen Kilpatrick

POTATO DIJON

4 cups quartered small new potatoes
2 cups chicken broth
salt and freshly ground black pepper to taste
2 cups non-fat yogurt
1 tablespoon Dijon mustard
3 tablespoons chopped parsley or 2 tablespoons dried parsley

Combine potatoes and broth in large saucepan or skillet. Bring to a boil and cook, partially covered, over medium heat for about 20 minutes or until potatoes are done. Drain liquid. Season with salt and black pepper. Add yogurt, mustard and parsley, stirring to coat well. Serve immediately. Potatoes are good accompaniment to lamb. Serves: 4.

Pat Thomas

CHEESY HASH BROWN CASSEROLE

1 (32 ounce) package frozen
  hash brown potatoes, thawed
1 cup chopped onion
½ cup margarine, melted
2 cups sour cream
1 (10¾ ounce) can cream of
  chicken soup, undiluted
1 cup water
1 cup (4 ounces) grated
  Cheddar cheese
salt and black pepper to taste

Combine potatoes, onion, margarine, sour cream, soup and water, mixing well. Season with salt and black pepper. Spread potato mixture in buttered 13x9x2-inch baking dish. Sprinkle with Cheddar cheese. Bake at 350 degrees for 1 hour. Serves: 8 to 10.

Vicki Murchison

POTATO CROQUETTES

4 cups mashed potatoes
2 eggs, beaten
2 to 4 tablespoons milk
3 tablespoons chopped chives
1 teaspoon salt
¼ teaspoon white pepper
1½ cups round buttery cracker
  crumbs
½ cup butter, melted
½ teaspoon paprika

The day before serving, assemble croquettes. Combine potatoes, eggs, milk, chives, salt and black pepper, mixing well. Divide mixture in 8 portions and shape into croquettes. Roll in crumbs and place on lightly greased 15x10x1-inch jelly roll pan. Chill, covered, overnight. Combine butter and paprika. Drizzle over croquettes. Bake at 375 degrees for 20 to 25 minutes or until golden brown. Croquettes are nice alternative to stuffed potatoes and are good accompaniment for beef or ham. Serves: 8.

Joyce Romine

RED NECK POTATOES

4 pounds small new potatoes,
   quartered
water
salt and black pepper to taste
Cajun seasoned salt to taste
1 (16 ounce) bottle ranch style
   salad dressing
1 bunch green onions, chopped
4 cups (16 ounces) grated
   Cheddar cheese

Cook potatoes in water until tender. Drain and place in 13x9x2-inch baking dish. Season with salt, black pepper and Cajun seasoned salt. Pour dressing over potatoes, add green onions and mix until potatoes are well coated. Sprinkle with Cheddar cheese. Bake at 350 degrees for 15 minutes or until cheese is bubbly. Serves: 10 to 12.

Kim Johnson

SAVORY RUTABAGAS

1 large rutabaga, peeled and
   sliced
2½ cups water
1 tablespoon bacon grease
2 tablespoons butter
1 tablespoon sugar
2 tablespoons soy sauce
1 tablespoon lemon juice
1 teaspoon Worcestershire
   sauce
salt and black pepper to taste

Cook rutabaga in boiling water with bacon grease for 15 to 20 minutes or until tender. Drain well. Melt butter in small saucepan. Add sugar, soy sauce, lemon juice, Worcestershire sauce, salt and black pepper to butter. Cook, stirring until thoroughly heated; do not boil. Pour sauce over rutabaga, stirring gently. Serves: 6.

Evie Posey

CREAMED SPINACH GOURMET

2 (10 ounce) packages frozen
  chopped spinach
2 tablespoons water
¼ cup butter, divided
1 teaspoon lemon juice
1 teaspoon anisette or ouzo
  liqueur
½ teaspoon sugar
½ teaspoon salt
¼ teaspoon freshly ground
  black pepper
⅛ teaspoon nutmeg
3 tablespoons minced onion
2 tablespoons all-purpose flour
½ cup milk
½ cup chicken broth
2 hard-cooked eggs
¼ cup pine nuts, toasted

Cook spinach in water. Drain in colander, return to pan and cook to evaporate excess moisture. Add 2 tablespoons butter, stirring until melted. Stir in lemon juice, anisette or ouzo, sugar, salt, black pepper and nutmeg. In separate pan, sauté onion in 2 tablespoons butter until softened. Remove from heat, add flour and cook, stirring to blend, for about 1 minute. Remove from heat, blend in milk and broth and cook, stirring frequently, for 4 to 5 minutes or until thickened. Pour sauce over spinach and mix thoroughly. Discarding egg yolks, chop whites and sprinkle with pine nuts on spinach for garnish. Spinach dish is recommended with wild duck or lamb, as a base for eggs Florentine or as filling for omelet. Serves: 6.

Pat Thomas

SPINACH WITH SOUR CREAM AND FETA CHEESE

2 (10 ounce) packages frozen
  chopped spinach
salt and black pepper to taste
red pepper to taste
cinnamon to taste
2 tablespoons butter
½ cup plus 2 tablespoons sour
  cream
½ cup (2 ounces) crumbled wet-
  packed feta cheese

Prepare spinach according to package directions and drain well. Season with salt, black pepper, red pepper and cinnamon. Add butter, stirring until melted. Add sour cream and feta cheese, mixing well. Spread mixture in greased 8x8x2-inch baking dish. Bake at 350 degrees for 10 minutes. Serves: 6.

G.F. Thomas, Jr.

SPINACH ARTICHOKE CASSEROLE

1 (14 ounce) can artichoke
  hearts, drained, rinsed and
  cut in bite-sized pieces
4 (10 ounce) packages frozen
  chopped spinach
½ cup chopped onion
1½ cups plus 2 tablespoons
  margarine, divided
2½ (8 ounce) packages cream
  cheese, softened
¼ cup lemon juice

Topping:
¼ cup butter, melted
1½ cups commercial
  breadcrumbs

Place artichoke hearts in greased 13x9x2-inch baking pan. Prepare spinach according to package directions and drain very well. Sauté onion in 2 tablespoons margarine until softened. Add onion to spinach. Combine cream cheese, 1½ cups margarine and lemon juice in top of double boiler. Cook over hot water, whisking to blend until smooth. Add sauce to spinach, mixing well, and pour over artichokes. Prepare topping by mixing butter and breadcrumbs. Sprinkle on spinach sauce. Bake, uncovered, at 325 degrees for 25 minutes or until bubbly. Serves: 8.

Cindy Smith

ZUCCHINI CASSEROLE

1 small onion, chopped
½ cup butter or margarine,
  divided
3 to 5 carrots
6 zucchini squash, sliced
water
1 (10¾ ounce) can cream of
  chicken soup
½ cup sour cream
1 (6 ounce) package croutons
½ cup sliced almonds

Sauté onion in ¼ cup plus 2 tablespoons butter until softened. While onion cooks, parboil carrots and zucchini in water until softened. Add soup and sour cream to onion and butter. Drain zucchini and carrots and add with 1 cup croutons to sauce, mixing well. Pour mixture into 13x9x2-inch baking dish. Bake at 350 degrees for 20 to 25 minutes. While vegetables bake, melt 2 tablespoons butter. Add remaining croutons and almonds. Sprinkle on partially baked vegetables and bake for additional 10 minutes. Yellow squash can be substituted for zucchini and cream of mushroom soup can be substituted for cream of chicken soup. Serves: 6 to 8.

Marguerite Picou

GREEN AND GOLD SQUASH PIE

1 unbaked 10-inch pastry shell
2 tablespoons butter
2 medium zucchini squash,
   thinly sliced
2 medium-sized yellow squash,
   thinly sliced
½ medium-sized onion,
   chopped
2 green onions, sliced
1 large clove garlic, minced
1 medium tomato, peeled and
   chopped
1 medium-sized green bell
   pepper, finely chopped
¾ teaspoon salt
¼ teaspoon black pepper
½ teaspoon basil
3 eggs, beaten
½ cup whipping cream
¼ cup (1 ounce) grated
   Parmesan cheese

Prick pastry shell with fork tines. Bake at 450 degrees for 8 minutes or until lightly browned. Melt butter in large skillet. Add zucchini, yellow squash, onion, green onions, garlic, tomato, bell pepper, salt, pepper and basil. Sauté until vegetables are softened. Spoon vegetable mixture into pastry shell. Combine eggs and cream, mixing well. Pour over vegetables. Sprinkle with Parmesan cheese. Bake at 350 degrees for 30 minutes or until firm. Vegetable can be used as side dish or as luncheon main dish. Serves: 6 to 8.

Debbie McBride

STUFFED SQUASH

4 yellow squash
½ cup cooked bulk pork
   sausage
½ cup chopped onion
½ cup breadcrumbs
½ cup sour cream
2 tablespoons margarine
1 to 2 tablespoons chopped
   parsley

Cut squash into halves, scrape to remove pulp, then cube. Steam squash for 6 minutes. While squash cooks, cook sausage, drain and set aside. Sauté onion in sausage drippings until softened. Combine squash, sausage, onion, breadcrumbs, sour cream and margarine, mixing lightly. Spoon mixture into squash shells and sprinkle with parsley. Bake at 375 degrees for 20 to 25 minutes. Serves: 8.

Debbie Murphy

SWEET POTATOES WITH ORANGE SLICES

6 medium-sized sweet potatoes
water
1 cup sugar
½ cup water
pinch of salt
1 orange, sliced

Cook unpeeled sweet potatoes in water until tender. Drain, let stand until cool, peel and cut into serving pieces. Place in greased 13x9x2-inch baking dish. Combine sugar, water and salt in saucepan. Bring to a boil, add orange slices and cook for 5 minutes. Place orange slices on sweet potatoes and pour syrup over both. Bake at 350 degrees until thoroughly heated. Serves: 6 to 8.

Marti Vienne

SWEET POTATO CASSEROLE

3 cups mashed sweet potatoes
¼ cup margarine, melted
2½ tablespoons sweetened
  condensed milk
1 cup sugar
1 egg
½ teaspoon vanilla extract
½ teaspoon nutmeg
½ teaspoon cinnamon

Topping:
½ cup margarine, melted
½ cup firmly packed sugar
⅓ cup chopped pecans
1 cup corn flakes, crushed

Combine potatoes, margarine, milk, sugar, vanilla, nutmeg and cinnamon, mixing well. Spread mixture in 8x8x2-inch baking dish. Bake at 400 degrees for 15 minutes. While potatoes are baking, prepare topping. Combine margarine, sugar, pecans and corn flakes, mixing well. Spread mixture on potatoes and bake for additional 15 minutes. Serves: 8 to 10.

Laura Lavespere

TOMATO PIE

1 unbaked 9-inch pastry shell
2 tablespoons finely chopped
  green bell pepper
2 tablespoons minced onion
8 to 10 mushrooms, finely
  chopped
¼ cup butter, divided
2 or 3 medium tomatoes, sliced
all-purpose flour
pinch of thyme
2 eggs
1 cup half and half
1 teaspoon seasoned salt
cayenne pepper to taste
grated Parmesan cheese

Prick pastry shell with fork tines. Bake at 450 degrees for 8 minutes or until lightly browned. Sauté bell pepper, onion and mushrooms in 2 tablespoons butter in skillet until vegetables are softened. Remove from skillet. Add 2 tablespoons butter to skillet. Dredge tomato slices in flour and fry in butter, turning to brown on each side and adding more butter if needed. Remove tomatoes from skillet and arrange in bottom of pastry shell. Spread sautéed vegetables on tomatoes and sprinkle with thyme. Combine eggs, half and half, salt and cayenne pepper, beating to blend. Pour over vegetables. Sprinkle with Parmesan cheese. Bake at 375 degrees for 40 minutes. Let stand for 10 minutes before cutting and serving. Tomatoes fresh from the garden make this pie delicious. Serves: 6.

Juanita Murphy

BROILED TOMATO SLICES

1 (12 ounce) package bacon
1 large onion, chopped
2 cups (8 ounces) grated
  Gruyère cheese
¼ cup minced parsley
1 tablespoon chopped basil
6 large tomatoes (homegrown
  preferred), cut in ½-inch
  slices
salt and black pepper

Fry bacon until crisp, drain on paper towel and crumble. Retaining ¼ cup bacon drippings in skillet, sauté onion until very soft. Remove onion from drippings. Combine onion, bacon, Gruyère cheese, parsley, basil, salt and black pepper, tossing to mix thoroughly. Place tomato slices on baking sheet. Spoon small amount of mixture on each slice. Broil until cheese is melted and tomato is slightly browned. Serves: 8 to 10.

Twylla Seaman

HELLEY HOT

3 slices bacon
1 cup sliced okra
1 large onion, minced
1 cup chopped celery
6 tomatoes, finely chopped
1 green bell pepper, chopped
1 chili pepper, minced
1 (16 ounce) can cream-style
  corn

Fry bacon in large skillet until crisp, remove from skillet, drain and crumble. Sauté edges of okra in bacon drippings. Add onions and celery. Sauté until translucent; do not brown. Stir in tomatoes, bell pepper and chili pepper. Cook until tomatoes are well done. Add corn and cook for 20 minutes. Sprinkle bacon on vegetable mixture before serving. Serves: 8 to 10.

Marteel Henry

RATATOUILLE

1 large or 2 medium eggplants,
  unpeeled and thinly sliced
salt
2 medium-sized onions, thinly
  sliced
½ cup olive oil
2 cloves garlic, thinly sliced
4 or 5 small or 2 large zucchini
  squash, thinly sliced
1 red or green bell pepper,
  thinly sliced
4 or 5 tomatoes, peeled, seeds
  removed and chopped, or 1
  (29 ounce) can Italian plum
  tomatoes, drained
2 teaspoons salt
1 teaspoon freshly ground black
  pepper
1 teaspoon ground basil
½ teaspoon ground coriander

Sprinkle eggplant with salt and let stand for 1 hour. Rinse and blot with paper towel. Sauté onion in oil in large skillet until softened. Add garlic, eggplant and zucchini to onion, mixing well. Cook over medium heat for 5 minutes. Add bell pepper and cook, covered, over medium heat for 15 minutes, removing cover once or twice to stir. Add tomatoes and simmer, uncovered, for 45 minutes to 1 hour or until vegetables are well blended and liquid is reduced. Season with salt, black pepper, basil and coriander. Cook for a few additional minutes. Check seasoning. Serves: 12.

Sarah Luster

Rice
and Pasta

LINGUINE AND VEGETABLE SUPREME

½ (12 ounce) package uncooked
  linguine
2 cups grated zucchini squash
½ cup grated carrots
½ cup chopped onion
2 tablespoons butter or
  margarine
½ cup half and half
2 tablespoons dry white wine
  (optional)
½ teaspoon salt
⅛ teaspoon garlic powder
⅛ teaspoon basil
1 cup (4 ounces) shredded
  mozzarella cheese

Prepare linguine according to package directions, cooked in boiling salted water. Drain, rinse with hot water and set aside. Sauté zucchini, carrots and onion in butter or margarine in large skillet over medium heat for 3 minutes, stirring occasionally. Add cooked linguine, half and half, wine, salt, garlic powder and basil, tossing to mix thoroughly. Sprinkle with mozzarella cheese. Serves: 3 or 4.

Jane Johnson

FETTUCCINE À LA STEPHEN

1 (8 ounce) package uncooked
  fettuccine
1 (10 ounce) package frozen
  chopped broccoli
1 medium-sized onion, chopped
2 tablespoons butter
½ pound fresh mushrooms,
  sliced
4 to 6 slices ham, chopped
1 cup whipping cream
grated Parmesan cheese to taste
salt and black pepper to taste

Begin preparation of fettuccine, according to package directions, and steaming broccoli at same time. While those are cooking, sauté onion in butter until softened. Add mushrooms and ham. Drain fettuccine, returning to pan. Add broccoli, ham mixture, whipping cream, Parmesan cheese, salt and black pepper, tossing to mix. Heat thoroughly. Serves: 6.

Anna Harrington

EASY MACARONI AND SWISS CHEESE

2 cups uncooked macaroni
1 small onion, thinly sliced
½ cup sour cream
½ cup (2 ounces) grated Swiss
　　cheese

Prepare macaroni according to package directions, cooking in salted water just until tender. Drain well. In 1½-quart casserole, layer ½ each of macaroni, onion, sour cream and Swiss cheese; repeat layers. Bake at 350 degrees for 35 minutes. Serves: 6.

Shirley Smiley

ZUCCHINI NOODLE BAKE

1 (8 ounce) package wide egg
　　noodles
2 tablespoons butter or
　　margarine
2 tablespoons all-purpose flour
salt and black pepper to taste
2 cups milk
1 cup (4 ounces) grated
　　Cheddar cheese
1 cup (4 ounces) grated Swiss
　　cheese
1½ pounds zucchini squash,
　　thinly sliced
½ cup breadcrumbs
1 tablespoon butter or
　　margarine, melted

Prepare noodles according to package directions. While noodles are cooking, prepare sauce. Melt 2 tablespoons butter in saucepan. Blend in flour, salt and black pepper. Gradually add milk and cook, stirring frequently, until thickened. Add Cheddar cheese and Swiss cheese, stirring until melted. Drain noodles. Spread ½ of noodles in bottom of 10x10x2-inch baking dish. Layer ½ of zucchini on noodles and top with ½ of sauce; repeat layers. Mix breadcrumbs and 1 tablespoon melted butter or margarine, mixing well. Sprinkle crumbs on sauce layer. Bake at 350 degrees for 30 minutes. Broccoli can be substituted for zucchini. Serves: 6.

JoKay Boyle

SEBASTIAN RICE

2 green onions, chopped
several sprigs parsley, chopped
2 tablespoons butter
½ cup slivered almonds,
  toasted
2 cups cooked regular rice
¼ cup Sebastian or Zinfandel
  white wine

Sauté green onions and parsley in butter until softened. Add almonds, rice and wine. Cook over medium heat, stirring briskly to separate and fluff rice, until wine liquid is evaporated. Serves: 4.

Twylla Seaman

NAKATOSH RICE CASSEROLE

1 cup uncooked converted rice
2 bunches green onions,
  chopped
1 large green bell pepper,
  chopped
1 to 2 tablespoons vegetable oil
½ cup margarine
2 (4 ounce) cans sliced
  mushrooms, drained
2 (3 ounce) jars diced pimiento,
  drained
1 tablespoon soy sauce
1 tablespoon Worcestershire
  sauce
salt to taste
¼ teaspoon black pepper
1½ teaspoons Italian seasoning
1 teaspoon dry parsley flakes

Prepare rice according to package directions. Sauté green onions and bell pepper in oil and margarine until softened. Combine sautéed vegetables, rice, mushrooms, pimiento, soy sauce, Worcestershire sauce, salt, black pepper, Italian seasoning and parsley, mixing well. Spread mixture in 2-quart casserole. Bake at 350 degrees until hot and bubbly. Unbaked casserole can be stored in refrigerator for up to 2 days. Serves: 8.

Shirley Smiley

GREEN CHILI CHEESE RICE

3 to 4 cups uncooked rice
2 cups sour cream
salt to taste
2 cups (8 ounces) grated
 Monterey Jack cheese
4 (4 ounce) cans chopped green
 chilies
butter

Prepare rice according to package directions. Combine rice and sour cream. Season with salt. Spread ½ of rice mixture in buttered 3-quart casserole. Layer 1 cup Monterey Jack cheese and chilies on rice, top with remaining rice, sprinkle with 1 cup cheese and dot with butter. Bake at 350 degrees for 30 minutes. Serves: 10.

Cele Cook

FRESH TOMATO CHEESY RICE CASSEROLE

2 (6 ounce) boxes long grain
 and wild rice mix
1 (8 ounce) can chopped
 mushrooms, drained and
 juice reserved
1 (10¾ ounce) can cream of
 mushroom soup, undiluted
1 (10¾ ounce) can onion soup,
 undiluted
4 firm medium tomatoes, cut in
 bite-sized wedges
2 cups (8 ounces) grated
 Cheddar cheese

Prepare rice according to package directions, using mushroom liquid as part of cooking liquid. Stir in mushrooms. Combine mushroom soup and onion soup and add to rice mixture. Fold tomatoes into rice. Spread mixture in 3-quart casserole and sprinkle with cheese. Bake, covered, at 350 degrees for 30 minutes, remove cover and bake for additional 15 minutes. Serves: 10 to 12.

Sarah Luster

RICE DRESSING WITH SPICY TOMATOES

1 pound lean ground beef
2 stalks celery, chopped
1 small onion, chopped
½ small green bell pepper,
　chopped
1 clove garlic, minced
1 tablespoon butter or
　margarine
1 envelope onion soup mix
2 cups uncooked rice
1 (10 ounce) can tomatoes with
　green chilies, drained and
　juice reserved
water

Cook ground beef, stirring to crumble, until browned. Drain excess grease. Sauté celery, onion, bell pepper and garlic in butter or margarine in large saucepan, cooking until onion is translucent. Add beef and onion soup mix. Stir in rice. Add enough water to reserved tomato liquid to measure 4 cups. Add liquid and tomatoes to rice mixture. Bring to a boil, stirring well, then reduce heat and simmer, covered for 20 to 25 minutes; do not lift pan lid while rice is cooking. Serves: 8 to 10.

Rebecca Lavespere

CHILLED RICE AND ARTICHOKES

1 (7½ ounce) package chicken
　flavored rice mix
2 green onions, chopped
½ green bell pepper, chopped
¼ cup sliced pimiento-stuffed
　green olives or to taste
2 (6 ounce) jars marinated
　artichokes, drained and
　liquid reserved
¼ teaspoon curry powder
½ cup mayonnaise

Prepare rice according to package directions but omit butter. Let stand until cool. Add onions, bell pepper, olives and artichokes to rice, stirring to blend. Combine curry powder, mayonnaise and reserved artichoke liquid to rice mixture, mixing well. Chill before serving. Serves: 6.

Kay Foshee

EASY MOCK DIRTY RICE

1 pound ground beef
2 tablespoons cooking oil
2 cups uncooked regular rice
1 cup chopped green onions
　with tops
1 (10 ounce) package frozen
　chef seasoning: minced onion,
　celery and bell pepper
　mixture
2 tablespoons parsley flakes
2 (10¾ ounce) cans onion soup,
　undiluted
2 (10¾ ounce) cans beef broth
1 (10 ounce) can diced tomatoes
　with green chilies
2 tablespoons red or white wine
　or lemon juice
2 tablespoons Worcestershire
　sauce
salt to taste

Cook beef in oil in Dutch oven or heavy roasting pan, stirring to crumble, until browned. Drain excess grease. Add rice, green onions, chef seasoning, parsley, onion soup, broth, tomatoes, wine or lemon juice, Worcestershire sauce and salt. Simmer, covered, for about 20 minutes or until rice is tender, stirring occasionally. Serves: 16.

Beverly Giering

DOWN AND DIRTY RICE DRESSING

½ pound ground beef
salt to taste
red pepper to taste
1 tablespoon butter
1 cup chopped parsley
1½ cups chopped green onions
2 cups uncooked regular rice
4½ cups chicken broth
black pepper

Season beef with salt and red pepper. Cook in butter, stirring to crumble, until browned. Add parsley and green onions. Cook until vegetables are softened. Stir in rice and add broth. Bring to a boil, reduce heat and simmer for 1 hour. Sprinkle surface of rice with black pepper before serving. For variety, use 1 cup wild rice with 1 cup regular rice. Serves: 8.

Melba Ackel

SOUTHWEST CORNBREAD DRESSING

2 (8½ ounce) packages
   cornbread mix
turkey giblets
water
1 cup chopped celery
½ cup chopped green bell
   pepper
1 cup chopped green onions
1 clove garlic, minced
½ cup butter or margarine
1 (10¾ ounce) can chicken
   broth
2 slices bread
3 eggs, lightly beaten
6 tamales, mashed
½ teaspoon salt
crushed red pepper flakes
   to taste

Prepare cornbread according to package directions. Let stand until cool, then crumble into mixing bowl and set aside. Combine giblets with water to cover in saucepan. Bring to a boil, reduce heat and simmer, covered, until tender. While giblets cook, sauté celery, bell pepper, green onions and garlic in butter or margarine. Add to cornbread. Separate liver from other giblets, reserving those to make gravy. Chop liver and add to cornbread mixture. Stir in ⅓ cup giblet cooking liquid. Soak bread in broth and add to cornbread mixture. Stir in eggs, tamales, salt and red pepper. Spoon mixture into greased 2-quart casserole. Bake at 350 degrees for 30 to 35 minutes. Serves: 8.

Marteel Henry

CORNBREAD DRESSING

1 (6 ounce) package cornbread
   mix
½ pound hot flavored bulk pork
   sausage
¾ cup chopped celery
¾ cup chopped onion
½ medium green bell pepper,
   chopped
½ cup fresh rye breadcrumbs
¾ cup canned chicken broth
½ teaspoon poultry seasoning
Creole seasoning to taste

Prepare cornbread mix according to package directions. Let stand until cool, then crumble. Cook sausage, stirring to crumble, until almost done. Add celery, onion and bell pepper. Cook until tender and drain. Add cornbread crumbs, breadcrumbs, broth, poultry seasoning and Creole seasoning. Spoon mixture into 1½-quart casserole. Bake at 350 degrees until well browned. Serves: 4.

Sara Nell Williams

CORNBREAD AND SAUSAGE DRESSING

1 cup chopped celery
1 cup chopped yellow onion
1 pound hot flavored bulk pork
  sausage
1 pound ground turkey or lean
  beef
6 cups water
1 (6 ounce) package cornbread
  mix
4 hard-cooked eggs, chopped
1 cup minced green onions
salt and black pepper to taste

Combine celery, onion, sausage, turkey or beef and water in saucepan. Bring to a boil and cook until vegetables are tender. While vegetables and meat are cooking, prepare cornbread according to package directions or use own recipe, baking in 9x9x2-inch baking pan. Let stand until cool, then crumble. Reserving cooking liquid, strain vegetables and meat and add to cornbread. Stir in eggs, green onions, salt and black pepper. Add reserved liquid to cornbread mixture, mixing to stiff consistency for stuffing or to soft, not soupy, consistency for baking separately. Spread dressing in 2-quart casserole. Bake at 350 degrees until browned. Reserved cooking liquid can be used to make gravy with addition of cornstarch and bottled brown bouquet sauce. The secret of this dressing is the small amount of cornbread used so the meat will dominate the flavor and texture. Serves: 12.

Reverend Samuel J. Pollizzi

Seafoods

TERRY'S BROILED SHRIMP

3 pounds large or jumbo
  shrimp, in shell
1 cup Worcestershire sauce
1 cup olive oil
½ cup white or red wine
1 tablespoon crab boil
3 cloves garlic, crushed
salt and black pepper to taste
3 lemons, cut in halves

Layer shrimp in large baking pan. Combine Worcestershire sauce, oil, wine, crab boil, garlic, salt and black pepper, mixing well. Pour over shrimp. Squeeze lemons over shrimp and liquid. Stir well. Bake at 350 degrees, checking and turning frequently to prevent shrimp from drying, for 30 to 35 minutes; shell will separate from shrimp slightly when done. Check shrimp for doneness. Serves: 4.

Lana Scott

SHRIMP AND ARTICHOKES IN CHEESE SAUCE

2 tablespoons margarine
3 tablespoons all-purpose flour
salt to taste
½ teaspoon red pepper
1 cup whipping cream
1 cup milk
1 tablespoon ketchup
juice of ½ lemon
1 tablespoon Worcestershire
  sauce
3 tablespoons sherry
2 cups (8 ounces) grated sharp
  cheese
1 (14 ounce) can artichoke
  hearts, drained
2 pounds cooked shrimp,
  peeled and deveined

Melt margarine in 12-inch skillet. Stir in flour, salt and red pepper. Cook to form smooth paste. Gradually add cream and milk, stirring constantly. Simmer until well blended and thickened. Add ketchup, lemon juice, Worcestershire sauce, sherry and cheese, mixing well. Add artichoke hearts and shrimp. Heat thoroughly. Serve in pastry shells or over rice. Serves: 6 to 8.

Elizabeth Post

SHRIMP ST. DENIS

1 cup chopped green onions
½ cup chopped celery
½ cup unsalted butter
1 pound peeled, deveined
  shrimp
1 tablespoon Creole seasoning
2 cups whipping cream
1 (12 ounce) package fettuccine,
  cooked

Sauté onions and celery in butter for 2 to 3 minutes. Add shrimp and seasoning. Sauté for 2 minutes. Stir in whipping cream and cook over medium heat for 5 to 7 minutes or until sauce is thickened. Serve shrimp sauce over fettuccine. Serves: 4.

JoKay Boyle

SHRIMP CREOLE

1 cup chopped onion
¼ cup chopped green onions
½ cup chopped green bell
  pepper
⅓ cup vegetable oil
⅓ cup bacon grease
1 (15 ounce) can tomato sauce
1 (29 ounce) can tomatoes
3 tablespoons Worcestershire
  sauce
1 small clove garlic, minced
1 tablespoon chopped parsley
1 teaspoon sugar
2 teaspoons salt
¼ teaspoon black pepper
¼ teaspoon red pepper
1 teaspoon chili powder
½ teaspoon seasoning salt
3 bay leaves
2 pounds peeled and deveined
  shrimp
1 tablespoon cornstarch
¼ cup cold water

Cook onion, green onions and bell pepper in oil and bacon grease in Dutch oven over low heat until vegetables are softened. Add tomato sauce, tomatoes, Worcestershire sauce, garlic, parsley, sugar, salt, black pepper, red pepper, chili powder, seasoning salt and bay leaves. Simmer for 30 minutes. Add shrimp and simmer for 20 minutes. Dissolve cornstarch in cold water and add to shrimp mixture, cooking until slightly thickened. Serve over rice. Serves: 6.

Marion Salter

SHRIMP DELIGHT

1 medium-sized onion, chopped
1 medium-sized green bell
  pepper, chopped
¾ cup butter or margarine
1 (10½ ounce) can onion soup,
  undiluted
1 (10¾ ounce) can cream of
  chicken soup, undiluted
1 (10 ounce) can tomatoes with
  green chilies
2 cups uncooked regular rice
1½ pounds peeled and
  deveined shrimp
2 tablespoons parsley
salt and black pepper to taste

Sauté onion and bell pepper in butter or margarine until onion is translucent. Combine sautéed vegetables, onion soup, cream of chicken soup, tomatoes, rice, shrimp, parsley, salt and black pepper. Spread mixture in 13x9x2-inch baking dish. Bake at 350 degrees for 1 hour, stirring after 30 minutes. Serves: 6 to 8.

Cathy Seymour

SHRIMP LINGUINE

2 cloves garlic, crushed
1 stalk celery, finely chopped
½ pound fresh mushrooms,
  sliced
⅓ cup butter
⅓ cup olive oil
2 pounds shrimp, peeled and
  deveined
Creole seasoning to taste
½ cup white wine
¼ cup chopped parsley
1 (8 ounce) package linguine
½ to ¾ cup (2 to 3 ounces)
  grated Parmesan cheese
1 to 2 cups half and half

Sauté garlic, celery and mushrooms in butter and oil until vegetables are tender. Add shrimp and Creole seasoning. Cook, stirring often, until shrimp are pink and curled. Add wine and parsley. Simmer shrimp mixture while preparing linguine according to package directions. Drain linguine, add shrimp mixture and toss to mix. Sprinkle with cheese. Add half and half. Serve immediately. Serves: 4.

Cathy Seymour

CRAB AND SHRIMP ALMONDINE

1 cup chopped green onions
½ cup chopped green bell
   pepper
⅓ cup butter
3 tablespoons all-purpose flour
salt and black pepper to taste
2 cups half and half
1 teaspoon grated lemon peel
2 tablespoons fresh lemon juice
1 cup thinly sliced celery
2 tablespoons sliced pimiento
2 hard-cooked eggs, coarsely
   chopped
½ cup slivered almonds
4 cups cooked shrimp, peeled
   and deveined
1 pound King or lump crabmeat
buttered breadcrumbs
paprika for garnish
lemon wedges
parsley sprigs for garnish

Sauté green onions and bell pepper in butter in heavy saucepan over low heat until vegetables are softened. Add flour, salt and black pepper, stirring to blend. Add half and half and simmer until slightly thickened. Remove from heat. Gradually add lemon peel and juice. Stir in celery, pimiento, eggs, almonds and shrimp. Fold crabmeat into shrimp mixture. Spoon into individual ramekins. Sprinkle with breadcrumbs, then paprika. Bake at 350 degrees until browned and bubbly. Serve with lemon wedges and garnish with parsley. Serves: 8 to 10.

Betty Ledet

FRENCH FRIED SHRIMP

1 cup all-purpose flour
½ teaspoon sugar
½ teaspoon salt
1 cup ice water
2 tablespoons melted vegetable
   shortening
1 egg
2 pounds shrimp
vegetable oil for deep-frying

Combine flour, sugar, salt, ice water, shortening and egg, blending well to form batter. Peel shrimp, leaving last section of shell and tail intact. Cut slit through center back of each, without severing either end, and remove vein. Blot shrimp with paper towel. Dip shrimp in batter and deep-fry in oil until golden brown. Drain on paper towel. Serves: 6 to 8.

Rhonda Guidroz

SHRIMP SCAMPI

½ cup margarine
2 green onions, minced
2 teaspoons Worcestershire
  sauce
2 teaspoons Italian salad
  dressing
½ teaspoon garlic salt
½ teaspoon lemon pepper
½ teaspoon parsley flakes
1 shake of paprika
1 shake of Cajun seasoning salt
juice of ½ lime
1½ pounds peeled and
  deveined shrimp

Combine margarine, green onions, Worcestershire sauce, salad dressing, garlic salt, lemon pepper, parsley, paprika, seasoning salt and lime juice in large skillet. Simmer for 20 minutes. Add shrimp and simmer for 5 to 10 minutes or until shrimp turns pink. Serve with rice or noodles. Serves: 4.

Claudia Triche

SHRIMP OR CRAWFISH FETTUCCINE

⅓ cup chopped parsley
⅓ cup chopped green onions
1 pound peeled shrimp or
  crawfish
½ cup butter
1½ teaspoons salt
⅓ teaspoon black pepper
⅓ teaspoon white pepper
½ teaspoon cayenne pepper
½ teaspoon garlic powder
1 (12 ounce) package fettuccine
  or egg noodles
2 cups half and half, divided
⅔ cup (2⅔ ounces) grated
  Parmesan cheese, divided
nutmeg to taste

Sauté parsley, green onions and shrimp or crawfish in butter and seasonings in Dutch oven over low to medium heat for 15 to 20 minutes. Using slotted spoon, remove shrimp or crawfish, retaining seasoned butter in Dutch oven. In large saucepan or pot, prepare fettuccine or egg noodles according to package directions. While pasta cooks, add 1 cup half and half and ⅓ cup Parmesan cheese to seasoned butter. Bring to a boil. Add cooked pasta and shrimp or crawfish to cream sauce. Add 1 cup half and half and ⅓ cup Parmesan cheese, tossing to mix. Sprinkle with nutmeg just before serving. Serve with green salad and bread. Serves: 4 to 6.

Frances Conine

SENSATIONAL SHRIMP AND OKRA

1 pound okra, sliced
1 tablespoon olive oil
1 medium-sized onion, chopped
½ cup chopped celery
½ small green bell pepper,
  chopped
2 cloves garlic, chopped
1 (16 ounce) can stewed
  tomatoes, undrained
salt and black pepper
1 tablespoon Worcestershire
  sauce
1 or 2 dashes hot pepper sauce
1 pound shrimp, peeled and
  deveined
2 tablespoons butter

Sauté okra in oil until no longer stringy. Add onion, celery, bell pepper and garlic and small amount of oil if needed. Cook until vegetables are softened. Add tomatoes and simmer for 25 minutes, stirring occasionally. Season with salt, black pepper, Worcestershire sauce and hot pepper sauce. In separate pan, sauté shrimp in butter for 2 to 3 minutes or until pink. Add shrimp to vegetables. Simmer, covered, for 15 minutes or until shrimp are done, adding liquid if needed. Serves: 4.

Mary Jean Thomas

MARINATED SHRIMP KABOBS

boiling water
1 large green bell pepper, cut in
  1-inch pieces
1 (8 ounce) can unsweetened
  pineapple chunks, drained
  and juice reserved
¼ cup prepared mustard
1 pound large shrimp, peeled
  and deveined
12 to 16 cherry tomatoes
1 pound fresh mushrooms
1 large onion, cut in chunks

Pour boiling water over bell pepper in heat-proof dish, let stand for 5 minutes and drain. Combine reserved pineapple juice and mustard in baking dish. Add shrimp. Chill for 3 to 4 hours, stirring occasionally. Remove shrimp from marinade, reserving marinade. Alternate shrimp, pineapple, tomatoes, mushrooms and onion on skewers and brush with sauce. Grill 4 inches from heat source for 3 to 4 minutes on each side or until shrimp are done, brushing frequently with marinade. If using wooden skewers, soak in water for 30 minutes before using to prevent burning on grill. Serves: 4.

Debbie Maynard

DILLY SHRIMP WITH ASPARAGUS

2 pounds fresh asparagus,
  tough ends trimmed
water
¼ cup plus 2 tablespoons
  butter, divided
2 pounds large shrimp, peeled
½ pound fresh mushrooms,
  sliced
½ cup chopped green onions
2 cups milk
2 tablespoons cornstarch
¼ cup lemon juice
1 tablespoon dillweed or fresh
  chopped dill

Cook asparagus in boiling water for 7 to 10 minutes or until crisp-tender. Drain and set aside, keeping warm. Sauté shrimp in ¼ cup butter in large skillet until pink. Remove shrimp with slotted spoon and set aside. Add 2 tablespoons butter to skillet. Sauté mushrooms and green onions for 2 minutes. Combine milk and cornstarch in small bowl, blending until smooth. Add to sautéed vegetables and bring to a boil, stirring constantly. Reduce heat and simmer for 1 minute. Add lemon juice and dillweed. Stir in shrimp and heat thoroughly. Place asparagus on serving plate. Spoon shrimp sauce over asparagus. Shrimp sauce can be served on toast or pasta instead of asparagus. Serves: 4 to 6.

Margaret Wheat

HAZEL'S SHRIMP JAMBALAYA

½ pound salt meat
vegetable shortening
2 medium-sized onions,
  chopped
1 cup chopped green onions
½ cup chopped celery
1 pound medium or small
  shrimp, peeled and deveined
1½ cups uncooked regular rice
2 cups water
½ cup chopped chives
1 clove garlic, crushed
dash of hot pepper sauce or 1
  hot pepper

Sauté salt meat in shortening in 5-quart Dutch oven. Remove meat and add onion, green onions and celery. Cook over medium heat, stirring constantly, until mixture is browned; do not burn. Add shrimp and salt meat and cook for 15 minutes. Stir in rice, water, chives, garlic and hot pepper sauce. Bring to a boil, reduce heat and simmer, covered, for about 30 to 40 minutes or until liquid is absorbed, stirring occasionally. Serves: 6 to 8.

Juanita Murphy

QUICK AND EASY BARBECUE SHRIMP

1 cup butter
1 cup vegetable oil
1 teaspoon fresh lemon juice
2 teaspoons minced garlic
½ teaspoon salt
¾ teaspoon freshly ground
   black pepper
4 bay leaves, finely crushed
1 tablespoon paprika
2 teaspoons finely crushed
   rosemary
½ teaspoon dried basil
½ teaspoon oregano
½ teaspoon cayenne pepper
2 pounds shrimp with heads

Combine butter, oil, lemon juice, garlic, salt, black pepper, bay leaves, paprika, rosemary, basil, oregano and cayenne pepper in large saucepan over medium heat, mixing well. Reduce heat and simmer for 8 minutes. Set aside for 30 minutes. Add whole shrimp to seasoned sauce and cook over medium heat for 6 to 8 minutes or until shrimp turn pink. Pour into 2-quart casserole. Bake, uncovered, at 450 degrees for 10 minutes. Serves: 4.

Frances Conine

BARBECUED SHRIMP

¼ cup chopped onion
1 tablespoon brown sugar
1 tablespoon dry mustard
¼ teaspoon garlic powder
1 tablespoon white vinegar
½ cup ketchup
dash of hot pepper sauce
2 tablespoons chopped fresh
   rosemary
24 jumbo fresh shrimp, peeled
   and deveined
1 lemon, cut in wedges

Sauté onion in non-stick skillet, prepared with vegetable cooking spray, over low heat until onion is softened. Stir in brown sugar, dry mustard, garlic powder, vinegar, ketchup, hot pepper sauce and rosemary, blending well. Remove from heat and let stand until cool. Place shrimp in bowl, add marinade and chill for 1 hour. Drain shrimp. Place on skewers and grill over medium hot coals for 3 to 4 minutes. Squeeze lemon on shrimp and serve. Serves: 4.

Vanessa Robertson

SHRIMP SCAMPI

½ cup margarine
2 green onions, minced
2 teaspoons Italian salad
   dressing
2 teaspoons Worcestershire
   sauce
juice of ½ lime
½ teaspoon garlic salt
½ teaspoon lemon pepper
½ teaspoon parsley
shake of paprika
1½ pounds shrimp, peeled and
   deveined

Combine margarine, green onions, salad dressing, Worcestershire sauce, lime juice, garlic salt, lemon pepper, parsley and paprika in large saucepan. Simmer for 20 minutes. Add shrimp and simmer for 5 to 10 minutes or until shrimp turns pink. Serve with rice or pasta. Serves: 4.

Claudia Triche

DIJON SHRIMP

½ cup butter, melted
2 tablespoons vegetable oil
juice of 1 lemon
2 tablespoons Dijon mustard
½ teaspoon Worcestershire
   sauce
2 cloves garlic, chopped
1 pound medium-large shrimp

Combine butter, oil, lemon juice, mustard, Worcestershire sauce and garlic. Place shrimp in 13x9x2-inch baking dish. Pour marinade over shrimp. Chill for 2 to 3 hours. Broil for 5 to 8 minutes. Serves: 3 or 4.

Kathryn Smith

SHRIMP OR CRAWFISH ENCHILADA

⅔ cup chopped onion
1 cup chopped green onions
1 (4 ounce) can mild or hot
   flavored chili peppers
¾ cup chopped green bell
   pepper
¾ cup chopped red bell pepper
1 cup margarine
salt and black pepper to taste
cayenne pepper to taste
1 teaspoon oregano
2 cloves chopped garlic
3 cups whipping cream
1 cup sour cream
2½ cups (10 ounces) grated
   Monterey Jack cheese,
   divided
2 pounds shrimp or crawfish
   tails
8 to 10 flour tortillas
vegetable oil

Sauté onion, green onions, chili peppers and bell peppers in margarine for about 10 minutes. Season with salt, black pepper, cayenne pepper, oregano and garlic. Add whipping cream. Bring to a boil, reduce heat and simmer for 10 minutes. Stir in sour cream and whisk for about 3 minutes. Add 1½ cups Monterey Jack cheese and stir until melted. Set aside. Sauté shrimp or crawfish for about 6 minutes or until done. Fry tortillas in oil until crisp. Arrange tortillas, whole or broken, to cover bottom of 13x9x2-inch baking dish. Spoon ½ of shrimp, then ½ of sauce on tortillas. Repeat layers, ending with sauce and sprinkling with 1 cup cheese. Bake at 350 degrees for 15 to 20 minutes. Serves: 8 to 10.

Sandra McCullen

CRABMEAT AND SHRIMP CASSEROLE

1 (16 ounce) package long grain
  wild rice
1 medium-sized onion, chopped
1 cup chopped celery
1 large green bell pepper,
  chopped
½ cup butter
2 pounds shrimp, cooked and
  peeled
2 (6 ounce) packages frozen
  crabmeat, thawed
3 (10¾ ounce) cans cream of
  celery soup, undiluted
2 (4 ounce) cans sliced
  mushrooms, drained
1 cup breadcrumbs, divided

Prepare rice according to package directions. Sauté onion, celery and bell pepper in butter until vegetables are softened. Stir in rice, shrimp, crabmeat, soup and mushrooms. Spoon mixture into 2 greased 2-quart casseroles. Sprinkle with breadcrumbs. Bake at 350 degrees for 35 to 40 minutes or until bubbly. Serves: 12 to 14.

Molly Collins

CRABMEAT AND BROCCOLI CASSEROLE

½ cup chopped onion
½ cup chopped celery
1 tablespoon margarine
1 (2 ounce) can sliced
  mushrooms, drained and
  liquid reserved
salt and black pepper to taste
2 cups cooked rice
6 to 8 ounces canned or fresh
  crabmeat
1 (10 ounce) package frozen
  chopped broccoli, cooked and
  drained
1 (10¾ ounce) can cheese soup,
  undiluted
¼ cup chopped almonds

Sauté onion and celery in margarine until vegetables are tender. Add mushrooms, salt, black pepper, rice and crabmeat. Spread ½ of mixture in greased 1-quart casserole. Spoon ½ of broccoli over rice mixture. Combine reserved mushroom liquid with cheese soup, blending well. Spread ½ soup mixture on broccoli. Repeat layers. Top with almonds. Bake at 350 degrees for 20 minutes or until hot. Serves: 4.

Libby Swafford

PASTA, SHRIMP AND CRABMEAT

1 (12 ounce) package spaghetti, fettuccine or vermicelli, cooked and drained
1 pound shrimp, peeled and deveined
¼ cup butter
2 tablespoons vegetable oil
2 bunches green onions with tops, sliced
3 cloves garlic, minced
1 (4 ounce) can sliced mushrooms, drained
1 to 2 tablespoons all-purpose flour
1 cup chicken broth or milk, warmed
1 pound white or claw crabmeat, drained
½ cup chopped parsley
1 teaspoon salt
1 teaspoon black pepper
¼ teaspoon red pepper
1 tablespoon Worcestershire sauce
hot pepper sauce to taste
½ cup (2 ounces) grated Parmesan cheese

Prepare pasta according to package directions. While pasta cooks, prepare sauce. Sauté shrimp in butter and oil in Dutch oven until shrimp turn pink. Add green onions, garlic and mushrooms. Sprinkle flour on shrimp and vegetables, blending well; do not brown. Add broth or milk and cook to thin consistency, stirring to keep smooth. Add crabmeat and cook over medium heat for 2 minutes. Stir in parsley, salt, black pepper, red pepper, Worcestershire sauce and hot pepper sauce. Drain pasta and combine with seafood sauce, mixing well. Serve with Parmesan cheese. Serves: 6.

Gerald F. Thomas, Jr.

CRABMEAT DELIGHT

½ pound fresh mushrooms,
  sliced
butter
1 (14 ounce) can artichoke
  hearts, drained and quartered
1 pound crabmeat
¼ cup butter
2½ tablespoons all-purpose
  flour
1 cup half and half
½ teaspoon salt
1 teaspoon Worcestershire
  sauce
¼ cup medium-dry sherry
paprika to taste
ground red pepper to taste
¼ cup (1 ounce) grated
  Parmesan cheese

Sauté mushrooms in butter until tender. Set aside. Place artichokes in 1-quart casserole. Sprinkle crabmeat on artichokes and top with mushrooms. Melt butter (stove top or microwave method). Stir in flour to form smooth paste and cook until bubbly. Add half and half, salt, Worcestershire sauce, sherry, paprika and red pepper. Cook until thickened. Check seasoning. Pour sauce over mushroom layer in casserole. Sprinkle cheese on sauce. Bake at 375 degrees for 20 minutes. Serve with salad, French bread and white wine. Serves: 6 to 8.

Sarah McElwee

CANE RIVER CRABMEAT CASSEROLE

8 slices white bread, crusts trimmed
3 cups crabmeat, drained
¾ cup mayonnaise
1 medium-sized onion, grated
1 cup finely chopped green bell pepper
1 cup finely chopped celery
3 cups milk
4 eggs, beaten
1 teaspoon salt
1 teaspoon black pepper
1 (10¾ ounce) can cream of mushroom soup, undiluted
1 cup (4 ounces) grated American cheese
1 teaspoon paprika

Dice bread and place in 2-quart casserole. Combine crabmeat, mayonnaise, onion, bell pepper and celery. Spoon mixture on bread. Combine milk, eggs, salt and black pepper, blending well. Pour milk mixture over crabmeat layer. Chill overnight. Spread soup over layered ingredients. Sprinkle with cheese and paprika. Chill for 1 hour. Bake at 325 degrees for 1 hour. Serves: 6 to 8.

Anne Giering

DEVILED CRAB

½ chopped green onion
½ cup chopped celery
⅓ cup chopped green bell
  pepper
¼ cup butter
1 pound crabmeat, drained
½ cup cracker crumbs
salt and black pepper to taste
red pepper to taste
dash of hot pepper sauce
¼ teaspoon dry or prepared
  mustard
cracker crumbs
melted butter

White Sauce:
2 tablespoons butter
2 tablespoons all-purpose flour
1 cup milk
salt and black pepper to taste
¼ to ½ teaspoon paprika

Sauté green onion, celery and bell pepper in butter in saucepan until tender. Stir in crabmeat and ½ cup cracker crumbs. Season with salt, black pepper, red pepper, hot pepper sauce and mustard. Set aside. Prepare white sauce by melting butter in small saucepan. Blend in flour; do not scorch. Add milk, stirring and cooking until smooth and thickened. Season with salt, black pepper and paprika. Combine crabmeat mixture and white sauce. Spoon mixture into 1½-quart casserole or crab shells. Sprinkle with additional cracker crumbs. Drizzle butter over crumbs. Bake at 350 degrees for 30 minutes or until browned. Serves: 4.

Marteel Henry

CRAWFISH BOIL FOR A DOZEN

**2 (30 to 35 pound) sacks live
  crawfish**
water
salt
1 (16 ounce) bottle crab boil
**3 (16 ounce) packages
  powdered crawfish-crab-
  shrimp seasoning mix,
  divided**
4 pounds small new potatoes
16 ears corn on cob
6 small onions, cut in quarters
Cajun seasoning salt

Rinse crawfish in sack with water. If de-sired, purge crawfish by placing sacks in ice chest, cover with water, add ½ (16 ounce) box salt, let stand for 5 to 10 min-utes, drain and rinse well. Using 15-gallon pot equipped with wire basket, fill about half full with water. Place on propane jet burner and turn flame to high setting. Add ⅓ (16 ounce) box salt, liquid crab boil, 2 packages seasoning mix and potatoes to water. Cover and bring to a boil. Add 1 sack crawfish, corn and onion to boiling water. Sprinkle with ½ package seasoning mix. Stir with large utensil such as boat paddle. Bring to a boil. Cook for 3 minutes if craw-fish are to be placed in ice chest until served or cook for 5 minutes if crawfish are to be served immediately. Check potatoes; if not yet tender, retain in pot to cook with second sack of crawfish. Pour crawfish, corn, potatoes (if tender) and onions on table. Sprinkle with Cajun seasoning salt. Repeat procedure for second sack of craw-fish. Seasoning amounts will accommo-date about 200 pounds of crawfish; add ½ package seasoning mix to each batch as cooked and adjust corn, potato and onion quantities for number of guests to be served. Serves: 12.

David M. Walker

FRIED CRAWFISH TAILS

2 eggs
2 cups milk
2 (1 pound) packages crawfish
  tails, undrained
all-purpose flour
1½ teaspoons salt
1 tablespoon black pepper
1½ teaspoons Creole seasoning
vegetable oil for deep-frying

Combine eggs and milk in large bowl and beat until blended. Add crawfish tails with liquid. Let stand for at least 1 hour and up to 8 hours. Combine flour, salt, black pepper and seasoning in brown paper bag. Heat oil for deep-frying to 330 degrees. Drain crawfish tails, add to flour mixture and shake to coat thoroughly. Drop crawfish by handfuls into oil and cook for 1 to 2 minutes or until golden brown. Serve immediately. For appetizer, serve with honey-mustard dressing. Serves: 4 to 6.

Kim Johnson

CREOLE CRAWFISH CASSEROLE

2 large onions, chopped
3 stalks celery, chopped
1 green bell pepper, chopped
½ cup margarine
1 pound cooked crawfish tails,
  peeled
1 egg
1 tablespoon minced parsley
3 cups cooked rice
1 (10¾ ounce) can cream of
  mushroom soup, undiluted
1½ cups (6 ounces) grated
  mozzarella cheese, Cheddar
  cheese or pasteurized process
  cheese spread
Cajun seasoning salt or salt and
  black pepper to taste
breadcrumbs

Sauté onion, celery and bell pepper in margarine in large saucepan until vegetables are softened. Add crawfish and cook for several minutes. Stir in egg, parsley and rice, mixing well. Add soup and cheese. Season with seasoning salt or salt and black pepper. Spread crawfish mixture in 2-quart casserole and sprinkle with breadcrumbs. Bake at 375 degrees for 25 minutes. Serves: 6.

Claudia Triche

CRAWFISH FETTUCCINE

2 cups chopped onion
3 cloves garlic, chopped
2 cups chopped green bell
  pepper
2 cups chopped celery
½ cup butter
½ cup all-purpose flour
1 to 2 pounds crawfish tails
1 (16 ounce) package hot
  flavored Mexican or jalapeño
  pasteurized process cheese,
  cubed
4 cups half and half
1 (16 ounce) package fettuccine
grated Parmesan cheese
  (optional)

Sauté onion, garlic, bell pepper and celery in butter until vegetables are softened. Remove from heat and blend in flour. Cook, covered, for 10 to 15 minutes. Add crawfish tails and cook, stirring occasionally, for 15 minutes. Stir in cheese and cook until melted. Gradually add half and half. Simmer for 15 to 20 minutes, stirring occasionally. Prepare fettuccine according to package directions and drain well. Add to crawfish sauce and toss to mix. Serve immediately or pour into casserole and bake at 350 degrees for 10 to 12 minutes. Serve with Parmesan cheese. Serves: 10 to 12.

Toni Gwinn

ROY'S CRAWFISH PIE

1 cup margarine
½ cup all-purpose flour
1 onion, chopped
4 cloves garlic, chopped
1 green bell pepper, chopped
1 cup chopped celery
3 tablespoons tomato sauce
3 cups water
3 pounds crawfish tails
2 tablespoons cornstarch
¼ cup cold water
2 bunches green onions,
  chopped
1 bunch parsley, chopped
salt and black pepper to taste
cayenne pepper to taste
3 baked 9-inch pastry shells

Melt margarine in Dutch oven. Add flour and cook until lightly browned. Add onion, garlic, bell pepper, celery and tomato sauce. Simmer for 1 hour, stirring frequently. Add 3 cups water and simmer for several hours, adding water if sauce thickens beyond creamy consistency. Add crawfish and cook for 30 minutes or until crawfish is tender. If sauce thins, dissolve cornstarch in cold water and add to sauce. Stir in green onions and parsley. Season with salt, black pepper and cayenne pepper. Pour mixture into pastry shells. For appetizer servings, spoon mixture into 1-inch patty shells. Serves: 18

Roy J. Delatte, Jr.

CRAWFISH PIES

2 pounds crawfish tails
2 teaspoons salt, divided
1 cup chopped onion
1 cup chopped green onions
½ cup chopped celery
½ cup chopped green bell
  pepper
½ cup vegetable oil
1 teaspoon hot pepper sauce or
  ½ teaspoon cayenne pepper
1 tablespoon Worcestershire
  sauce
2 tablespoons cornstarch
1 cup cold water
2 tablespoons chopped parsley

Pastry:
5 cups all-purpose flour
½ teaspoon baking powder
2 teaspoons salt
2 cups vegetable shortening
1 egg, beaten, plus egg whites to
  measure 1 cup liquid
1 teaspoon vinegar

Sprinkle crawfish tails with 1 teaspoon salt and set aside. Sauté onion, green onions, celery and bell pepper in oil until onion is translucent. Stir in 1 teaspoon salt, hot pepper sauce or cayenne pepper and Worcestershire sauce. Add crawfish tails and simmer for 3 to 5 minutes. Dissolve cornstarch in cold water. Add to crawfish mixture and simmer until sauce begins to thicken. Add parsley. Let stand until cool, then chill. Prepare pastry by sifting flour, baking powder and salt together. Using pastry blender, cut shortening into dry ingredients. Add liquid and mix to form dough. Roll and cut dough to fit 8 pot pie pans or 11 to 12 muffin-sized pans plus circles for upper crust. Fit dough in pans, fill with crawfish mixture and add top pastry, sealing edges well. Prick with fork tines to vent steam. Bake at 425 degrees for 45 minutes. Extra pastry dough can be stored in refrigerator or frozen. Serves: 8 to 12.

Betty Ledet

SEAFOOD JAMBOREE

2 tablespoons butter
1 tablespoon olive oil
½ cup chopped green onions
¼ pound crabmeat, shell
   removed
¼ pound shrimp, peeled and
   deveined
¼ pound small scallops
2 tablespoons all-purpose flour
1 (4 ounce) can mushroom
   stems and pieces, well
   drained
¾ cup milk
dash of hot pepper sauce
1 teaspoon Worcestershire
   sauce
2 tablespoons chopped parsley
salt and black pepper to taste
6 flounder, trout, whitefish or
   sole fish fillets

Melt butter with oil in skillet over medium heat, stirring to blend. Sauté green onions in butter-oil mixture for 3 to 5 minutes or until softened. Add crabmeat, shrimp and scallops. Sauté for about 3 minutes. Add flour, blending well with seafood mixture, and cook for 2 minutes; do not brown. Stir in mushrooms and add milk. Simmer, stirring constantly, until creamy sauce consistency. Add hot pepper sauce, Worcestershire sauce and parsley. Simmer until thickened. Season with salt and black pepper. Place fillets in single layer in 13x9x2-inch baking dish. Pour sauce over fillets. Bake at 350 degrees for 20 minutes or until fish flakes easily when pierced with fork tines. Serves: 6.

Gerald F. Thomas Jr.

SEAFOOD SPECTACULAR

½ pound fresh mushrooms,
   sliced
¾ cup chopped onion
¾ cup chopped celery
¾ cup butter
½ cup all-purpose flour
2 cups half and half
1½ cups dry vermouth
1 cup (4 ounces) grated
   Cheddar cheese
1 cup (4 ounces) grated
   Monterey Jack cheese
2 (14 ounce) cans artichoke
   hearts, drained and quartered
1 (8 ounce) can sliced water
   chestnuts, drained
Konriko spicy seasoning to
   taste
garlic powder to taste
lemon pepper to taste
juice of 1 lemon
2 pounds large shrimp, peeled
   and deveined
1 bunch green onions with tops,
   chopped
1 pound fresh crabmeat
¾ cup sliced almonds
patty shells or cooked pasta

Sauté mushrooms, onion and celery in butter until vegetables are softened. Stir in flour and cook; do not brown. Add half and half and vermouth. Cook, stirring constantly, until thickened and creamy. Add Cheddar cheese, Monterey Jack cheese, artichoke hearts and water chestnuts. Season with Konriko seasoning, garlic powder and lemon pepper. Stir in lemon juice and shrimp. Simmer for 30 minutes, stirring frequently. Add green onions, crabmeat and almonds. Simmer for 15 minutes. Serve seafood sauce in patty shells or over pasta. Serves: 8.

Sara Nell Williams

PLANTATION OYSTERS

1 large onion, chopped
3 cloves garlic, chopped
½ cup butter
½ teaspoon salt
¼ teaspoon black pepper
¼ teaspoon red pepper
1 teaspoon oregano
½ teaspoon thyme
4 (10 ounce) jars oysters,
   drained and liquid reserved
1 cup Italian seasoned
   breadcrumbs
1 cup (4 ounces) freshly grated
   Parmesan cheese

Sauté onion and garlic in butter until softened. Add salt, black pepper, red pepper, oregano, thyme and oysters. Cook until oyster edges begin to curl, adding oyster liquid as needed. Fold breadcrumbs into oyster mixture. Spread in 9-inch pie plate and sprinkle with Parmesan cheese. Bake at 350 degrees for 15 to 20 minutes. Serves: 6.

Susan Cloutier

OYSTER LOAF

1 (16 ounce) loaf French bread
¼ cup butter, melted
2 dozen select oysters, drained
salt to taste
2 eggs, beaten
1 cup cracker meal
vegetable oil
½ cup ketchup
1 tablespoon Worcestershire
   sauce
¼ teaspoon prepared
   horseradish
⅓ cup chopped green onion
   tops

Cut slice from top ⅓ of bread loaf, reserving slice. Remove bread from bottom section in cubes, leaving shell. Brush cut surfaces of both top and bottom with butter. Broil until lightly browned. Sprinkle oysters with salt. Dip oysters in egg, then cracker meal and repeat. Fry oysters in oil for 2 to 3 minutes or until golden brown. Drain on paper towels. Combine ketchup, Worcestershire sauce and horseradish. Place oysters in bread shell, spoon ketchup mixture over oysters, sprinkle with green onions and top with bread slice. Cut loaf crosswise in 4 sections and serve immediately. Serves: 4.

Marteel Henry

SCALLOPS AU GRATIN

1 green bell pepper, chopped
1 large onion, chopped
1 bunch green onions, chopped
 3 tablespoons chopped parsley
½ cup butter
1 pound scallops
1 pound shrimp, peeled and
  deveined
½ pound lump crabmeat
  (optional)
2 cups soft breadcrumbs
2 cups whipping cream
2 eggs, beaten
1 teaspoon chicken bouillon
  granules
1 teaspoon red pepper
1 cup (4 ounces) grated
  Cheddar cheese

Sauté bell pepper, onion, green onions and parsley in butter until vegetables are softened. Add scallops, shrimp and crabmeat. Cook for 2 to 3 minutes. Place breadcrumbs in mixing bowl. Pour cream and eggs on breadcrumbs, add seafood mixture and toss lightly. Add bouillon granules and red pepper. Spoon mixture into 8 to 10 individual ramekins. Bake at 350 degrees for 30 minutes. Sprinkle with cheese and bake at 425 degrees for additional 10 minutes. Serves: 8 to 10.

Rosemary Baker

FROG LEGS WITH TOMATO SAUCE

8 pairs medium-sized frog legs
3 cups milk
salt and black pepper
all-purpose flour
2 to 3 tablespoons olive oil
2 cloves garlic, crushed

Tomato Sauce:
1 (16 ounce) can stewed
  tomatoes, coarsely chopped,
  or 2 cups chopped fresh
  tomatoes
½ cup minced onion
2 cloves garlic, minced
salt and black pepper to taste
¼ cup chopped parsley

Soak frog legs in milk, seasoned with salt and black pepper, for 1 hour. Drain, then lightly dust frog legs with flour. Sauté legs and garlic in olive oil in skillet over medium heat for 4 to 5 minutes, turn and sauté on second side for 4 to 5 minutes. While legs cook, prepare sauce by combining tomatoes, onion, garlic, salt, black pepper and parsley in saucepan. Cook, uncovered, until thickened. Spoon sauce over frog legs or serve on side. Serves: 4.

Pat Thomas

OVEN-BLACKENED CATFISH

4 catfish fillets
Worcestershire sauce
white wine Worcestershire
  sauce
lemon pepper seasoning
liquid butter
lemon slices
parsley sprigs

Place fillets in broiler-safe baking dish. Coat with Worcestershire sauces and sprinkle with lemon pepper. Drizzle small amount of butter on fillets. Bake at 400 degrees for 15 minutes. Broil fillets until dark brown, nearly burned. Remove from oven, turn fillets and season with Worcestershire sauces, lemon pepper and butter. Broil until very brown. Serve garnished with lemon slices and parsley. Serves: 4.

Linda Burke

CATFISH MARGUERY

4 catfish fillets
lemon pepper to taste
salt-free herb blend seasoning
    to taste
salt to taste
paprika to taste
3 tablespoons olive oil

Sauce:
2 egg yolks, beaten
1 cup butter, melted
1 tablespoon lemon juice
1 cup chopped cooked shrimp
½ cup crabmeat
½ cup sliced mushrooms
¼ cup dry white wine
salt and black pepper to taste

Season fillets with lemon pepper, herb seasoning, salt and paprika. Pan-fry fillets in olive oil in electric skillet for about 20 minutes or until golden brown and fish begins to flake. While fillets cook, prepare sauce. Place egg yolks in top of double boiler over hot (not boiling) water. Gradually add melted butter and stir constantly until thickened. Add lemon juice, shrimp, crabmeat, mushrooms and wine. Season with salt and black pepper. Cook, stirring often, for 15 minutes or until sauce is thoroughly heated. Place fried fillets on oven-safe platter or individual plates and top with sauce. Broil until lightly browned. Serves: 4.

Cindy Smith

CATFISH EVANGELINE

¼ cup margarine, melted
2 teaspoons fresh lemon juice
4 catfish fillets (1½ pounds total)
lemon pepper to taste
3 to 4 cups cooked rice

Crawfish Sauce:
1¼ cups chopped onion
½ cup chopped celery
½ cup chopped green bell pepper
1 clove garlic, minced
¼ cup margarine
1 teaspoon salt
¼ teaspoon black pepper
¼ teaspoon cayenne pepper
¼ teaspoon sugar
1 tablespoon tomato paste
2 teaspoons cornstarch
¾ cup cold water
1 to 2 cups cooked crawfish tails or shrimp
1 green onion, chopped

Prepare sauce 1 day in advance. Sauté onion, celery, bell pepper and garlic in margarine until softened. Stir in salt, black pepper, cayenne pepper, sugar and tomato paste. Simmer, stirring occasionally, for 20 minutes. Dissolve cornstarch in cold water and add to vegetable mixture. Cook until thickened. Add crawfish or shrimp and green onion. Chill overnight. Reheat when ready to serve. Prepare fish by combining margarine and lemon juice. Dip each fillet in mixture and sprinkle with lemon pepper. Grill over hot coals. Serve fillets on rice topped with crawfish sauce. Serves: 4.

Gwen Taylor

STUFFED BAKED CATFISH

4 catfish fillets
1 teaspoon lemon juice
¼ teaspoon black pepper
8 slices bacon
lemon wedges

Stuffing:
1 cup breadcrumbs
3 tablespoons cream cheese,
  softened
1 tablespoon lemon juice
1 tablespoon finely chopped
  celery
1 tablespoon minced onion
1 tablespoon parsley flakes
¼ teaspoon salt
¼ teaspoon black pepper
1 teaspoon ground thyme

Sprinkle fillets with lemon juice and black pepper. Set aside. Prepare stuffing by combining breadcrumbs, cream cheese, lemon juice, celery, onion, parsley, salt, black pepper and thyme, mixing well. Spoon ¼ of breadcrumb mixture on each fillet. Roll up, wrap with 2 slices bacon and secure with wooden picks. Place stuffed fillets seam side down in lightly greased baking dish. Bake, uncovered, at 350 degrees for 25 minutes or until fish flakes easily when pierced with fork tines. Remove wooden picks. Serve with lemon wedges on stuffed fillets. Serves: 4.

Debbie Maynard

RAY'S FISH FRANCAISSE

1 (3 to 6 pound) whole fish with
  head and tail
1 head iceberg lettuce,
  shredded
parsley sprigs, sliced hard-
  cooked eggs, stuffed olives,
  vegetables or fruits for
  garnish

Prepare poaching liquid. Press 4 cloves in each onion. Combine onion, water, wine, vinegar, carrots, celery, parsley, salt, peppercorns, bay leaves, allspice and thyme in oblong poaching pan. Bring to a boil and cook for 45 to 50 minutes. Set aside. Prepare mayonnaise. Using food processor, chop garlic, green onions and parsley to fine consistency. With processor running, gradually add oil, then egg, lemon juice,

(continued on next page)

(continued)

Poaching Liquid:
3 onions
12 whole cloves
3 quarts water
1 quart white wine
½ cup wine vinegar
4 carrots, quartered
3 stalks celery, quartered
6 sprigs parsley
2 tablespoons salt
12 whole black peppercorns
3 bay leaves
2 tablespoons allspice
1 teaspoon thyme

Green Mayonnaise:
6 cloves garlic
4 green onions
1 bunch parsley
2 cups vegetable oil
1 egg, lightly beaten
juice of ½ lemon
1 tablespoon vinegar
2 dashes Worcestershire sauce
2 dashes hot pepper sauce
½ teaspoon sugar
1 teaspoon salt
1 tablespoon dry mustard

vinegar, Worcestershire sauce, hot pepper sauce, sugar, salt and mustard. Store in refrigerator. Wrap fish in cheesecloth for easier handling. Simmer in poaching liquid for 7 minutes per pound or until fork tender; do not boil. When done, remove fish and let stand until comfortable to handle. Place on tray or baking sheet, unwrap cheesecloth and remove skin on upper side. Turn fish on back and split lengthwise. Remove and discard exposed back bones. Remove head and tail, reserving for later user. Place top ½ of fish, cut side down, on cutting board of tray. Turn first half of cut side down and remove skin. Let both halves of fish cool until aspic (gelatinous matter) becomes firm. Spread first ½ with green mayonnaise and place, cut side up, on serving base. Surround and support with lettuce to keep thin edges of fish from splitting. Garnish lettuce fringe with parsley. Coat cut surface of second ½ of fish with green mayonnaise and place on top of other ½ to reconstruct fish. Place head and tail in position. Fish can be chilled overnight. Garnish with parsley, eggs, olives, vegetables or fruits before serving. Serves: 20 to 40.

Jo Ann Ford

SMOKED SALMON PASTA WITH CAVIAR

1 (16 ounce) package spinach
   fettuccine
1 medium-sized onion, minced
1 clove garlic, minced
¼ cup plus 2 tablespoons
   unsalted butter
¾ pound smoked salmon, cut in
   thin 1½-inch long strips
1 large tomato, peeled, seeds
   removed and diced
salt and black pepper to taste
¼ cup vodka
2 tablespoons brandy
2 cups whipping cream
2 tablespoons caviar
2 tablespoons chopped parsley
¼ cup (1 ounce) freshly grated
   Parmesan cheese

Prepare fettuccine according to package directions. While fettuccine cooks, prepare sauce. Sauté onion and garlic in butter over medium-high heat until softened. Add salmon, tomato, salt and black pepper. Cook, stirring frequently, for about 2 minutes. Add vodka and brandy. Cook until liquid is reduced by ½. Stir in cream and cook, stirring constantly, until thickened. Drain fettuccine, add sauce and toss gently. Sprinkle individual servings with caviar, parsley and Parmesan cheese. Serve immediately. Serves: 4 to 6.

Eugenie Watson

194

Meats

CELEBRATION STEAKS

1 (4-inch thick) beef tenderloin,
   cut into 2 (2-inch thick)
   steaks, fat trimmed
Worcestershire sauce
2 green onions, chopped
½ pound fresh mushrooms,
   sliced
2 tablespoons butter
1 teaspoon parsley flakes
1 teaspoon green peppercorns
dash of hot pepper sauce
2 tablespoons brandy
1 cup whipping cream

Sprinkle steaks with Worcestershire sauce and set aside. Sauté onions and mushrooms in butter until vegetables are tender. Add parsley, peppercorns and hot pepper sauce. In separate saucepan, warm brandy. Ignite and pour into vegetable sauce, stirring until flames subside. Add cream and cook over high heat, stirring constantly, until thickened. Set sauce aside. Grill steaks to desired doneness. Reheat sauce and ladle over steaks. Serves: 2.

Tanya Conlay

MEXICAN STEAK

1¼ pounds boneless round
   steak
2 tablespoons margarine
1 (4 ounce) can chopped green
   chilies, drained
1 (8 ounce) jar taco sauce
½ cup (2 ounces) shredded
   Monterey Jack cheese

Cut steak into 4 pieces and pound to ¼-inch thickness. Sauté steak in margarine over medium heat, turning to brown on both sides. Place in greased 9x9x2-inch baking dish. Spoon chilies and taco sauce on steaks. Bake, covered, at 350 degrees for 40 minutes. Sprinkle Monterey Jack cheese on steaks and bake, uncovered, for additional 5 minutes. Serves: 4.

Vicki Methvin

PEPPER STEAK

1 pound lean round or sirloin
  beef steak, cut ½-inch thick
1 tablespoon paprika
2 tablespoons margarine
2 cloves garlic, crushed
1½ cups beef broth
1 cup sliced green onions with
  tops
2 green bell peppers, sliced
2 tablespoons cornstarch
¼ cup water
¼ cup soy sauce
2 tomatoes, each cut in
  8 wedges

Place steak between wax paper sheets and pound to ¼-inch thickness. Cut into ¼-inch wide strips. Season with paprika and let stand for a few minutes. Sauté beef in margarine, tossing to brown on all sides. Add garlic and broth. Cook, covered, for 30 minutes. Stir in green onions and bell peppers. Cook, covered, for 5 minutes. Blend cornstarch, water and soy sauce. Add to beef mixture and cook, stirring until thickened, for about 2 minutes. Add tomatoes and heat thoroughly. Serve over rice. Serves: 4.

Mary Jean Thomas

ROYAL HAWAIIAN STEAKS

4 ribeye steaks or steaks of
  choice
1 (46 ounce) can pineapple
  juice
1 (10 ounce) bottle soy sauce
¼ cup sugar

Pierce steaks with fork tines several times. Place in 13x9x2-inch baking dish and set aside. Combine pineapple juice and soy sauce. Pour over steaks, completely covering. Sprinkle sugar on juice mixture and steaks. Marinate in refrigerator for at least 72 hours, turning steaks after 36 hours. Drain steaks and grill to desired doneness. Serves: 4.

Christopher L. Ingram

VEAL CORDON BLEU

6 medium-thin slices cooked
  ham
6 medium-thin slices baby
  Swiss cheese
6 (6x4-inch) slices veal
¼ cup butter, melted
1 cup Italian seasoned
  breadcrumbs
3 tablespoons grated Parmesan
  cheese

Layer ham and Swiss cheese on veal. Roll up, securing with wooden pick. Dip in butter and roll in breadcrumbs mixed with Parmesan cheese. Place in 9x9x2-inch baking dish brushed with melted butter. Bake at 325 degrees for 35 minutes, basting once with melted butter. Do not bake at higher oven temperature because cheese will melt too quickly. Sprinkle veal rolls with Parmesan cheese. Serves: 6.

Joyce Romine

VEAL PICCATA

1 pound thin sliced veal, cut in
  3x4-inch pieces
¼ cup all-purpose flour
¼ cup vegetable oil
2 tablespoons butter
2 lemons, cut in halves
¼ cup dry white wine
salt and black pepper to taste

Dredge veal in flour, coating both sides. Heat oil and butter in skillet until bubbly. Sauté veal for about 3 minutes, turn and sauté second side for 3 minutes, squeezing lemon juice over veal as it cooks. Place on warm platter. Add wine to drippings in skillet and cook to reduce to a few tablespoons. Spoon sauce over veal and season with salt and black pepper. Serve immediately. Serves: 4.

Rose Marie Salim

VEAL VERMOUTH

2 pounds veal cutlets, cut in
   serving-sized pieces
salt and black pepper to taste
grated Parmesan cheese
butter
2 large onions, chopped
4 or 5 carrots, sliced
1 cup sliced fresh mushrooms
3 chicken bouillon cubes
½ cup boiling water
½ cup vermouth or dry white
   wine

Season veal with salt, black pepper and Parmesan cheese. Sauté veal in butter in heavy skillet, turning to brown on both sides. Place in 3-quart casserole. Sauté onion, carrots and mushrooms in skillet, adding more butter if needed, until vegetables are softened. Dissolve bouillon cubes in boiling water, add wine and pour over vegetables. Spoon vegetables with liquid on veal. Bake, covered, at 325 degrees for 1 hour. Serve gravy over noodles, rice or potatoes. Serves: 4 to 6.

Cathy Sutton

STUFFED PORK CHOPS

1½ cups cornbread dressing
   mix or breadcrumbs
¾ teaspoon salt
¼ teaspoon black pepper
1½ tablespoons minced parsley
1 tablespoon grated onion
1 egg
3 tablespoons milk
4 thick pork chops, slit to form
   pockets
butter

Combine dressing mix or breadcrumbs, salt, black pepper, parsley, onion, egg and milk, mixing well. Spoon stuffing into pockets in chops. Sauté stuffed chops in butter, turning to brown on both sides. Place in 9x9x2-inch baking dish. Bake at 350 degrees for 1 to 1½ hours. Serves: 4.

Marion Salter

PORK ROAST WITH STUFFING

1 (6 pound) rolled boneless
  pork roast
salt and black pepper to taste
garlic powder to taste
6 slices bacon

Stuffing:
½ pound hot-flavored bulk
  pork sausage
½ cup chopped celery
½ cup chopped green bell
  pepper
½ cup chopped onion
1 cup chopped peeled apples
1 cup golden raisins
2 cups fresh breadcrumbs

Roux:
½ cup butter
¼ cup plus 2 tablespoons all-
  purpose flour
1 large onion, chopped
2 cups hot water
6 beef bouillon cubes

Prepare stuffing by frying sausage until browned, stirring to crumble. Drain excess grease. Add celery, green bell pepper and onion to sausage and sauté until vegetables are softened. Add apples, raisins and breadcrumbs. Season pork roast with salt, black pepper and garlic powder. Stuff roast with sausage mixture and secure with heavy string at 2 to 3 inch intervals. Arrange bacon on roast and secure with wooden picks. Place in large roasting pan or casserole. Prepare roux by melting butter in saucepan. Add flour and cook, stirring constantly, until dark brown. Sauté onion in roux. Add hot water and bouillon cubes. Pour roux into roasting pan. Bake, uncovered, at 325 degrees until bacon is crisp, then cover with aluminum foil and continue baking for total baking time of 3½ hours. Serves: 8.

Sara Nell Williams

PORK CHOPS AND SOUTHERN STYLE GRAVY

12 center cut pork chops
lemon pepper to taste
Creole seasoning to taste
garlic powder to taste
1¼ cups all-purpose flour,
   divided
1 cup butter
1 large onion, chopped
3 cups water
9 beef bouillon cubes

Season both sides of pork chops with lemon pepper, Creole seasoning and garlic powder. Dredge in ¾ cup flour, coating both sides. Sauté chops in butter, turning to brown on both sides. Remove chops and set aside. Add ½ cup flour to butter and cook, stirring constantly, to form dark brown roux. Add onion and sauté for 2 minutes. Stir in water and bouillon cubes. Bring to a boil, then reduce heat. Add chops and simmer, stirring occasionally, for 1⅓ hours. Serve over rice. Serves: 12.

Sara Nell Williams

POLYNESIAN PORK CHOPS

6 medium pork chops
salt and black pepper to taste
1½ cups barbecue sauce
½ cup pineapple preserves

Season pork chops with salt and black pepper. Layer chops in 1½-quart casserole. Combine barbecue sauce and preserves. Spread ½ of sauce over chops, layer chops again and pour remaining sauce over top. Bake, covered, at 350 degrees for 50 to 60 minutes. Chops may be prepared 1 day in advance. Serves: 6.

Claudia Triche

SEAFOOD STUFFED PORK CHOPS

20 (1-inch thick) pork chops
salt and coarsely ground black
  pepper to taste
red pepper to taste
6 green onions, chopped
1 large onion, chopped
½ cup chopped parsley
1 medium-sized green bell
  pepper, chopped
1 cup margarine or butter
1 cup cooked rice
1 cup fresh cornbread crumbs
1 (8 ounce) package herb
  seasoned stuffing mix
3 teaspoons chicken bouillon
  granules
2 cups chopped cooked large
  shrimp or unchopped small
  shrimp
1 pound lump crabmeat

Using knife, slit 1 side of each chop to form pocket. Season chops with salt, black pepper and red pepper. Sauté green onions, onion, parsley and bell pepper in margarine or butter until softened. Add rice, cornbread crumbs, stuffing mix and bouillon granules, then add shrimp and crabmeat, mixing well. Spoon seafood mixture into pockets of chops, stuffing full but not protruding. Place chops in roasting pan. Bake at 350 degrees for about 45 minutes. Or grill chops for about 1 hour, turning frequently with tongs. Stuffing can be used to fill 12 pork chops and 8 chicken breasts or jumbo butterfly shrimp, wrapping the shrimp with bacon slices and broiling them. Serves: 20.

Rosemary Baker

CHICKEN IN PATTY SHELLS

4 chicken breast halves
water
salt and black pepper to taste
red pepper to taste
1 bay leaf
½ cup chopped onion
1 clove garlic, diced
½ cup chopped green bell
    pepper
½ cup chopped celery
¼ cup margarine
2 tablespoons all-purpose flour
1 teaspoon bottled brown
    bouquet sauce
1 tablespoon chopped parsley
1 tablespoon chopped green
    onion tops
1 (4½ ounce) jar mushrooms,
    drained
patty shells

Place chicken in stock pot and add water to cover. Season with salt, black pepper, red pepper and bay leaf. Cook until tender. Reserving 3 cups broth, remove chicken. When cool to touch, cut chicken in bite-sized pieces and set aside. Discard bay leaf from broth. Sauté onion, garlic, bell pepper and celery in margarine until vegetables are softened. Stir in flour, mixing thoroughly. Add bouquet sauce and reserved broth. Simmer for about 1 hour; sauce should be thickened. Add chicken, parsley, green onions and mushrooms, mixing well. Cook for about 20 minutes. Spoon chicken mixture into patty shells or serve over hot cooked rice. Serves: 6 to 8.

Marteel Henry

CHEESE CHICKEN

8 chicken breast halves, skin
    removed and boned
⅔ cup barbecue sauce
1 cup (4 ounces) shredded
    Cheddar cheese
1 cup (4 ounces) shredded
    mozzarella cheese
1 large tomato, cut in 8 slices
½ cup chopped green onions
sour cream (optional)

Cook chicken on grill or in oven, basting on both sides with barbecue sauce. Place cooked chicken in single layer in 13x9x2-inch baking dish. Combine Cheddar cheese and mozzarella cheese and sprinkle on chicken. Arrange tomato slices on cheese layer and sprinkle green onions on tomatoes. Broil for about 5 minutes or until cheese is bubbly. Serve with dollop of sour cream on each chicken piece. Serves: 4 to 6.

Renee Donahue

STOVE TOP CHICKEN

2 pounds chicken legs and
  thighs
vegetable oil
1 (10¾ ounce) can golden
  mushroom soup, undiluted
1 (10¾ ounce) can cream of
  chicken soup, undiluted
1 cup water
2 stalks celery, finely chopped
2 onions, thinly sliced
¼ cup vegetable oil
2 cloves garlic, chopped
1 teaspoon salt substitute
½ teaspoon black pepper
2 tablespoons white
  Worcestershire sauce

Sauté chicken legs and thighs in oil, turning to brown on all sides. Place chicken in large saucepan. Add mushroom soup, cream of chicken soup, water, celery, onion, ¼ cup oil, garlic, salt substitute, black pepper and Worcestershire sauce. Bring to a boil, reduce heat and simmer for 55 minutes to 1 hour or until meat separates from bones. Serve sauce over rice or potatoes. Serves: 4.

Lawrence Lawton

SUNDAY CHICKEN

8 chicken breast halves, skin
  removed and boned
½ cup butter, softened
¼ cup fresh lemon juice
3 tablespoons ketchup
1 tablespoon prepared mustard
¼ cup Worcestershire sauce
1 teaspoon hot pepper sauce
1 clove garlic, minced
1 small onion, chopped
¼ teaspoon black pepper
¼ teaspoon red pepper

Place chicken in 13x9x2-inch baking dish. Combine butter, lemon juice, ketchup, mustard, Worcestershire sauce, hot pepper sauce, garlic, onion, black pepper and red pepper in saucepan. Cook over low heat until butter is melted and ingredients are well mixed. Pour sauce over chicken. Bake, uncovered, at 350 degrees for 1 to 1½ hours or until chicken is tender. Serves: 8.

Tanya Conlay

CRAWFISH-STUFFED CHICKEN BREAST WITH GARLIC SAUCE

3 tablespoons butter, divided
⅓ cup all-purpose flour
¼ cup Marsala wine
⅔ cup half and half
6 cloves garlic, minced
1 cup chicken broth
6 chicken breasts, skin removed and boned
½ large white onion, minced
½ pound crawfish tails, peeled and finely chopped
8 fresh mushrooms
⅛ teaspoon salt or to taste
⅛ teaspoon black pepper
⅛ teaspoon hot pepper sauce
¼ cup chopped parsley

Prepare sauce by melting 2 tablespoons butter in heavy skillet over low heat. Add flour and stir until smooth. Add wine, half and half, garlic and broth. Cook, stirring constantly to prevent burning, for 3 minutes. Remove from heat and set aside. Place chicken pieces between wax paper sheets and pound to ¼-inch thickness. Sauté onion in 1 tablespoon butter in heavy skillet until onion is translucent. Add 2 tablespoons garlic sauce, crawfish, mushrooms, salt, black pepper, hot pepper sauce and chopped parsley, mixing to make stuffing. Place ⅙ stuffing mixture on each chicken piece, fold ends over stuffing and place, folded side down, in greased 13x9x2-inch baking dish. Pour sauce over chicken. Bake, uncovered, at 350 degrees for 45 minutes. Serve over pasta or rice with crisp green salad and garlic bread. For garlic lovers. Serves: 6.

Peter Cloutier

CRAWFISH STUFFED CHICKEN BREAST

8 chicken breasts, skin removed
   and boned
salt and black pepper to taste
1 large onion, chopped
1 green bell pepper, chopped
½ cup chopped celery
½ cup margarine
1 pound frozen crawfish tails,
   rinsed in hot water to remove
   fat
red pepper to taste
lemon pepper to taste
3½ cups Italian seasoned
   breadcrumbs
¼ cup plus 1 tablespoon
   chopped parsley
¼ cup plus 1 tablespoon
   chopped green onion tops

Place chicken pieces between wax paper sheets and pound to ¼-inch thickness. Season with salt and black pepper. Sauté onion, bell pepper and celery in margarine in saucepan until onion is translucent. Add crawfish and cook over medium heat for about 10 minutes. Season with salt, black pepper, red pepper and lemon pepper. Add breadcrumbs to desired stuffing consistency. Stir in parsley and green onions. Place ⅛ stuffing mixture on each chicken piece, fold ends over stuffing and secure with wooden pick. Place in 13x9x2-inch baking dish. Bake, covered with aluminum foil, at 375 degrees for 45 minutes. Remove foil and bake for additional 15 minutes, allowing chicken to brown. Place chicken on serving platter and remove wooden picks. Serves: 8.

Becky Luster

EASY CHICKEN MARSALA

6 chicken breast halves, skin
   removed and boned
¼ cup all-purpose flour
¼ teaspoon dried basil
¼ teaspoon dried oregano
3 tablespoons butter
¼ cup plus 2 tablespoons dry
   Marsala wine
¼ cup plus 2 tablespoons
   chicken broth
¼ teaspoon salt
¼ teaspoon black pepper
parsley for garnish

Place chicken pieces between wax paper sheets and pound with flat side of large knife. Combine flour, basil and oregano. Dredge chicken in seasoned flour. Sauté chicken in butter in skillet over medium to high heat until golden brown. Add wine, broth, salt and black pepper. Cook until chicken is tender. Place chicken on serving platter, pour cooking liquid over chicken and garnish with parsley. Veal or turkey fillets can be substituted for chicken. Serves: 6.

Pam DeBlieux

206

CHICKEN MARSALA

5 chicken breast halves, skin removed, boned and cut in ½-inch cubes
salt and black pepper to taste
all-purpose flour
3 tablespoons olive oil
2 cups sliced fresh mushrooms
½ teaspoon minced garlic
1 (16 ounce) can tomatoes, undrained, crushed
1 (8 ounce) can tomato sauce
⅓ cup Marsala wine
½ teaspoon basil
1 (16 ounce) package linguine

Season chicken with salt and black pepper and dredge lightly in flour. Sauté chicken in oil in Dutch oven for 10 minutes, turning to brown on all sides. Remove chicken from Dutch oven and set aside. Sauté mushrooms and garlic for 2 to 3 minutes. Add tomatoes, tomato sauce, wine and basil. Cook for 1 to 2 minutes. Add chicken to tomato mixture and simmer for 15 minutes. While chicken simmers, prepare linguine according to package directions. Drain. Serve chicken and sauce over hot linguine. Serves: 5 or 6.

Cathy Seymour

BREAST OF CHICKEN WITH CAPERS

4 chicken breast halves, skin removed and boned
½ cup all-purpose flour
1 tablespoon dried tarragon
¼ cup olive oil
¼ cup dry white wine
¾ cup chicken broth
¼ cup Dijon mustard
2 tablespoons lemon juice
2 tablespoons drained capers

Place chicken pieces between wax paper sheets and flatten with meat pounder to ⅛-inch thickness. Dredge chicken lightly with flour and sprinkle with tarragon. Sauté in oil over medium-high to high heat, turning to brown lightly on both sides. Combine wine, broth, mustard and lemon juice. Pour over chicken and cook over medium heat for 5 to 10 minutes or until sauce is slightly thickened. Place chicken on serving platter and keep warm. Strain sauce, pour over chicken and sprinkle with capers. Serves: 4.

Pat Thomas

CHICKEN BEER BAKE

¼ cup all-purpose flour
salt and black pepper to taste
6 chicken breast halves, skin
   removed
vegetable oil
2 (10¾ ounce) cans cream of
   chicken soup
1 tablespoon soy sauce
¼ cup slivered almonds,
   toasted, divided
½ cup beer
1 (4 ounce) can sliced
   mushrooms, drained, or ⅓
   cup cooked sliced fresh
   mushrooms

Combine flour, salt and black pepper. Dredge chicken in seasoned flour. Sauté in oil over medium heat, turning to brown on all sides. Place chicken in 13x9x2-inch baking dish. Combine soup, soy sauce, 2 tablespoons almonds, beer and mushrooms. Pour sauce over chicken. Bake, uncovered, at 350 degrees for 1 hour, basting occasionally with cooking liquid. Remove chicken from oven and sprinkle with 2 tablespoons almonds. Serves: 6.

Vicki Parrish

ORANGE CHICKEN

¼ cup margarine
3 tablespoons orange juice
1 tablespoon Worcestershire
   sauce
1 tablespoon soy sauce
1 tablespoon honey
4 chicken breast halves, skin
   removed and boned

Combine margarine, orange juice, Worcestershire sauce, soy sauce and honey in saucepan. Heat until margarine is melted. Place chicken in 13x9x2-inch baking dish. Pour sauce over chicken. Bake, uncovered, at 350 degrees for about 1 hour, basting occasionally with cooking liquid. Serves: 4.

Beverly Giering

LIGHT GRILLED CHICKEN BREASTS

3 tablespoons horseradish
1 cup fat-free ranch-style salad
  dressing
10 chicken breast halves, skin
  removed and boned
garlic powder to taste
onion powder to taste
lemon pepper to taste
seasoning salt to taste
grated orange peel (optional)
Szechwan seasonings (optional)

Combine horseradish and salad dressing. Lightly season both sides of chicken pieces with garlic powder, onion powder, lemon pepper and seasoning salt. Marinate chicken in salad dressing mixture for 24 hours. Drain chicken. Grill over medium heat for 8 to 10 minutes, turning once or twice during cooking. Serve on sesame seed buns with sandwich accompaniments. Fat-free Catalina salad dressing can be substituted for the horseradish-ranch dressing mixture. Serves: 10.

Shirley Walker

CAJUN FRIED CHICKEN

1 (2½ to 3 pound) broiler-fryer
  or 6 chicken breast halves
salt and black pepper to taste
red pepper to taste
3 or 4 jalapeño peppers
2 eggs, beaten
all-purpose flour
vegetable oil for deep-frying

Season chicken with salt, black pepper and red pepper. Using food processor, puree jalapeño peppers. Blend puree and eggs. Marinate chicken in egg mixture for 1 to 2 hours. Dredge chicken pieces with flour and deep fry in oil until crispy and cooked. Serves: 4 to 6.

Lynn Pierson

COUNTRY-STYLE CHICKEN KIEV WITH SAUCE

⅔ cup butter
½ cup fine breadcrumbs
2 tablespoons Parmesan cheese
¼ teaspoon salt
½ teaspoon garlic salt
1 teaspoon basil
1 teaspoon oregano
4 chicken breast halves
¼ cup white dry vermouth
¼ cup chopped green onions
¼ cup chopped parsley

Melt butter in heavy 2-quart saucepan. Combine breadcrumbs, Parmesan cheese, salt, garlic salt, basil and oregano on wax paper sheet. Dip chicken pieces in melted butter, then roll in crumb mixture to coat. Place skin side up in ungreased 13x9x2-inch baking dish. Bake at 375 degrees for 50 to 60 minutes or until golden brown and tender. Add wine, green onions and parsley to remaining melted butter. Pour butter sauce over chicken and bake for additional 3 to 5 minutes or until sauce is hot. Boneless chicken breasts can be used; bake for 45 minutes. Serves: 4.

Jeanne McGlathery

SAVORY CRESCENT CHICKEN

1 (3 ounce) package cream
  cheese, softened
3 tablespoons margarine,
  divided
2 cups cubed cooked chicken or
  2 (5 ounce) cans chicken
2 tablespoons milk
¼ teaspoon salt
⅛ teaspoon black pepper
1 tablespoon chopped chives or
  green onions
1 tablespoon chopped pimiento
1 tablespoon chopped green
  bell pepper
1 (8 ounce) can refrigerated
  crescent rolls
¾ cup crushed seasoned
  croutons

Blend cream cheese and 2 tablespoons margarine. Add chicken, milk, salt, black pepper, chives or green onions, pimiento and bell pepper, mixing well. Separate roll dough into 4 squares, pressing to seal perforations. Spoon equal amounts of chicken mixture into center of each square. Pull corners to center and press to seal. Melt 1 tablespoon margarine. Brush top of pastry with melted margarine and dip into crouton crumbs. Place on ungreased baking sheet. Bake at 350 degrees for 20 to 25 minutes. Chicken squares can be assembled and frozen. Extend baking time slightly. Serves: 4.

Claudia Rees

EVE'S ASIAN CHICKEN

1 (3½ pound) broiler-fryer,
   cut in serving pieces, or 3½
   pounds chicken pieces of
   choice
2 tablespoons peanut oil
1 clove garlic, coarsely chopped
red pepper to taste
¾ cup distilled white vinegar
¼ cup soy sauce
3 tablespoons honey

Sauté chicken in oil in large heavy skillet, turning to brown on all sides and adding garlic and red pepper toward end of cooking time. Add vinegar, soy sauce and honey. Cook over medium-high heat until chicken is done and sauce has been reduced; do not burn or allow all of sauce to evaporate. Remove light meat before dark meat to avoid drying. Chicken will be slightly glazed. Serve sauce with chicken. Serves: 4.

Susan Cloutier

CHICKEN FLORENTINE

4 bunches spinach or 2 (10
   ounce) packages frozen
   chopped spinach, thawed
8 chicken breast halves, skin
   removed and boned
½ cup butter, melted
all-purpose flour
1 teaspoon salt
¼ teaspoon white pepper
1 cup whipping cream
⅔ cup (2⅔ ounces) grated
   Parmesan or Romano cheese

If using fresh spinach, wilt in skillet over low heat. Let stand until cool and squeeze dry. Using food processor with knife blade, chop spinach. If using frozen spinach, squeeze to remove excess moisture. Spread spinach in bottom of buttered au gratin dish. Cut chicken breasts in halves, then cut horizontally in halves to form thin cutlets. Dredge each chicken piece in flour, then dip in butter and place on spinach. Season with salt and white pepper. Pour cream over chicken and sprinkle with cheese. Bake at 400 degrees for 20 minutes or until chicken is done. Serve with white Chardonnay wine and fresh fruit salad. Serves: 8.

Christina Smith

HOME STYLE CHICKEN AND DUMPLINGS

**4 large chicken breasts, skin
  removed, boned and cut in
  1-inch pieces**
1 tablespoon vegetable oil
**1 (16 ounce) jar whole onions,
  drained**
2 large cloves garlic, crushed
**¼ pound medium-sized fresh
  mushrooms, quartered**
¼ cup butter or margarine
¼ cup all-purpose flour
**1 packet instant chicken broth
  mix**
3 cups water
**1 (16 ounce) can whole baby
  carrots, drained**
1 (9 ounce) package frozen peas
1¾ cups buttermilk biscuit mix
¼ cup chopped parsley
½ cup milk

Sauté chicken in oil in 12-inch skillet over medium-high heat for about 5 minutes or until golden brown, stirring frequently. Add onion, garlic and mushrooms. Cook, stirring frequently, for about 5 minutes or until vegetables are tender. Place chicken mixture in bowl and keep warm. Melt butter or margarine in same skillet over medium heat. Add flour and cook, stirring constantly, for 5 minutes or until mixture is golden brown. Add broth mix. Gradually stir in water and cook, stirring constantly, for about 10 minutes or until mixture is smooth and slightly thickened. Add carrots, peas and chicken mixture. Cover and bring to a boil. Combine biscuit mix and parsley in mixing bowl. Add milk, stirring with fork just until biscuit mix is moistened. Divide dough in 8 round dumplings. Remove lid from skillet. Using tablespoon and fork, drop dumplings into boiling chicken mixture. Return to boil, reduce heat and simmer, covered, for 10 minutes or until dumplings are light, fluffy and gently firm to touch. Serves: 4.

Karen Townsend

BACON LACED CHICKEN

6 chicken breast halves, skin
  removed and boned
salt and black pepper to taste
onion powder to taste
1½ cups (6 ounces) grated
  Swiss cheese
6 slices bacon, partially cooked
1 (10¾ ounce) can cream of
  mushroom soup, undiluted
1 cup sour cream

Place chicken pieces between wax paper sheets and pound to flatten. Season chicken with salt, black pepper and onion powder. Place ¼ cup cheese in center of each chicken piece and roll up. Wrap each with bacon slice and secure with 2 wooden picks. Place chicken in 13x9x2-inch baking dish. Combine soup and sour cream. Spread on chicken rolls. Bake, covered, at 325 degrees for 30 minutes, remove cover and bake for additional 15 minutes. Serves: 6.

Claudia Rees

COMPANY CORNISH HENS

6 (2 pound) Rock Cornish game
  hens
¾ cup butter
½ cup all-purpose flour
1 cup chopped onion
1 cup chopped celery
½ pound fresh mushrooms,
  sliced
1½ cups dry white vermouth
½ cup water
8 chicken bouillon cubes
black pepper to taste
garlic powder to taste

Using twine, secure legs of hens. Sauté hens in butter in Dutch oven over medium heat, turning to brown on all sides. Remove hens. Add flour to butter and cook, stirring constantly, to form dark brown roux. Add onion and celery and sauté until vegetables are softened. Stir in mushrooms, vermouth, water and bouillon cubes. Season with black pepper and garlic powder. Bring to a boil, add hens, reduce heat and simmer for 1 to 1¼ hours. Serve hens with wild rice. Serves: 6.

Sara Nell Williams

CORNISH HENS WITH HERBED BUTTER AND MANDARIN RICE

4 Rock Cornish game hens
salt and black pepper to taste
¾ cup butter (not margarine), softened
1 cup chopped chives or ¼ cup dried chives
1 cup chopped parsley or ½ cup parsley flakes
1 tablespoon dried rosemary
1 tablespoon dried thyme
3 tablespoons dried sage, divided
3 tablespoons olive oil

Rice:
1 (6 ounce) package wild rice mix
1 cup small native pecans or 1 cup broken pecans
1 (11 ounce) can mandarin oranges, drained

Season cavities of hens with salt and black pepper. Using food processor, combine butter, chives, parsley, rosemary, thyme and 1 tablespoon sage, blending to form smooth paste. Gently separate skin from breast of each hen to form a pocket. Stuff each with 2 to 3 tablespoons butter mixture. Divide remaining butter into 4 portions and rub in cavities of hens. Rub oil on outside of hens and sprinkle with 2 tablespoons sage. Place hens in roasting pan. Bake at 450 degrees for 20 minutes, basting after 10 minutes. Reduce oven temperature to 350 degrees and continue baking for about 45 minutes or until leg bone turns easily; baste hens every 10 to 15 minutes to assure moistness. While hens bake, prepare rice according to package directions. Stir pecans into cooked rice and fold in oranges just before serving. Carefully place hens on bed of rice and top with 1 or 2 spoons cooking liquid. Serves: 4.

Tanya Conlay

HOLIDAY ROAST DUCKLING WITH ALMOND APRICOT SAUCE

water
1 (14½ ounce) can chicken
  broth
1 Long Island duckling
1 tablespoon honey
1 tablespoon soy sauce
1 tablespoon hot water
½ teaspoon ground ginger

Almond-Apricot Sauce:
¼ cup thinly sliced green
  onions
¼ cup butter
3 tablespoons lemon juice
⅓ cup orange juice
½ teaspoon grated orange peel
1 tablespoon Dijon mustard
1 (17 ounce) can apricot halves,
  drained
salt and freshly ground black
  pepper to taste
½ cup amaretto liqueur
1 tablespoon cognac
¼ cup slivered almonds,
  toasted

Pour water to 1-inch depth in Dutch oven. Add broth and bring to a boil. Using fork tines, pierce skin of duck in several places. Place duck on rack over broth liquid. Simmer, covered, for 1 to 1½ hours or until duck is tender and thoroughly cooked. Duck fat will be rendered during cooking process. Cooked duck can be stored in refrigerator for 1 day or frozen. Prepare sauce by briefly sautéing green onions in butter. Add lemon juice, orange juice, orange peel, mustard, apricots, salt and black pepper. Simmer, stirring occasionally, for about 15 minutes or until well blended. Stir in amaretto and cognac. Continue cooking for 30 minutes. While sauce cooks, complete preparation of duck. Combine honey, soy sauce, hot water and ginger. Baste duck liberally and place duck directly on center rack in oven, covering lower rack with aluminum foil to catch drippings. Bake at 425 degrees for about 20 minutes or until duck is browned. Using sharp knife, cut duck in quarters. Add toasted almonds to sauce and serve over duck and wild rice. Serves: 4.

Pat Thomas

215

ROAST WILD DUCK

4 (2 to 3 pound) ducks
2 onions, quartered
4 apples, quartered
salt and black pepper to taste
red pepper to taste
2 cups dry white wine
8 slices bacon

Stuff cavities of ducks with onions and apples. Season ducks with salt, black pepper and red pepper. Place ducks in roasting pan. Add wine to 1½-inch depth in pan. Place 2 bacon slices in cross shape on each duck. Bake, covered, at 300 degrees for 2 to 3 hours, checking after 1 hour and basting often. Add more wine if necessary. Red wine can be substituted for white wine. Serves: 6 to 8.

Lana Scott

PRAIRIE LAKE DUCKS

4 duck breasts and legs
all-purpose flour
salt and black pepper to taste
garlic powder to taste
onion salt to taste
4 slices bacon, cut in halves
1 onion, sliced in rings
1 cup red wine and vinegar
    salad dressing

Dredge duck pieces lightly in flour, shaking to remove excess. Season with salt, black pepper, garlic powder and onion salt. Place 2 slices bacon on each duck and top with onion rings. Place side by side in roasting pan. Pour salad dressing over ducks. Bake, covered, at 325 degrees for 2½ hours. Basting is unnecessary. Serves: 4.

Mickey Hennigan

HELEN'S BAKED WILD DUCK

4 or 5 ducks or teal
salt to taste
lemon pepper to taste
red pepper to taste
2 medium-sized onions, cut in
  halves
4 stalks celery, cut in 1-inch
  pieces, divided
vegetable oil
3 carrots, cut in 1-inch pieces
4 small turnips (optional)
1 (14 ounce) can mushrooms,
  drained
1 packet dry onion soup mix
1 (10¾ ounce) can cream of
  mushroom soup, undiluted
¼ cup chopped parsley
1 cup water
1 cup dry red wine
1 cup cola flavored carbonated
  drink

Season ducks inside and out with salt, lemon pepper and red pepper. Place onion half and 2 pieces celery in cavity of each duck. Using enough oil to coat bottom of iron pot, sauté ducks, turning to brown on all sides. Combine remaining celery, carrots, turnips, mushrooms, soup mix, soup, parsley, water, wine and cola in roasting pan, stirring to mix. Place ducks in vegetable mixture. Bake, covered, at 375 degrees for about 4 hours or until legs separate from duck, basting frequently. Serve ducks and vegetables over rice. Duck may be cooked on stove top over medium-low heat; additional liquid may be required during cooking time. For beef roast, sear beef on all sides in oil. Chop onion and celery and add to same vegetable mixture (as for duck) in roasting pan. Place roast in center and season with 1 teaspoon ground oregano. Bake at 375 degrees for 4 hours, basting often. Serves: 4 or 5.

Kay Aaron

DAVID DAILY'S ALLIGATOR AND SHRIMP SAUCE

2 pounds alligator, cut in 1-inch
  cubes
milk
1½ large onions, chopped
2 large green bell peppers,
  chopped
½ cup margarine
1 tablespoon vegetable oil
½ cup all-purpose flour
1 (14½ ounce) can chicken
  broth
2 (8 ounce) cans tomato sauce
2 cups ketchup
2 cups water
1 tablespoon salt (optional)
1 tablespoon black pepper
1 tablespoon seasoned salt
1 tablespoon lemon pepper
1 tablespoon garlic powder
1 tablespoon paprika
1 tablespoon chopped parsley
½ teaspoon Creole seasoned
  salt, preferably Tony
  Chachere's
1 pound large shrimp, peeled
  and deveined
2½ cups regular rice

Marinate alligator chunks in milk in refrigerator for 2 to 3 hours. Sauté onion and green bell pepper in margarine, oil and flour until vegetables are softened. Add broth, tomato sauce, ketchup and water. Simmer for 10 minutes. Stir in salt, black pepper, seasoned salt, lemon pepper, garlic powder, paprika, parsley and Creole seasoned salt, adding additional seasoning if desired. Drain alligator chunks and add to sauce. Simmer for 1½ hours, adding shrimp for final 12 minutes of cooking time. While sauce cooks, prepare rice according to package directions. Serve sauce over rice. Serves: 6.

Linnye Daily

Main Dishes

ROLLED STEAK

1 (2 to 2½ pound) round beef
  steak
salt and black pepper
1 small Irish potato, thinly
  sliced
1 small onion, thinly sliced
1 clove garlic, minced
2 tablespoons grated Parmesan
  or Romano cheese
1 teaspoon chopped parsley
1 tablespoon vegetable oil
1 (32 ounce) jar prepared
  spaghetti sauce
1 (16 ounce) package spaghetti

Place steak on work surface. Season upper side with salt and black pepper. Spread potatoes, onion, garlic, Parmesan or Romano cheese, parsley and oil evenly on steak and season with salt and black pepper. Roll, jelly-roll fashion, and secure with cord. Sear steak roll in oil in large skillet, turning to brown on all sides. Pour spaghetti sauce into Dutch oven. Place steak roll in sauce. Simmer for 2 hours. Prepare spaghetti according to package directions toward end of steak cooking time. Place steak roll on serving platter, remove cord and slice. Drain spaghetti and place around steak roll. Pour sauce over steak and spaghetti. Serve with green salad, French bread and red wine. Serves: 8.

Beverly Giering

SPICY STEAK AND CORN SOFT TACOS

1 medium-sized purple onion,
  sliced
1 red bell pepper, sliced
2 tablespoons olive oil
½ pound round, flank or skirt
  steak, cut in ¼-inch strips
¾ cup frozen corn, cooked and
  drained
½ teaspoon ground cumin
½ teaspoon chili powder
salt and freshly ground black
  pepper
1½ tablespoons minced cilantro
corn or flour tortillas
grated Cheddar cheese
chopped tomatoes
sour cream

Sauté onion and bell pepper in oil in heavy skillet over medium heat for about 10 minutes or until vegetables are softened. Remove vegetables. Sauté steak in skillet, stirring, for about 1 minute or until no longer pink. Add onion, bell pepper, corn, cumin and chili powder to steak and heat thoroughly. Season with salt and black pepper. Remove from heat and stir in cilantro. Place in heated dish and keep warm. Cook tortillas over gas flame or electric burner just until they begin to change color. Spoon steak mixture on each tortilla and garnish with Cheddar cheese, tomatoes and sour cream. Serve immediately. Serves: 2.

Linda Burke

MEXICAN TAMALE SQUARES

¾ cup all-purpose flour
¾ cup cornmeal
2 teaspoons baking powder
¾ cup milk
3 tablespoons margarine,
  melted
1 pound ground beef
¾ cup chopped green bell
  pepper
1 (8 ounce) jar pasteurized
  process cheese spread,
  divided
1 cup chopped fresh tomato,
  divided
1 tablespoon chili powder

Combine flour, cornmeal and baking powder. Add milk and margarine, beating until smooth. Pour batter into greased 8x8x2-inch baking dish. Cook beef until browned, stirring to crumble. Drain excess grease. Add bell pepper and cook until softened. Add ½ cup cheese spread, ½ cup tomatoes and chili powder to beef mixture, mixing well. Spoon beef mixture over batter. Bake at 375 degrees for 20 minutes. Top with ½ cup cheese spread and sprinkle ½ cup tomatoes and bake for additional 5 minutes. Cut into squares to serve. For variety, 1 (4 ounce) can chopped green chilies, drained, can be added to meat mixture for spicier flavor or jalapeño cheese spread can be substituted for regular flavor cheese spread. Serves: 6 to 8.

Karen Townsend

HOT TAMALES

Filling:
1 (5 to 6 pound) Boston butt
  pork roast
water
4 medium-sized onions,
  chopped
9 cloves garlic, chopped
4 stalks celery, chopped
4 medium-sized green bell
  peppers, chopped
1 bunch green onions, chopped
½ bunch parsley, chopped
2 to 3 tablespoons black pepper
2 to 3 tablespoons red pepper
2 tablespoons cumin
2 to 3 tablespoons chicken
  bouillon granules

Meal:
2 pounds stone ground
  cornmeal
4 medium-sized onions,
  chopped
1 bunch green onions, chopped
9 cloves garlic, chopped
4 stalks celery, chopped
4 medium-sized green bell
  peppers, chopped
½ bunch parsley, chopped
1 tablespoon black pepper
2 to 3 tablespoons red pepper
2 to 3 tablespoons chicken
  bouillon granules
2 to 4 (8 ounce) packages pre-
  packed corn shucks
water
1 cup vegetable oil

Prepare filling. Place pork roast in Dutch oven with water to cover. Bake at 300 degrees overnight or until tender. Remove roast from pan, reserving broth. Discard bone. Using food processor, chop meat. Place meat in clean Dutch oven. Add onion, garlic, celery and bell pepper, stirring to mix. Add green onions and parsley, mixing by hand if necessary. Stir in black pepper, red pepper, cumin and bouillon granules. Set aside. Prepare meal mixture. Combine pork broth, cornmeal, onion, green onions, garlic, celery, bell pepper and parsley, mixing well. Add black pepper, red pepper and bouillon granules. Simmer, covered, for 1 to 2 hours or until meal is cooked, stirring frequently. Set aside. Boil shucks in water for about 1 hour or until soft and pliable. Add oil to meal mixture, mixing well. Flatten shuck. Place ⅓ cup meal mixture on shuck, spreading to 4x3-inch rectangle. Spoon about ¼ cup meat mixture in center of meal. Roll 1 turn, tuck ends under and continue to roll to form tamale. A small string of shuck may be necessary to hold tamale wrapper together. Steam assembled tamales for about 3 hours. Makes 96.

Rosemary Baker

223

SOUTH OF THE BORDER LASAGNA

2 pounds ground chuck beef
1 onion, chopped
2 cloves garlic, chopped
3 tablespoons butter or
   margarine
¼ cup chili powder
3 cups low-salt tomato sauce
½ teaspoon sugar
1 tablespoon parsley flakes
1 teaspoon dried oregano
1 (6 ounce) can sliced black
   olives with jalapeño peppers
1 (4 ounce) can chopped green
   chilies
12 corn tortillas, cut in quarters
2 cups low-fat cottage cheese
1 large egg, beaten
2 cups (8 ounces) grated
   Monterey Jack cheese
1 cup (4 ounces) grated sharp
   Cheddar cheese
chopped green onions
sour cream
sliced black olives

Fry beef, stirring to crumble, until browned. Drain excess grease and set aside. Sauté onion and garlic in butter or margarine until softened and slightly translucent. Add beef to vegetables. Stir in chili powder, tomato sauce, sugar, parsley, oregano, olives with jalapeños and chilies. Simmer for 10 to 15 minutes. Combine egg and cottage cheese. In 14x10x2-inch lasagna pan, layer ⅓ of meat mixture, ½ of tortillas, ½ of egg mixture and ½ of Monterey Jack cheese; repeat layers, top with remaining meat mixture and sprinkle with Cheddar cheese. Bake at 350 degrees for about 30 minutes or until thoroughly heated and bubbly. Serve hot, allowing guests to add green onions, sour cream and olives as desired. Serves: 8.

Tanya Conlay

SMOTHERED BURRITOS

1 pound ground beef
1 (16 ounce) can refried beans
8 to 10 soft flour tortillas
2 cups chopped fresh tomatoes
½ cup diced onion
1 (16 ounce) package Cheddar
   cheese or Monterey Jack
   cheese, melted
sour cream (optional)

Green Pepper Chili:
1 pound hot or mild flavored
   bulk pork sausage
3 (4 ounce) cans chopped green
   chilies
1 (16 ounce) can stewed
   tomatoes, chopped
1 cup water

Prepare chili by frying sausage, stirring to crumble, until browned. Drain excess grease. Add chilies, tomatoes and water. Simmer for 30 minutes. While chili cooks, fry ground beef, stirring to crumble, until browned. Drain excess grease. Set aside and keep warm. To assemble burrito, spread refried beans on soft tortillas. Layer beef, chili, fresh tomatoes, onion, Cheddar or Monterey Jack cheese and sour cream on beans. Roll up, place on serving plate and top with more chili and cheese, remelting cheese by microwaving at high setting for about 30 seconds, if necessary. Serves: 6.

Lynne Johnson

MARGARET'S CURRY PILAF

1 onion, chopped
2 cloves garlic, chopped
1 green bell pepper, chopped
2 stalks celery, chopped
2 tablespoons oil
1 pound ground beef
2 tablespoons curry powder
1 (16 ounce) can stewed
   tomatoes
1 cup beef or chicken bouillon
1 cup uncooked regular rice

Sauté onion, garlic, bell pepper and celery in oil until softened. Remove vegetables from skillet and set aside. Cook beef until browned, stirring to crumble. Drain excess grease. Add vegetables to beef. Stir in curry powder, tomatoes, bouillon and rice. Simmer, covered, for 18 to 20 minutes. Let stand for 10 minutes before serving. Serves: 8.

Sarah Luster

NATCHITOCHES MEAT PIES

Filling:
1½ pounds ground beef
1½ pounds ground pork
1 cup chopped green onions
  with tops
1 tablespoon salt
1 teaspoon coarsely ground
  black pepper
1 teaspoon coarsely ground red
  pepper
½ teaspoon cayenne pepper
⅓ cup all-purpose flour

Crust:
⅓ mounded cup vegetable
  shortening
2 cups self-rising flour, sifted
1 egg, beaten
¾ cup milk

Prepare filling. Combine beef, pork, green onions, salt, black pepper, red pepper and cayenne pepper in Dutch oven. Cook over medium heat, stirring often, until meat is no longer red; do not overcook. Sift flour over meat mixture and stir to mix well. Remove from heat, place in colander to drain excess grease and juice and let stand until room temperature. Prepare crust. Cut shortening into flour. Add egg and milk, mixing to form dough. Shape dough into a ball. Using about ⅓ of dough at a time, roll on lightly floured surface. Cut into 5 to 5½-inch circles. Stack circles on baking sheet, separating with wax paper. Assemble meat pies by placing a rounded tablespoon of meat filling at 1 side of pastry circle. Using fingertips dipped in water, moisten edge of circle, fold top over meat and crimp to seal with fork tines dipped in water. Prick upper surface twice with fork tines. Assembled pies can be frozen. To cook, deep-fry meat pies in oil heated to 350 degrees until golden brown. If using frozen pies, do not thaw before frying. For cocktail meat pies, use cutter and 1 teaspoon filling. Makes 26 to 28.

Mary Fulton

MEAT PIES

Filling:
1 pound ground beef
1 pound ground pork
1 bunch green onions, chopped
1 clove garlic, minced
1 green bell pepper, chopped
salt and black pepper to taste
red pepper to taste
1 teaspoon vegetable shortening
1 tablespoon all-purpose flour

Crust:
4 cups all-purpose flour
1 teaspoon baking powder
2 teaspoons salt
½ cup vegetable shortening
1 egg, beaten
1 cup milk

Prepare filling. Sauté beef, pork, green onions, garlic and bell pepper with salt, black pepper and red pepper in shortening, stirring to crumble meat, until meat is browned but not dry. Remove from heat. Drain excess liquid. Stir in flour. Prepare crust. Sift flour, baking powder and salt together. Cut shortening into dry ingredients. Combine egg and milk. Gradually add liquid to dry ingredients until dough consistency. Break into small pieces and roll very thin. Cut into circles, using saucer as guide. Assemble meat pies by placing 1 tablespoon meat filling at 1 side of pastry circle. Fold top over meat and crimp to seal with fork tines. To cook, deep-fry meat pies in oil until golden brown. Drain and serve hot. Makes about 18.

Gay Melder

EGGPLANT CASSEROLE

2 medium eggplants, peeled
  and sliced
1 medium-sized onion, sliced
1 green bell pepper, sliced
water
1 (6 ounce) package Mexican
  cornbread mix
1 pound ground beef
½ cup (2 ounces) grated
  Cheddar cheese, divided
salt and black pepper to taste
garlic powder to taste

Steam eggplant, onion and bell pepper with small amount of water until vegetables are softened. Prepare cornbread according to package directions. Fry beef, stirring to crumble, until browned. Drain excess grease. Combine vegetables, cornbread, beef, ¼ cup Cheddar cheese, salt, black pepper and garlic powder, mixing well. Pour into 12x7x2-inch baking dish. Sprinkle with ¼ cup cheese. Bake at 350 degrees for 30 minutes. Serves: 8 to 10.

Cathy Sutton

ARTICHOKE CHICKEN

8 chicken breast halves, skin
  removed and boned
salt and black pepper to taste
all-purpose flour
¼ cup butter
½ cup chopped onion
2 or 3 cloves garlic, chopped
1 (10 ounce) can tomatoes with
  green chilies
1 (14 ounce) can artichoke
  hearts, drained and quartered
1 (4 ounce) can sliced
  mushrooms, drained
3 tablespoons Sauterne wine

Season chicken with salt and black pepper and dredge in flour. Sauté chicken in butter, turning to lightly brown on both sides. Place chicken in 13x9x2-inch baking dish prepared with vegetable cooking spray. Sauté onion and garlic in butter until softened. Add tomatoes with green chilies, artichoke hearts, mushrooms and wine. Cook until thickened. Pour sauce over chicken. Bake, covered, at 350 degrees for 40 minutes. Remove cover and bake for 15 to 20 additional minutes. Serves: 8.

Ginger Horton

CHICKEN CRESCENT ROLLS

1 (8 ounce) package cream
  cheese, softened
1 (10¾ ounce) can cream of
  chicken soup, undiluted
¼ to ½ (10 ounce) package
  frozen chopped broccoli,
  cooked and well drained
2 cups chopped cooked chicken
¼ cup chopped black olives
2 tablespoons minced onion
1 tablespoon lemon juice
2 teaspoons lemon pepper
2 (8 ounce) cans refrigerated
  crescent roll dough
¾ cup (3 ounces) grated
  Cheddar cheese

Combine cream cheese and soup, blending until smooth. Stir in broccoli and add chicken, olives, onion, lemon juice and lemon pepper. Cover a baking sheet with aluminum foil and spray foil with vegetable cooking spray. Unroll ½ crescent roll dough on baking sheet, arranging to form 2 long rectangles and pressing perforations to seal. Place ½ of chicken mixture on each rectangle, leaving ½-inch margin along edges. Sprinkle with cheese. Separate second can of crescent roll dough into 2 long rectangles, place over chicken filling, press to seal perforations and seal edges with fork tines. Bake at 350 degrees for 25 to 30 minutes or until golden brown. Slice to serve. Serves: 8 to 10.

Elizabeth Post

CHICKEN CROISSANTS

1 (6 ounce) can chunk chicken
   or 1½ cups chopped cooked
   chicken, drained and liquid
   reserved
1 (8 ounce) can crushed
   pineapple, drained and liquid
   reserved
half and half
¼ cup butter, melted
3 tablespoons all-purpose flour
1 tablespoon brown sugar
2 tablespoons mayonnaise
1 cup (4 ounces) shredded
   Swiss cheese
1 cup (4 ounces) shredded
   Monterey Jack cheese
salt and black pepper to taste
6 croissants

Combine liquid from chicken and pine-apple. Add enough half and half to measure 1 cup liquid. Set aside. Flake chicken into saucepan. Add butter, flour and brown sugar. Cook, stirring frequently, over medium heat until browned. Add half and half liquid and cook until thickened. Combine pineapple, mayonnaise, Swiss cheese, Monterey Jack cheese, salt and black pepper. Add to chicken mixture and cook until cheese is melted. Spread on croissants and place on baking sheet. Bake at 350 degrees for 10 to 12 minutes. Serves: 6.

Lynne Johnson

CHICKEN AND ASPARAGUS

4 small chicken breast halves,
   skin removed, boned and cut
   in ½-inch strips
1 tablespoon dried rosemary
12 to 16 stalks fresh asparagus,
   cut diagonally in 1-inch
   pieces
2 medium-sized onions, sliced
12 to 16 fresh mushrooms,
   sliced
¼ cup water
2 teaspoons lemon juice
salt and black pepper to taste
garlic powder to taste

In 2-quart casserole, layer ¼ each of chicken, rosemary, asparagus, onion and mushrooms; repeat layers 3 times. Pour water and lemon juice over layers and season with salt, black pepper and garlic. Bake, covered, at 450 degrees for 25 to 30 minutes. Serve with green salad and crusty bread for low-calorie meal. Serves: 4.

Cathy Seymour

CHICKEN EPICUREAN

8 chicken breast halves, skin
  removed and boned
⅔ cup brandy
1 cup butter or margarine
1 tablespoon Worcestershire
  sauce
1 teaspoon garlic salt
½ cup chopped fresh
  mushrooms
½ cup sliced carrots
1 cup seedless green grapes
salt and black pepper to taste
⅓ cup all-purpose flour
6 to 8 slices bread, toasted
parsley sprigs

Marinate chicken in brandy for 30 minutes. Drain chicken. Sauté chicken in butter in skillet over low heat, cooking until lightly browned on both sides. Add Worcestershire sauce, garlic salt, mushrooms, carrots, grapes, salt and black pepper. Simmer, covered, for 15 to 20 minutes. Remove chicken and keep warm. Add flour to vegetable mixture in skillet and cook, stirring constantly, until thickened. Place chicken on toast slices and spoon sauce over chicken. Garnish with parsley. Serves: 6 to 8.

Linda Burke

CHICKEN LOAF

2 envelopes unflavored gelatin
½ cup cold water
warm water
3½ to 4 cups finely chopped
  cooked chicken
1 cup finely chopped celery
6 finely chopped hard-cooked
  eggs
1 (3 ounce) bottle sliced
  pimiento-stuffed green olives
1 cup chicken broth, heated
1 cup mayonnaise
1 (10 ounce) bottle mustard-
  mayonnaise sandwich and
  salad sauce
salt and black pepper to taste

Soften gelatin in cold water in small bowl. Place bowl in warm water to dissolve; do not allow warm water to mix with gelatin. Combine chicken, celery, eggs, olives, broth, mayonnaise, salad sauce, salt and black pepper. Stir in dissolved gelatin. Pour mixture into two 9x5x3-inch loaf pans or one 13x9x2-inch baking pan or 24 individual molds. Chill until firm. Serves: 12 to 24.

Mary Lee Posey

CHICKEN WITH SQUASH

5 chicken breast halves
salt and black pepper to taste
  (optional)
3 tablespoons vegetable oil
1 onion, chopped
2 cloves garlic, crushed
2 (16 ounce) cans stewed
  tomatoes
1 teaspoon salt
¼ teaspoon black pepper
½ teaspoon thyme
2 small zucchini squash, sliced
5 small yellow squash, sliced

Season chicken with salt and black pepper. Sauté chicken in oil in large skillet, turning to lightly brown on both sides. Add onion, garlic, tomatoes, salt, black pepper and thyme to chicken. Simmer, stirring occasionally, for 15 minutes. Add zucchini and yellow squash. Cook for 10 minutes or until chicken and vegetables are tender. Serves: 5.

Renee Donahue

CRISPY WALNUT CHICKEN

3 cups crispy rice cereal
½ cup walnuts, cashews or
  pecans
½ cup butter, melted
½ teaspoon salt
½ teaspoon black pepper
1 teaspoon garlic powder
3 pounds chicken pieces, skin
  removed

Using food processor, process cereal and nuts to fine crumb consistency. Combine butter, salt, black pepper and garlic powder. Dip chicken pieces in butter mixture, then in cereal crumbs and place on 15x10x1-inch jelly roll pan. Pour remaining butter mixture over chicken. Bake at 350 degrees for 1 hour or until chicken is done. Chicken is best when prepared the same day as served. Serves: 6.

Vanessa Robertson

MEXICAN CHICKEN LASAGNA

3 cups chopped cooked chicken
　or turkey
1 (15 ounce) can tomato sauce
1 cup picante sauce
1 (14 ounce) can artichoke
　hearts, drained and quartered
½ cup chopped green onions
1 clove garlic, minced
1 green bell pepper, chopped
1 teaspoon ground cumin
12 corn tortillas
2 cups (8 ounces) shredded
　Monterey Jack cheese,
　divided

Combine chicken or turkey, tomato sauce, picante sauce, artichoke hearts, green onions, garlic, bell pepper and cumin in 10-inch skillet. Bring to a boil, reduce heat and simmer for 15 minutes, stirring occasionally. Spread thin layer of chicken mixture in lightly greased 13x9x2-inch baking dish. Place 6 tortillas on sauce, overlapping to cover bottom of dish. Spread ½ of remaining chicken mixture on tortillas, sprinkle with 1 cup cheese, add 6 tortillas and top with remaining chicken mixture. Bake, tightly covered with aluminum foil, at 350 degrees for 25 minutes. Sprinkle with 1 cup cheese and let stand for 10 minutes before cutting to serve. Lasagna can be topped with shredded lettuce, chopped tomatoes, sliced olives and avocados and dollops of sour cream. Serves: 8.

Brenda Stamey

CHICKEN AND SQUASH CASSEROLE

1 cup minced green onions
2 tablespoons margarine
1 (10¾ ounce) can cream of
  celery soup
2 eggs
1 cup Italian seasoned
  breadcrumbs, divided
½ teaspoon salt
⅛ teaspoon black pepper
¼ teaspoon garlic powder
⅛ teaspoon oregano
1 tablespoon Worcestershire
  sauce
6 chicken breast halves, cooked
  and cubed
2 cups diced cooked yellow
  squash
1 cup (4 ounces) grated
  Cheddar cheese

Sauté green onions in margarine until softened. Combine green onions, soup, eggs, ½ cup breadcrumbs, salt, black pepper, garlic powder, oregano and Worcestershire sauce, mixing well. In 2½-quart casserole, layer ½ each of chicken, squash and soup mixture; repeat layers and sprinkle with ½ cup breadcrumbs and Cheddar cheese. Bake at 375 degrees for 30 minutes. Serves: 6 to 8.

Melissa Aldredge

LEEK-STUFFED CHICKEN BREASTS WITH WALNUT CREAM SAUCE

2 large leeks (about 1 pound),
  split lengthwise and cut in
  2-inch pieces
3 tablespoons unsalted butter
⅔ cup plus 3 tablespoons
  whipping cream, divided
1 tablespoon water
¼ teaspoon salt
freshly ground black pepper to
  taste
4 large chicken breast halves,
  skin removed and boned
salt to taste
2 teaspoons peanut oil
3 tablespoons chicken broth
¼ cup toasted walnuts

Sauté leeks in butter in heavy skillet over medium heat, cooking and stirring for about 15 minutes or until partially softened; do not brown. Add 3 tablespoons whipping cream, water, salt and black pepper. Cook for about 15 minutes or until leeks are softened and liquid is evaporated. Chill, covered, thoroughly. Leeks can be prepared 1 day in advance and stored in refrigerator until ready to use. Place chicken pieces between wax paper sheets. Using meat mallet or rolling pin, pound to ¼-inch thickness. Season with salt and black pepper. Spread 1 rounded teaspoon leek mixture on each chicken piece. Fold short edges of chicken over filling. Starting on 1 long side, roll tightly, jelly roll fashion. Secure with string. Reserve remaining leek mixture for sauce. Brush chicken rolls lightly with oil. Chicken rolls can be assembled up to 6 hours in advance; cover with plastic wrap and store in refrigerator. Return to room temperature before continuing with preparation. Arrange chicken rolls, seam side down, in oven-safe skillet or casserole. Bake at 400 degrees for about 25 minutes or until lightly browned and firm to touch. Transfer to serving platter, discard strings and cover rolls with aluminum foil to keep warm. Do not clean skillet or casserole. Add ⅔ cup cream, broth and reserved leek mixture to skillet. Boil for about 5 minutes or until reduced to measure ⅔ cup. Stir in walnuts,

(continued on next page)

(continued)

reserving several pieces for garnish. Check seasoning, adding salt and black pepper if necessary. Spoon 1 tablespoon sauce on each individual plate. Cut each chicken piece crosswise in 5 slices and overlap slices on sauce. Spoon remaining sauce over chicken. Garnish with reserved walnuts. Serves: 4.

Linda Burke

CHICKEN IMPERIAL

12 pieces chicken
2 cups sherry
6 cups breadcrumbs
2½ cups (10 ounces) grated
  Parmesan cheese
3 cloves garlic, crushed
1½ cups chopped blanched
  almonds
2 tablespoons salt
⅜ teaspoon black pepper
1½ cups butter, melted

Soak chicken in sherry for at least 2 hours. Combine breadcrumbs, Parmesan cheese, garlic, almonds, salt and black pepper. Drain chicken. Dip pieces in butter, then dredge in breadcrumbs, coating well on all sides. Place chicken in roasting pan and top each with small amount of butter. Bake at 350 degrees for 1½ hours. Serves: 6 to 8.

Linda Burke

CRABMEAT IMPERIAL

2 teaspoons finely chopped
   green bell pepper
½ teaspoon salt
¼ teaspoon white pepper
1 egg, well beaten
½ cup mayonnaise
½ teaspoon English mustard
1 pound fresh crabmeat
paprika

Combine bell pepper, salt and white pepper. Add egg, mayonnaise and mustard, mixing well. Add crabmeat, mixing by hand to retain lumps. Spoon mixture into 8 crab shells or other small baking dishes, mounding slightly. Sprinkle lightly with paprika. Bake at 350 degrees for 15 to 20 minutes. Serve with green salad. Bell pepper can be omitted. Serves: 4.

Reneva Trahant

MUSHROOM AND SPINACH MANICOTTI

1 (8 ounce) package manicotti
  shells
1 clove garlic, minced
2 tablespoons olive oil
2 tablespoons butter
1 pound fresh mushrooms
1 bunch spinach
salt and black pepper to taste
½ teaspoon basil
½ teaspoon oregano
1 (16 ounce) carton ricotta
  cheese

Sauce:
2 onions, chopped
2 cloves garlic, minced
¼ cup olive oil
2 (16 ounce) cans stewed
  tomatoes
2 (15 ounce) cans tomato sauce
1 tablespoon plus 1 teaspoon
  sugar
2 tablespoons basil
1 teaspoon oregano
red pepper to taste
1 cup beef bouillon
4 cups (16 ounces) grated
  mozzarella cheese
grated Parmesan or Romano
  cheese

Prepare manicotti shells according to package directions. While shells cook, prepare filling. Sauté garlic in oil and butter. Using food processor, mince mushrooms and spinach. Add to garlic. Season with salt, black pepper, basil and oregano. Sauté over medium heat until mushrooms are cooked. Let stand until cool. Drain shells. Add ricotta cheese to cooled vegetable mixture. Spoon mixture into shells. Chill until sauce is prepared or store in refrigerator overnight or freeze. Prepare sauce by sautéing onion and garlic in oil until softened. Add stewed tomatoes, tomato sauce, sugar, basil, oregano, red pepper and bouillon. Simmer for 1½ hours. Pour thin layer of sauce in two 12x7x2-inch baking dishes. Arrange stuffed shells on sauce in single layer. Pour additional sauce over shells and cover with mozzarella cheese. Sprinkle with Parmesan or Romano cheese. Bake at 300 degrees until thoroughly heated. Serves: 8 to 10.

Juanita Murphy

PIZZERIA PIZZA

Crust:
1 packet rapid rise yeast
1 cup lukewarm (105 to 115
  degrees) water
3 cups all-purpose flour
2 tablespoons olive oil

Tomato Sauce:
1 (29 ounce) can crushed
  tomatoes with added puree
1 clove garlic, minced
black pepper to taste
1 teaspoon basil
1 teaspoon oregano
dash of red wine vinegar

Toppings:
shredded mozzarella, Cheddar,
  Monterey Jack or Parmesan
  cheese
grilled green bell peppers or
  onions
mushrooms, sautéed in olive oil
ground beef or pork sausage,
  browned and crumbled
pepperoni slices
Canadian bacon slices
olives

Dissolve yeast in warm water in mixing bowl. Add 1½ cups flour, mixing well. Add oil, stirring to blend. Stir in 1½ cups flour. Using dough hook attachment on electric mixer or hands, knead dough for about 10 minutes or until smooth and elastic, adding more flour if necessary to more easily handle dough. Cover dough and let stand in warm place for about 45 minutes or until doubled in bulk. While dough rises, prepare tomato sauce. Combine tomatoes, garlic, black pepper, basil, oregano and vinegar in saucepan. Simmer for 30 minutes. Punch down dough and divide into 2 portions. Let rise again for 15 minutes. On lightly floured surface, roll and shape each portion to 12-inch round. Place on baking sheets which have been lightly brushed with olive oil and dusted with cornmeal. Layer tomato sauce on dough, then top with preferred cheese, vegetables, meat and additional cheese. Preheat oven at 450 degrees to assure crispy crust. Bake for 15 to 20 minutes or until crust is golden and cheese is bubbly. Cheese can be almost any kind, depending on personal preference. One combination is equal amounts of mozzarella, sharp Cheddar and Monterey Jack, sprinkled on tomato sauce, and Parmesan sprinkled on vegetable and meat layers. Vegetables, except for olives and canned mushrooms, should be pre-cooked to avoid soggy pizza. Grilling gives bell pepper and onions a unique flavor. Ground

(continued on next page)

(continued)

meats must be cooked and drained; cured meats such as pepperoni and Canadian bacon can be added without cooking. Basic dough and sauce recipe can be used to make an endless variety of pizzas. A fun party is to prepare dough and sauce and provide a variety of toppings to allow guests to build their own pizzas. Makes: two 12-inch pizzas.

Tanya Conlay

CHILE RELLENO

4 cups (16 ounces) coarsely grated Monterey Jack cheese
3 (4 ounce) cans chopped green chilies
4 eggs, separated
⅔ cup half and half
1 tablespoon all-purpose flour
½ teaspoon salt
⅛ teaspoon black pepper
2 medium tomatoes, sliced

Combine Monterey Jack cheese and chilies. Spread mixture in well-buttered shallow 2-quart casserole. Using electric mixer, beat egg whites until stiff peaks form. In small bowl, combine egg yolks, half and half, flour, salt and black pepper, blending well. Fold egg whites in yolk mixture. Pour egg mixture over cheese in casserole, gently probing cheese with fork tines to allow liquid to seep through. Bake at 325 degrees for 30 minutes. Arrange tomatoes around edge of partially-baked cheese mixture. Bake for additional 30 minutes. Serves: 8.

Christina Smith

Desserts

ST. DENIS KING'S CAKE

King cakes have been an important part of Mardi Gras lore for at least 100 years. Traditionally, they are simple coffee cakes with the dough shaped or braided into a ring to represent a crown. The brilliant bands of granular sugar in green, yellow and purple represent the Mardi Gras colors and are the jewels in the crown. The finder of the baby doll becomes the king or queen and must provide the King's Cake for the next party.

1 cup boiling water
⅔ cup instant potato flakes
3 cups plus 2 tablespoons milk, divided
1½ cups unsalted butter, divided
2 packages active dry yeast
1 cup sugar
¾ cup lukewarm (105 to 115 degrees) water
6 eggs
10 cups bread flour
2 tablespoons salt
2 teaspoons nutmeg
2 teaspoons grated lemon peel
1 teaspoon cinnamon
1 large dried bean or small plastic toy baby

Topping:
1 (16 ounce) package powdered sugar
1 teaspoon almond extract
¼ cup plus 3 tablespoons whipping cream
1 cup sugar
red, blue, green and yellow food coloring

Combine boiling water, potato flakes, 2 tablespoons milk and 1 tablespoon butter, mixing well. In separate bowl, dissolve yeast and sugar in lukewarm water. Combine 1 cup butter and 3 cups milk in saucepan. Simmer until butter is melted. Add potato mixture to milk, stir, remove from heat and set aside to cool to lukewarm. Using heavy duty electric mixer at low speed, gradually add yeast mixture to potato liquid. Add eggs, 1 at a time, beating after each addition. Combine flour, salt, nutmeg and lemon peel, mixing until dough leaves side of bowl. Place dough on floured surface and knead for 20 minutes. Place in greased bowl, cover with dampened cloth and let rise for 1 hour. Punch down and let rise again for about 1 hour or until doubled in bulk. Melt ¼ cup plus 3 tablespoons butter and set aside. Combine 1 cup sugar with cinnamon. Punch dough down and divide in 3 portions. Using rolling pin, roll each portion of dough to ½-inch thickness in rectangles about twice as long as wide. Spread each portion with ⅓ of melted butter and ⅓ of cinnamon sugar, leaving 1-inch margin along edges. Starting from long

(continued on next page)

(continued)

side, roll each dough rectangle into cylinder, then braid the three together. Place on greased or parchment covered baking sheet and shape into a ring, pinching the ends of the cylinders together to form a circular braid. Bake at 350 degrees for 30 minutes or until browned and wooden pick inserted near center of braid comes out clean. Cool on baking sheet, invert and make a small hole in bottom of braid. Insert bean or doll and replace the bread plug. Prepare topping. Using an electric mixer, combine powdered sugar, almond extract and whipping cream, beating until smooth. Spread on top of braid. Place ⅓ cup sugar in 3 bowls. Add food coloring, a drop at a time, stirring to produce deep bright colors. Mix equal parts red and blue to produce purple. Spoon sugars on icing in 2-inch wide bands, alternating purple, green and yellow. Serves: 15.

Jim Dagar, Food Editor
Alexandria Town Talk

BUTTER CAKE

1 cup butter, softened
2 cups sugar
5 eggs
2 cups cake flour
1 teaspoon vanilla

Using electric mixer, cream butter and sugar together until smooth. Add eggs, 1 at a time, beating well after each addition. Add cake flour, 1 cup at a time. Stir in vanilla. Spread batter in greased and floured 10-inch tube pan. Bake at 300 degrees for 1 hour. Serves: 10 to 12.

Eula Henry

AMARETTO CAKE

1 (18½ ounce) package yellow
  cake mix with pudding
1 (3½ ounce) package instant
  vanilla pudding mix
4 eggs
½ cup water
½ cup vegetable oil
½ cup amaretto liqueur

Glaze:
¼ cup butter
2 tablespoons water
½ cup sugar
¼ cup amaretto liqueur

Combine cake mix, pudding mix, eggs, water, oil, and amaretto. Using electric mixer at medium speed, beat for 2 minutes. Pour batter into greased and floured 10-inch fluted tube pan. Bake at 350 degrees for 1 hour. While cake is baking, prepare glaze. Combine butter, water and sugar in saucepan. Bring to a boil and cook for 3 minutes. Remove from heat and stir in amaretto. Invert cake on wire rack. Using fork tines, make holes in top of cake. Spoon hot glaze over cake. Cake can be prepared up to 2 days in advance. Serves: 10 to 12.

Merita Brouillette

JOAN'S MOUNDS CAKE

1 (18½ ounce) package
  chocolate cake mix
1 (4 ounce) can piña colada mix

Frosting:
½ cup margarine
¼ cup cocoa
¼ cup plus 2 tablespoons milk
1 (16 ounce) package powdered
  sugar
2 teaspoons vanilla
½ cup nuts
1 cup flaked coconut

Prepare cake according to package instructions for a low-fat version. Bake in 13x9x2-inch baking pan. Just after removing cake from oven, use handle end of wooden spoon to make holes in surface. Drizzle piña colada mix evenly over cake. Melt margarine in saucepan. Add cocoa and milk. Bring to a full boil, remove from stove and add sugar and vanilla, mixing well. Stir in nuts and coconut. Spread frosting on cooled cake. Serves: 12.

Mimi Dyess

EASTER BUNNY CARROT CAKE

1½ cups vegetable oil
2 cups sugar
4 eggs
2½ cups all-purpose flour
2 teaspoons baking soda
2 teaspoons salt
2 teaspoons cinnamon
3½ cups coarsely grated carrots
1½ cups chopped pecans

Frosting:
1 (8 ounce) package cream
   cheese, softened
¼ cup margarine, softened
2 teaspoons vanilla
1 (16 ounce) package powdered
   sugar

Combine oil, sugar and eggs. Using electric mixer at medium speed, beat for 2 minutes. Combine flour, baking soda, salt and cinnamon. Add to creamed mixture and beat at low speed for 1 minute. Stir in carrots and pecans. Pour batter into 2 greased and floured 9-inch round baking pans. Bake at 300 degrees for about 1 hour. Cool in pans for 10 minutes, then invert on wire rack to complete cooling. Prepare frosting. Combine cream cheese and margarine, blending until smooth. Add vanilla. Gradually beat in powdered sugar, thinning with milk for spreading consistency if needed. To assemble cake, cut 1 layer into 3 parts to form 2 ears and bow tie (cut oval ears from sides and remaining center will form bow tie). Arrange ears and bow tie around uncut round layer to form bunny head. Frost cake, tinting frosting as necessary and adding colored decorations, to look like Easter bunny. Serves: 16.

Marian Keator

BLACK FOREST CAKE

2 egg whites
1½ cups sugar, divided
1¾ cups cake flour
¾ teaspoon baking soda
1 teaspoon salt
⅓ cup vegetable oil
1 cup milk
2 egg yolks
2 (1 ounce) squares
  unsweetened chocolate,
  melted
1 teaspoon vanilla
powdered sugar
maraschino cherries for garnish
chocolate curls for garnish

Filling:
1 (20 ounce) can pitted tart
  cherries, drained
½ cup port wine
2 tablespoons kirsch
½ teaspoon almond extract
1½ cups cherry juice
¼ cup cornstarch
1 cup sugar
¼ cup butter

Frosting:
½ cup butter, softened
2 cups powdered sugar
2 tablespoons whipping cream
1½ teaspoons vanilla

Beat egg whites until soft peaks form. Gradually add ½ cup sugar, beating until stiff peaks form. Sift flour, baking soda and salt together. Add oil and ½ cup milk to dry ingredients. Using electric mixer, beat for 1 minute. Add egg yolks, chocolate, vanilla and ½ cup milk. Beat for 1 minute. Gently fold egg whites into batter. Spread batter in 2 greased and floured 9-inch round baking pans. Bake at 350 degrees for 30 to 35 minutes. Cool in pans for 10 minutes, then remove and chill layers. Split cold layers in halves. Prepare filling by combining cherries, wine, kirsch and almond extract. Chill overnight. Drain cherries, reserving juice. Combine juice, cornstarch and sugar in saucepan. Cook until thickened. Stir butter into sauce. Cool, then add cherries. Prepare frosting by creaming butter with 1 cup powdered sugar. Beat in whipping cream and vanilla. Blend in 1 cup powdered sugar. Chill. Prepare mousse by melting chocolate with kirsch over low heat. Beat chocolate mixture into egg. Fold cream and sugar into chocolate mixture. Chill. Prepare cream by whipping cream. Add sugar and vanilla. Chill. To assemble cake, spread frosting on cut side of 1 layer, shaping to form collar about ½-inch wide and ¾-inch high around edge of cake. Form inner collar about 2 inches from outside edge. Chill, then fill with cherry filling. Spread second cake layer with chocolate

(continued on next page)

(continued)

Mousse:
3 (1 ounce) squares semisweet
   chocolate
3 tablespoons kirsch
1 egg, beaten
1 cup whipping cream,
   whipped
3 tablespoons sugar

Cream:
1½ cups whipping cream
¼ cup sugar
1½ teaspoons vanilla extract

mousse and place on top of first layer. Chill. Spread prepared cream on third layer and place on top of second layer. Chill, then top with fourth layer. Spread frosting on sides and top of cake. Sift powdered sugar on top of cake and garnish with prepared cream, maraschino cherries and chocolate curls. Serves: 10 to 12.

Rosemary Baker

CHOCOLATE POUND CAKE

1 cup butter, softened
½ cup vegetable shortening
3 cups sugar
5 eggs
3 cups sifted all-purpose flour
½ teaspoon baking powder
½ teaspoon salt
¼ cup cocoa
1 cup milk
1 teaspoon vanilla

Cream butter, shortening and sugar together until smooth. Add eggs, 1 at a time, beating well after each addition. Sift flour, baking powder, salt and cocoa together. Alternately add dry ingredients and milk to creamed mixture. Stir in vanilla. Pour batter into greased and floured 10-inch tube pan. Bake at 325 degrees for 1 hour, 20 minutes or until wooden pick inserted near center comes out clean. Recipe can be doubled and can be frozen for up to 1 month. Omission of cocoa produces a delicious yellow pound cake. Serves: 10 to 12.

Jan Harrington

FUDGE CAKE WITH FROSTING

4 (1 ounce) squares
  unsweetened chocolate
½ cup hot water
1¾ cups sugar, divided
1 teaspoon vanilla
1¾ cups sifted all-purpose flour
1 teaspoon baking soda
1 teaspoon salt
½ cup margarine, softened
3 eggs
¾ cup milk

Fudge Frosting:
½ cup vegetable shortening
2 cups sugar
3 (1 ounce) squares
  unsweetened chocolate
⅔ cup milk
½ teaspoon salt
2 teaspoons vanilla

Heat chocolate with water until melted and smooth. Add ½ cup sugar and cook, stirring often, for 2 minutes. Let stand until lukewarm. Stir in vanilla. Sift flour, baking soda and salt together. Cream margarine until smooth. Gradually add 1¼ cups sugar, beating until fluffy. Add eggs and beat thoroughly. Alternately add dry ingredients and milk to egg mixture, beating after each addition until smooth. Add chocolate liquid, blending thoroughly. Pour batter into 2 greased and floured 9-inch round baking pans. Bake at 350 degrees for 30 to 35 minutes. Cool in pan. Prepare frosting by combining shortening, sugar, chocolate, milk and salt in 1½-quart saucepan. Bring to a rolling boil, stirring occasionally, and cook for 1 minute without stirring. Place pan of frosting in bowl of ice and water. Beat frosting until smooth and spreading consistency. Stir in vanilla. Spread frosting on cake layers, covering top and sides. Serves: 12 to 14.

Vicki Methvin

MARSHMALLOW AND CHOCOLATE CHIP CAKE

1 cup butter, softened
2 cups sugar
4 eggs, lightly beaten
1½ cups plus 1 tablespoon all-
  purpose flour, divided
1½ teaspoons baking powder
¼ cup cocoa
1 cup miniature semisweet
  chocolate chips
1 cup chopped pecans
2½ teaspoons vanilla
3 cups miniature
  marshmallows

Topping:
1 (16 ounce) package powdered
  sugar
¼ cup cocoa
½ cup whipping cream
¼ cup butter, melted

Cream butter and sugar together until smooth. Add eggs, mixing well. Sift 1½ cups flour, baking powder and cocoa together. Add to creamed mixture, mixing thoroughly. Sprinkle chocolate chips with 1 tablespoon flour, tossing to lightly coat. Stir chocolate chips, pecans and vanilla into batter. Spread batter in greased 13x9x2-inch baking pan. Bake at 350 degrees for 40 minutes. Remove cake from oven. Spread marshmallows on hot cake and let stand for a few minutes to soften. Prepare topping by combining powdered sugar, cocoa, cream and butter, mixing until smooth. Pour topping over cake. Serves: 12.

Ronnell Whitehead

NUT CAKE

1 cup vegetable shortening
1 cup sugar
1 (16 ounce) package light
  brown sugar
7 eggs
4 cups sifted flour
1 teaspoon baking powder
1 teaspoon salt
4 cups chopped pecans
½ to ¾ cup whiskey

Cream shortening, sugar, brown sugar and eggs together until smooth. Combine flour, baking powder and salt. Add dry ingredients to creamed mixture, mixing well. Stir in pecans and whiskey. Pour batter into greased 9x5x3-inch loaf pan. Bake at 350 degrees for 45 minutes or until wooden pick inserted near center comes out clean. Remove loaf to wire rack and pour additional whiskey over it. Smaller loaf pans can be used to bake great gifts. Cakes can be frozen. Serves: 12 to 16.

Mimi Dyess

AUNTIE'S NUT CAKE

½ pound currants (not raisins)
water
1 cup butter, softened
2 cups sugar
6 eggs, separated
4 cups all-purpose flour
1 teaspoon baking powder
1 whole nutmeg, freshly ground
  or grated
1 cup whiskey
4 cups chopped pecans

Soak currants in water for 15 minutes, then drain and set aside. Cream butter and sugar until smooth. Add egg yolks, 1 at a time, beating after each addition. Combine flour, baking powder and nutmeg. Alternately add dry ingredients and whiskey to creamed mixture, mixing well after each addition. Dredge currants and pecans in small amount of flour and add to batter. Beat egg whites until peaks form, then fold into batter. Spread batter in 10-inch tube pan lined on bottom and sides with greased brown paper. Bake at 300 degrees, over a pan of water, for 2¼ to 2½ hours. Cake can be frozen. Serves: 12.

Elizabeth Post

LILLIAN GIERING'S NUT CAKE

1 cup butter, softened
2 cups sugar
4 cups all-purpose flour
2 teaspoons baking powder
½ teaspoon cinnamon
½ teaspoon nutmeg
1 (16 ounce) package candied
  cherries (optional)
1 (16 ounce) package candied
  pineapple, cut up
4 cups chopped pecans
6 eggs
1 cup whiskey

Cream butter and sugar together until smooth. Sift flour, baking powder, cinnamon and nutmeg together. Add cherries and pineapple to dry ingredients, tossing to coat thoroughly. Add pecans. Add creamed mixture, eggs and whiskey to dry ingredients, mixing thoroughly. Spread batter in greased and floured 10-inch fluted tube pan or spoon into foil-lined muffin pans. Bake cake at 275 degrees for 2 hours; bake cupcakes at 275 degrees for 1 hour. Serves: 12.

Lillian Giering

PISTACHIO NUT SWIRL CAKE

1 (18½ ounce) package yellow butter cake mix
1 (3½ ounce) package pistachio instant pudding mix
4 eggs
1 cup sour cream
½ cup vegetable oil
½ teaspoon almond extract
½ cup chopped nuts
½ cup sugar
1 tablespoon cinnamon

Combine cake mix, pudding mix, eggs, sour cream, oil and almond extract. Using electric mixer at medium speed, beat for 2 minutes. Combine nuts, sugar and cinnamon. Pour ⅓ of batter into greased and floured 10-inch regular or fluted tube pan. Sprinkle with ½ of nut mixture. Repeat layers and top with remaining batter. Bake at 350 degrees for 50 to 55 minutes. Cool in pan for 15 minutes. Serves: 12.

Sandra Thomas

LOUISE'S POUND CAKE

1 cup margarine, softened
½ cup vegetable shortening
3 cups sugar
5 eggs
1 teaspoon butter flavoring
1 teaspoon rum flavoring
1 teaspoon coconut flavoring
3 cups all-purpose flour
½ teaspoon baking powder
1 cup milk

Cream margarine and shortening together until smooth. Add sugar and beat well. Add eggs, 1 at a time, beating well after each addition. Blend in butter, rum and coconut flavorings. Sift flour with baking powder. Alternately add dry ingredients and milk to creamed mixture, mixing well. Spread batter in greased and floured 10-inch tube pan. Bake at 350 degrees for 1 hour. Serves: 10 to 12.

Karen Kilpatrick

POUND CAKE

1 cup butter, softened
½ cup vegetable shortening
3 cups sugar
5 eggs
3 cups sifted all-purpose flour
½ teaspoon baking powder
½ teaspoon salt
1 cup milk
1 tablespoon vanilla
⅓ cup vegetable oil

Cream butter, shortening and sugar together until smooth. Add eggs, 1 at a time, beating well after each addition. Sift flour, baking powder and salt together. Alternately add dry ingredients and milk to creamed mixture. Stir in vanilla and oil. Pour batter into greased and floured 10-inch tube pan. Bake at 325 degrees for 1½ hours or until wooden pick inserted at center comes out clean. Cake can be frozen. Serves: 10 to 12.

Jeanne McGlathery

CRÈME DE MENTHE CAKE

1 (18½ ounce) package white cake mix
½ cup plus 3 tablespoons crème de menthe liqueur, divided
3 eggs
½ cup water
⅓ cup vegetable oil
1 (8 ounce) carton frozen whipped topping, thawed
2 (8 ounce) jars fudge ice cream topping

Combine cake mix, ½ cup crème de menthe, eggs, water and oil. Using electric mixer, beat for 2 minutes. Pour batter into 2 greased and floured 9-inch round baking pans and bake according to cake mix package directions. Cool cake layers. Combine whipped topping and 3 tablespoons crème de menthe. Spread 1 jar fudge topping on each layer, spread ½ of whipped topping on each and stack layers. Chill before serving. Store in refrigerator. Serves: 12.

Ellen Hill

WHITE FRUIT CAKE

1 cup butter, softened
2 cups sugar
2 cups all-purpose flour
2 teaspoons baking powder
1 coconut, grated
1 cup almonds
1 cup English walnuts
1 cup pecans
2 cups golden raisins
½ cup candied pineapple
½ cup candied cherries
milk from coconut
2 teaspoons vanilla
7 egg whites, beaten

Cream butter and sugar together until smooth. Sift flour and baking powder together. Add coconut, almonds, walnuts, pecans, raisins, pineapple and cherries to creamed mixture, stirring to coat. Add dry ingredients, coconut milk, vanilla and egg whites to fruit mixture, mixing thoroughly. Spread batter in greased and floured 10-inch tube pan or in small loaf pans. Bake at 350 degrees for 3 hours. Serves: 10 to 12.

Nell Salim

PINEAPPLE COCONUT CAKE

1 (18½ ounce) package yellow cake mix
1 (16 ounce) package powdered sugar
1 cup sour cream
1 (8 ounce) can crushed pineapple, drained
1 (5 ounce) package frozen coconut, thawed
1 (8 ounce) carton frozen whipped topping, thawed

Prepare cake according to package directions, baking in 2 greased and floured 9-inch round baking pans. Cool, then split each layer. Combine powdered sugar, sour cream, pineapple and coconut, mixing well. Spread frosting on 3 layers and stack, topping with unfrosted layer. Add ½ of whipped topping to remaining frosting. Spread on top and sides of cake. Cake is better when made 1 day in advance. Store in refrigerator. Serves: 12.

Kay Aaron

CHOCOLATE SANDWICH COOKIE CHEESECAKE

Crust:
1¼ cups crushed graham crackers
¾ cup crushed creme-filled chocolate sandwich cookies
¼ cup firmly-packed brown sugar
⅓ cup melted butter

Filling:
4 (8 ounce) packages cream cheese, softened
1½ cups sugar
2 tablespoons all-purpose flour
⅓ cup whipping cream
4 eggs
2 egg yolks
2 teaspoons vanilla
1½ cups chopped creme-filled chocolate sandwich cookies

Topping:
2 cups sour cream
¼ cup sugar
1 teaspoon vanilla

Glaze:
1 cup whipping cream
1 (6 ounce) package semisweet chocolate chips
1 teaspoon vanilla
5 creme-filled chocolate sandwich cookies, separated in halves

Prepare crust by combining cracker crumbs, cookie crumbs, brown sugar and butter, mixing thoroughly. Press crumb mixture in bottom and about ½ depth of 10-inch springform pan. Chill. Prepare filling by combining cream cheese, eggs and egg yolks, blending well. Add sugar, flour and whipping cream, mixing thoroughly. Blend in vanilla. Pour ½ of filling into prepared crust, add layer of chopped cookies and top with remaining filling. Bake at 425 degrees for 14 minutes, reduce oven temperature to 225 degrees and bake for 50 minutes. Prepare topping by combining sour cream, sugar and vanilla. Without removing cake from oven, spread topping on cheesecake surface. Increase oven temperature to 350 degrees and bake for 8 minutes. Remove from oven and immediately place in refrigerator. Chill for at least 8 hours or overnight. Prepare glaze by heating whipping cream to boiling; pour in chocolate chips and vanilla, whisking quickly until melted. Remove from heat and let stand for 30 minutes. Spread glaze on top and sides of cheesecake. Garnish with cookie halves. Serves: 10 to 12.

Lynne Johnson

JACK'S CHEESECAKE

Crust:
1 cup graham cracker crumbs,
  divided
3 tablespoons sugar
¼ cup plus 2 tablespoons
  butter, melted

Filling:
5 (8 ounce) packages cream
  cheese, softened
1⅓ cups sugar
1½ teaspoons vanilla extract
3 tablespoons all-purpose flour
1 tablespoon lemon juice
5 eggs
2 egg yolks
¼ cup whipping cream
blueberries or cherries
  (optional)

Prepare crust by combining ¾ cup cracker crumbs, sugar and melted butter. Press crumb mixture on bottom of 10-inch springform pan to form crust. Place in freezer to harden. Grease sides of pan and sprinkle with ¼ cup cracker crumbs. Set aside. Prepare filling by combining cream cheese, sugar, vanilla, flour, lemon juice, eggs, egg yolks and whipping cream, mixing until smooth. Remove springform pan bottom from freezer and reassemble pan. Pour cream cheese mixture into pan. Bake at 500 degrees for 10 minutes or until top is light golden brown, reduce oven temperature to 250 degrees and bake for 1 hour. Cool in pan for 1½ hours. Remove from pan and top with blueberries or cherries. Serves: 10 to 12.

Karen Kilpatrick

MARJORIE'S CHEESECAKE

2 cups graham cracker crumbs
½ cup butter or margarine,
  softened
3 tablespoons sugar
¾ teaspoon cinnamon

Filling:
4 (8 ounce) packages cream
  cheese, softened
1½ cups sugar
1 cup sour cream
1 cup whipping cream
4 eggs
juice of 1 lemon

Prepare crust by combining crumbs, butter or margarine, sugar and cinnamon, mixing well. Press crumb mixture in bottom of 10-inch springform pan. Prepare filling by combining cream cheese, sugar, sour cream, whipping cream, eggs and lemon juice. Beat until smooth. Pour batter into prepared springform pan. Bake at 350 degrees for 1 hour. Cool at room temperature, then chill overnight. Top with favorite fruit filling. Serves: 16.

Shirley Smiley

CHOCOLATE RASPBERRY TRUFFLE CHEESECAKE

Crust:
1½ cups crushed creme-filled chocolate sandwich cookies
¼ cup butter or margarine, melted

Filling:
4 (8 ounce) packages cream cheese, softened
1¼ cups sugar
3 eggs
1 teaspoon vanilla
1 cup sour cream
1 (6 ounce) package semisweet chocolate chips, melted
⅓ cup seedless raspberry preserves

Topping:
2 cups sour cream
¼ cup sugar
1 teaspoon vanilla
½ (6 ounce) package semisweet chocolate morsels, melted
¼ cup whipping cream

Garnish:
whipped cream
raspberries
mint leaves

Prepare crust. Combine crumbs and melted butter or margarine. Press crumb mixture in 10-inch springform pan. Bake at 400 degrees for 5 to 10 minutes. Remove crust form oven and reduce oven temperature to 325 degrees. Prepare filling. Combine 3 packages cream cheese and sugar, creaming until smooth. Add eggs, 1 at a time, beating well after each addition. Stir in vanilla. Fold sour cream into cream cheese mixture. Combine 1 package cream cheese with melted chocolate and raspberry preserves. Pour ⅔ cream cheese filling on partially baked crust in springform pan. Drop chocolate mixture by rounded tablespoonfuls on filling and top with remaining filling. Bake at 325 degrees for 1 hour, 20 minutes. Prepare topping by blending sour cream, sugar and vanilla. Spread on partially baked cheesecake. Increase oven temperature to 375 degrees and bake for additional 5 minutes. Let cheesecake cool to room temperature. Combine melted chocolate and whipping cream. Remove rim from pan. Drizzle chocolate mixture on top and sides of cheesecake. Chill for several hours or overnight. Cheesecake can be prepared in advance and frozen. Garnish with whipped cream, raspberries and mint leaves. Serves: 12.

Rosemary Baker

BANANA SPLIT PIE

Crust:
2 cups graham cracker crumbs
¼ cup sugar
¼ cup margarine, melted

Filling:
1 (8 ounce) package cream
  cheese, softened
1 egg
3 cups powdered sugar
½ teaspoon vanilla
1 (16 ounce) can crushed
  pineapple, drained
2 large bananas, sliced
1 (16 ounce) carton frozen
  whipped topping, thawed

Topping:
1 pint fresh strawberries, sliced
1 cup chopped pecans
1 (8 ounce) can chocolate syrup
  (optional)

Prepare crust. Combine crumbs, sugar and margarine, mixing well. Press crumb mixture in bottom of 13x9x2-inch baking dish. Bake at 350 degrees for 15 minutes. Let stand until completely cooled. Prepare filling. Combine cream cheese, egg, powdered sugar and vanilla. Using electric mixer at high speed, beat until smooth. Spread filling on cooled crust. Spread pineapple on filling, add layer of sliced banana and spread with whipped topping, covering completely. For topping, arrange strawberries and pecans evenly on whipped topping layer. Chill for at least 2 hours. Cut into squares and drizzle each serving with chocolate syrup. Serves: 16.

Aimee Wright

SALLY'S PEANUT ICE CREAM PIE

1 quart vanilla ice cream,
  softened
1 graham cracker pie shell
½ cup light corn syrup
⅓ cup creamy peanut butter
⅔ cup chopped, salt-free, dry
  roasted peanuts

Press ½ of ice cream into pie shell. Combine syrup and peanut butter, blending well. Spread ½ of mixture on ice cream and sprinkle with ½ of peanuts; repeat layers. Freeze pie for 5 hours. Let stand for 5 minutes at room temperature before serving. Serves: 8.

Karen Kilpatrick

BUTTERMILK PIE

Crust:
1 cup all-purpose flour
1 tablespoon sugar
½ teaspoon salt
½ teaspoon grated orange peel
⅓ cup shortening
3 tablespoons cold orange juice

Filling:
1 cup sugar
3 tablespoons all-purpose flour
½ teaspoon salt
3 eggs, separated
2 cups buttermilk
¼ cup butter, melted

Prepare crust by combining flour, sugar, salt and orange peel. Cut shortening into dry ingredients. Add orange juice and mix to form dough. Shape into flattened ball and chill, enclosed in plastic wrap. On lightly floured surface, roll dough to fit 9-inch pie plate, place in plate and flute edges. Preheat oven to 450 degrees. Prepare filling. Combine sugar, flour and salt. Beat egg yolks and add with buttermilk and melted butter to dry ingredients. Beat egg whites until stiff and fold into buttermilk mixture. Pour into pastry shell. Reduce oven temperature to 350 degrees and bake pie for about 45 minutes. Serves: 8.

Rosemary Baker

LYDIA'S FROZEN CHOCOLATE PIE

½ cup butter, softened
1 cup plus 2 tablespoons
  powdered sugar, divided
6 (1 ounce) squares semisweet
  chocolate, melted and cooled
1 teaspoon vanilla
4 eggs
1 baked 9-inch pastry shell
1 cup whipping cream, chilled

Using electric mixer at low speed, beat butter and 1 cup powdered sugar until fluffy. Blend in melted chocolate and vanilla. Add eggs, 1 at a time, beating at high speed after each addition. Spread filling in pastry shell. Freeze, covered with plastic wrap, for several hours or until firm. In chilled bowl, beat whipping cream with 2 tablespoons powdered sugar until stiff. Mound whipped cream on frozen pie. Pie can be prepared and frozen up to 5 days in advance. One (6 ounce) package semisweet chocolate chips can be substituted for chocolate squares. Serves: 8 to 10.

Lydia Lee

BUTTERSCOTCH PIE

Pastry:
1 cup all-purpose flour
1 teaspoon sugar
¼ teaspoon salt
⅓ cup vegetable shortening
3 tablespoons ice water

Filling:
1½ cups sugar, divided
¼ cup plus 3 tablespoons
 cornstarch
pinch of salt
1½ cups milk
3 egg yolks
¼ cup butter
2 teaspoons vanilla

Meringue:
1 tablespoon cornstarch
2 tablespoons cold water
½ cup boiling water
3 egg whites
pinch of salt
¼ cup plus 2 tablespoons sugar

Prepare pastry. Combine flour, sugar and salt, mixing with fork. Add shortening, cutting in with fork tines until mixture is crumbly. Sprinkle ice water over mixture, stirring lightly with fork. Working by hand, form dough into ball and flatten into thick patty. Chill, enclosed in plastic wrap, for 20 minutes. On lightly floured surface, roll dough to 12-inch circle. Fold and fit loosely in 9-inch pie plate. Trim and flute edges. Prick bottom of pastry. Bake at 450 degrees for about 12 minutes. Cool on wire rack. Prepare filling. Combine ¾ cup sugar, cornstarch and salt. Add milk and mix until smooth. Pour ¾ cup sugar in skillet and cook until light caramel color. Add sugar to hot milk mixture, stirring and cooking until caramelized sugar is dissolved and mixture is thickened. Lightly beat egg yolks, add to custard and cook until thickened enough to hold shape. Stir in butter and vanilla. Let stand until cool. Pour filling into pastry shell. Prepare meringue. Dissolve cornstarch in cold water. Add boiling water and cook until thickened. Let stand until completely cooled. Beat egg whites until stiff. Gradually add salt and sugar, beating until stiff peaks form. Add cornstarch liquid and beat to blend thoroughly. Spread meringue on filling in pastry shell. Bake at 350 degrees for 5 to 7 minutes or until lightly browned. Serves: 8.

Rosemary Baker

MILE-HIGH LEMONADE PIE

3 tablespoons butter
1½ cups flaked coconut

Filling:
1 cup evaporated milk
1 envelope unflavored gelatin
¼ cup cold water
½ cup boiling water
⅔ cup sugar
1 (6 ounce) can frozen
   lemonade concentrate

Melt butter in large skillet. Add coconut and cook over medium heat, stirring constantly, until coconut is golden brown. Pour coconut into 9-inch pie pan and press firmly against bottom and sides of pan. Let stand to cool to room temperature. Prepare filling. Chill milk in freezer tray until liquid begins to freeze around edges. Soften gelatin in cold water. Add boiling water and stir until gelatin is dissolved. Add sugar and lemonade, stirring until lemonade is thawed. Chill until thickened but not firm. Using electric mixer at high speed, whip evaporated milk until stiff. Fold milk into chilled gelatin mixture. Pour filling into coconut crust and chill for about 3 hours or until firm. Serves: 6 to 8.

Lily Harkins

CHOCOLATE CHIP PIE

2 eggs
½ cup all-purpose flour
½ cup sugar
½ cup firmly-packed brown
   sugar
1 cup butter, melted and cooled
   to room temperature
1 (6 ounce) package semisweet
   chocolate chips
1 cup chopped pecans
1 unbaked 9-inch pastry shell
ice cream or whipped cream
chocolate chips for garnish

Beat eggs until foamy. Add flour, sugar and brown sugar, beating until well blended. Add melted butter, chocolate and pecans. Pour filling into pastry shell. Bake at 325 degrees for 1 hour or until filling is firm. Serve warm, topped with ice cream or whipped cream and garnished with chocolate chips. Serves: 8.

Vanessa Robertson
Beverly Harrell

CHOCOLATE PECAN PIE

1 unbaked 9-inch deep dish
  pastry shell
½ cup butter, melted
1⅓ cups sugar
3½ tablespoons cocoa
2 eggs
1 teaspoon vanilla extract
1 (5 ounce) can evaporated
  milk
1 cup chopped pecans
2 cups whipping cream,
  whipped

Bake pastry shell according to package directions until golden brown. Cream butter and sugar together until smooth. Add cocoa, eggs, vanilla, milk and pecans. Using electric mixer at medium speed, beat until well blended. Pour filling into pastry shell; some filling may be left over. Bake at 325 degrees for 30 minutes. Turn oven heat off; leave pie in oven for 2 hours. Let stand at room temperature to cool completely. Top with whipped cream. Serves: 8.

Melanie McCain

MELT-IN-YOUR-MOUTH PECAN PIE

1⅓ cups sugar
1 tablespoon all-purpose flour
4 eggs
¾ cup light corn syrup
1 tablespoon butter, melted
2 teaspoons vanilla
1½ cups chopped pecans
1 unbaked 9-inch pastry shell

Combine sugar, flour, eggs, syrup, butter, vanilla and pecans. Pour filling into pastry shell. Bake at 325 degrees for 50 to 55 minutes or until firm at center. Serves: 8.

Lynn Pierson

RUM PIE

4 eggs, separated
1 cup sugar, divided
½ teaspoon salt
½ cup hot water
1 envelope unflavored gelatin
¼ cup cold water
¼ cup rum
1 teaspoon nutmeg
1 baked 9-inch pastry shell

Combine egg yolks, ½ cup sugar and salt, beating well. Place in top of double boiler. Gradually add hot water and cook until thickened. Soak gelatin in cold water. Add to egg yolk mixture, mixing thoroughly. Remove from heat and let stand until cool. Add rum. Beat egg whites until stiff. Add nutmeg and ½ cup sugar. Fold egg whites into egg yolk mixture. Spread filling in pastry shell. Chill. Serves: 8 to 10.

Nell Salim

PLANTATION PIE

1½ cups cooked or canned
   sweet potatoes
1 cup plus 1 tablespoon firmly-
   packed brown sugar, divided
1 teaspoon cinnamon
½ teaspoon salt
3 eggs, separated
1 cup milk
2 tablespoons butter or
   margarine, melted
½ cup chopped walnuts
   (optional)
1 unbaked 9-inch pastry shell

Mash sweet potatoes until smooth. Add ½ cup brown sugar, cinnamon and salt, beating well. Beat egg yolks and add to sweet potatoes. Add milk, butter or margarine and walnuts, mixing well. Spread sweet potato mixture in pastry shell. Bake at 425 degrees for 10 minutes, reduce oven temperature to 350 degrees and bake for 30 minutes. Beat egg whites until stiff but not dry. Gradually add ½ cup plus 1 tablespoon sugar, beating constantly. Spread meringue on pie and bake for additional 20 minutes. Serves: 8 to 10.

Marti Vienne

CREAM CHEESE TARTS

2 (8 ounce) packages cream
  cheese, softened
2 cup sugar
2 eggs
1 teaspoon vanilla
2 dozen vanilla wafers
1 (21 ounce) can blueberry or
  cherry pie filling

Beat cream cheese until creamy. Gradually add sugar, beating until light and fluffy. Add eggs, one at a time, beating well after each addition. Stir in vanilla. Place a vanilla wafer in each paper-lined cup of muffin pan. Spoon cream cheese over wafer. Chill overnight or until firm. To serve, remove paper liners and top cheese filling with pie filling. Tarts can be prepared up to 2 days in advance and stored in refrigerator. Makes 24.

Jan Harrington

DEATH BY CHOCOLATE

1 (18½ ounce) package
  chocolate cake mix
1 cup Tia Maria or Kahlúa
  liqueur
2 (3 ounce) packages chocolate
  mousse pudding
1 (12 ounce) carton frozen
  whipped topping, thawed
6 chocolate-covered toffee
  candy bars, crushed

Prepare cake according to package directions, baking in 13x9x2-inch baking pan. Cool cake in pan. While cake is cooling, prepare pudding according to package directions and set aside. Using fork tines, makes holes in cooled cake. Pour liqueur over cake, then crumble by hand. In 13x9x2-inch baking dish, layer ½ of crumbled cake, ½ pudding, ½ of whipped topping and ½ of crushed candy; repeat layers. Chill, preferably overnight. Serves: 15.

Rhonda Guidroz

MOCHA MOUSSE CUPS

Chocolate Cups:
1 (12 ounce) package semisweet
   chocolate chips
2 tablespoons vegetable
   shortening

Mocha Mousse:
1 (6 ounce) package semisweet
   chocolate chips
½ cup sugar, divided
2 tablespoons water
2 tablespoons Tia Maria or
   Kahlúa liqueur
2 tablespoons instant coffee
   granules
2 egg yolks, beaten
3 egg whites
¾ cup whipping cream
1½ teaspoons vanilla extract

Prepare cups. Combine chocolate and shortening in top of double boiler over hot (not boiling) water. Stir until smooth and blended. Remove from heat but keep chocolate over hot water. Spoon rounded teaspoon of mixture into each of 12 foil baking cups. Rotating gently, use rubber spatula to coat sides with chocolate. Place in muffin pan. Chill for about 1 hour or until firm. Remove foil cups from pan and carefully peel away from chocolate. Place chocolate cups on baking sheet and chill. Prepare mousse. Combine chocolate, ¼ cup sugar, water, liqueur and coffee in top of double boiler over hot (not boiling) water, stirring until smooth. Remove from heat. Place egg yolks in bowl. Gradually add chocolate liquid, beating until smooth. Place bowl in ice bath for 10 to 15 minutes, stirring constantly, until mixture mounds from spoon. Remove from ice bath and set aside. Beat egg whites until soft peaks form. Gradually add ¼ cup sugar, beating until stiff peaks form. In small chilled bowl, beat whipping cream with vanilla until stiff peaks form. Fold small amount of sweetened egg white into chocolate mixture, then fold in remaining egg white and whipped cream. Spoon ⅓ cup mousse into each chilled chocolate cup. Chill for several hours. Garnish with chocolate curls. Serves: 12.

Rhonda Guidroz

B&B PUDDING AND SAUCE

½ loaf French bread
½ cup margarine, softened
1 cup sugar
3 eggs
1 (12 ounce) can evaporated
  milk
1 can water
1 teaspoon vanilla or more to
  taste
nutmeg to taste
cinnamon to taste
raisins (optional)

Sauce:
½ cup margarine, softened
1 cup sugar
¼ cup water
1 egg, beaten
1 tablespoon bourbon, rum or
  brandy or more to taste

Cut bread in 2-inch slices, then cut cross-wise. Place in 13x11x2-inch baking dish. Cream margarine, sugar and eggs together until smooth. Add milk, water, vanilla, nutmeg, cinnamon and raisins. Pour mixture over bread. Bake at 350 degrees for 45 minutes. Prepare sauce. Cream margarine until fluffy. Add sugar and water, then transfer to top of double boiler. Cook over hot water until sugar is dissolved. Add egg and whisk vigorously until sauce is smooth. Let stand to cool slightly and add liquor. Serve sauce over bread pudding. Serves: 12.

Jo Ann Ford

OLD FASHIONED RICE PUDDING

¼ cup cornstarch
1 cup plus 2 tablespoons sugar,
  divided
2 eggs, separated
1½ cups milk
1 tablespoon vanilla
2 cups cooked rice

Combine cornstarch, 1 cup sugar, egg yolks and milk in 2-quart saucepan. Bring to a boil over medium heat, stirring, until thick pudding consistency. Stir in vanilla. Let stand until cool. In deep dish, alternate layers of pudding and rice. Beat egg whites with 2 tablespoons sugar until soft peaks form. Spread on rice pudding. Bake at 300 degrees for 5 to 7 minutes. Cool before serving. Serves: 6.

Ida Conde

ALMOND CREME PARFAIT

1 envelope unflavored gelatin
¾ cup cold water
½ cup sugar
¾ cup boiling water
1¼ cups evaporated milk
½ teaspoon vanilla
½ teaspoon almond flavoring
2 kiwi, peeled and sliced
2 or 3 ripe strawberries, cut in halves

Soften gelatin in cold water and let stand for 1 minute. Add sugar, stirring to dissolve. Combine gelatin mixture and boiling water. Combine evaporated milk, vanilla and almond flavoring. Add to gelatin mixture. Pour into 4 to 6 parfait or champagne glasses. Chill for 3 hours. Garnish with kiwi and strawberries. Serves: 4 to 6.

Frances Conine

FRUIT TRIFLE

2 cups milk
4 egg yolks
½ cup sugar
¼ cup plus 1 tablespoon cornstarch
¼ teaspoon salt
2 tablespoons butter or margarine
1 teaspoon vanilla

Trifle:
1 (16 ounce) sponge cake cut in ½-inch slices
¼ to ½ cup Grand Marnier, kirsch, cream sherry or rum
combination of seasonal fruit: kiwi, strawberries, bananas, blueberries, melons, oranges and peaches

Topping:
2 cups whipped cream
¼ cup powdered sugar

Using food processor, combine milk, egg yolks, sugar, cornstarch and salt. Pour into microwave-safe bowl and cook at high setting for 6 to 7 minutes. Whisk in butter and vanilla. Chill, covered, until softly firm. To assemble trifle, brush cake slices generously with liquor. Arrange slices to cover bottom of trifle or deep glass bowl. Place sliced fruit against side of bowl, then fill center with same fruit to complete layer. Spread custard to cover fruit layer and top with layer of cake. Repeat layers, using different fruit for each fruit layer. Prepare topping. Combine whipped cream and powdered sugar. Spread on cake. Chill until firm. Recipe may be doubled. Serves: 20 to 25.

Tamara Ford

COLD LEMON SOUFFLÉ WITH RASPBERRY SAUCE

Lemon Soufflé:
1 tablespoon unflavored gelatin
¼ cup cold water
5 eggs, separated
¾ cup fresh lemon juice
2 teaspoons grated lemon peel
1½ cups sugar, divided
1 cup whipping cream

Raspberry Sauce:
2 (10 ounce) packages frozen
   raspberries, thawed
3 tablespoons powdered sugar
2 tablespoons Cointreau liqueur

Prepare soufflé. Soften gelatin in cold water. Combine egg yolks, lemon juice and peel and ¾ cup sugar in top of double boiler. Cook, stirring constantly, for about 8 minutes or until slightly thickened. Remove from heat and add gelatin, stirring until dissolved. Chill for 30 to 40 minutes. Beat egg whites until stiff, gradually adding ¾ cup sugar. Whip cream until stiff. Fold egg whites and whipped cream into yolk mixture until no white streaks are visible. Pour into 2-quart soufflé dish. Chill for at least 4 hours. Prepare sauce. Puree raspberries with powdered sugar in blender. Strain through sieve and add Cointreau. Chill before serving with soufflé. Sauce can also be made with blackberries or strawberries. Serves: 6.

Sarah Katherine Ahrens

STRAWBERRY CHIFFON SQUARES

½ cup butter, melted
1½ cups vanilla wafer crumbs
1 (3 ounce) package strawberry
   gelatin
¾ cup boiling water
1 (14 ounce) can sweetened
   condensed milk
1 (10 ounce) package frozen
   strawberries with syrup,
   thawed
4 cups miniature
   marshmallows
1 cup whipping cream

Combine butter and wafer crumbs. Press firmly in bottom of 11x7x2-inch baking dish. Chill. Dissolve gelatin in boiling water. Stir milk and undrained strawberries into gelatin. Fold in marshmallows and cream. Pour strawberry mixture into prepared dish. Chill for 2 hours before serving. Serves: 12.

Patti Wingo

STRAWBERRIES OVER SNOW

1 large angel food cake
1 (8 ounce) package cream
    cheese, softened
1 (8 ounce) carton frozen
    whipped topping, thawed
¾ cup milk

Glaze:
1 cup water
1 teaspoon lemon juice
1 cup sugar
2 tablespoons cornstarch
12 drops red food coloring
2 pints strawberries, cut in
    halves

Trim crust from cake. Tear into chunks and place in 13x9x2-inch baking dish. Combine cream cheese, whipped topping and milk, blending until smooth. Spread mixture over cake chunks. Chill. Prepare glaze. Combine water, lemon juice, sugar and cornstarch in saucepan. Bring to a boil, cook until thickened. Remove from heat. Add food coloring, mix well. Fold strawberries into glaze. Let stand until cool. Pour glaze over cake. Chill thoroughly. Serves: 8 to 10.

Shelley West

STRAWBERRY MOUSSE

2 pints fresh strawberries,
    pureed
1 cup sugar
1 envelope unflavored gelatin
¼ cup lemon juice
2 eggs whites
1½ cups whipping cream,
    divided
1 pint whole strawberries

Combine pureed strawberries and sugar. Soften gelatin in lemon juice in small bowl; place over hot water and stir until dissolved. Add gelatin to strawberry puree. Beat egg whites until foamy and add to puree. Freeze mixture for 45 to 60 minutes or until partially frozen. Using food processor, beat until pale pink. Transfer to mixing bowl. Whip 1 cup cream and fold into berry mixture. Spoon into parfait glasses or serving bowl. Chill for at least 2 hours or until firm. Whip ½ cup cream. Pipe cream or spoon dollops of cream on mousse servings, topping with whole strawberries. Serves: 8.

Marion Salter

CRISPY CRÊPES WITH APRICOT SAUCE

Crêpes:
1 cup all-purpose flour
3 eggs, beaten
1½ cups milk
¼ cup vegetable oil
vegetable oil for deep-frying
2 tablespoons sugar
2 tablespoons cinnamon
powdered sugar

Sauce:
¾ cup apricot preserves
¼ cup orange juice
3 whole cloves
1 small cinnamon stick
1 teaspoon brandy extract

Prepare crêpe batter. Combine flour and eggs, beating until smooth. Add milk, mixing to thin consistency. Chill, covered, for 1 hour. Prepare sauce by combining preserves, orange juice, cloves, cinnamon stick and brandy extract in saucepan. Simmer for 10 minutes. Remove cinnamon and cloves and keep warm. Heat 6-inch pan or skillet until sprinkle of water sizzles. Brush pan with oil before each crêpe is cooked. Pour 2 tablespoons batter into center of pan, tilting and rotating to spread batter evenly. Cook over medium heat for about 1 minute or until top of crêpe is dry and bottom is lightly browned; turn and cook other side about 20 seconds. Stack 6 crêpes and cut with sharp knife into 1-inch strips. Fry strips, a handful at a time, by deep-frying in oil for about 1 minute or until golden brown and crisp. Drain strips on paper towel. Sprinkle with mixture of sugar and cinnamon, then powdered sugar. Serve with apricot sauce. Serves: 16 to 18.

Pam DeBlieux

TOFFEE TORTE À LA BETSY

6 egg whites, at room
   temperature
1½ teaspoons vinegar
pinch of salt
1 cup sugar
2 cups whipping cream
8 small chocolate-covered toffee
   candy bars, ground

Beat egg whites until soft peaks form. Beating constantly, add vinegar, salt and sugar. Spread meringue on two 9-inch circles of brown paper on baking sheet. Bake at 250 degrees for 1 hour. Let stand until cool. Whip cream. Fold candy into whipped cream. Spread whipped cream on meringue layers, stack and frost as layer cake. Chill for at least 1 hour. Serves: 6 to 8.

Sarah Luster

LEMON-LIME SHERBET

4 oranges
2 limes
3 lemons
4 cups sugar
4 cups milk
4 cups whipping cream,
   whipped

Grate peels of 1 orange, 2 limes and 2 lemons. Squeeze juice of all oranges, limes and lemons. Add sugar to juice, stirring to dissolve. Add grated peel. Pour milk into ice cream freezer container. Fold in whipped cream. Add fruit juices to milk mixture, stirring while pouring to avoid curdling. Process according to ice cream freezer manufacturer's directions. Serves: 10 to 12.

Marion Salter

NON-FAT BERRY FREEZE

1 (10 ounce) package frozen
   strawberries or raspberries
1 (8 ounce) carton non-fat plain
   yogurt
¼ cup sugar
1 tablespoon vanilla

Combine strawberries or raspberries, yogurt, sugar and vanilla in blender. Blend until smooth. Pour into footed sherbet dishes. Freeze for several hours. For light luncheon dessert, serve with meringue cookies. Serves: 6 to 8.

Gayle Henry

FROZEN STRAWBERRY FLUFF

1 cup all-purpose flour
½ cup chopped pecans
½ cup margarine, melted
½ cup firmly-packed brown
  sugar
1 (10 ounce) package frozen
  strawberries, thawed
¾ cup sugar
2 teaspoons fresh lemon juice
2 egg whites
2 cups whipped topping
sliced fresh strawberries
  (optional)

Combine flour, pecans, margarine and brown sugar in 8x8x2-inch baking pan, mixing well. Bake at 350 degrees for 20 minutes, stirring occasionally. Let stand until cool. Combine strawberries, sugar, lemon juice and egg whites. Using electric mixer at high speed, beat for 10 to 20 minutes or until stiff peaks form. Fold whipped topping into strawberry mixture. Press about ⅔ of crumb mixture into 9-inch springform pan. Spread strawberry mixture in prepared pan and sprinkle with remaining crumbs. Freeze until firm. Garnish with fresh strawberries. Serves: 8 to 10.

Claudia Rees

NO SUGAR APPLE TOPPING

1 (12 ounce) can all natural
  frozen apple juice
  concentrate, thawed
½ cup water
2 tablespoons cornstarch
1 Red Delicious apple, cored
  and thinly sliced in circles

Heat apple juice concentrate in 2-quart saucepan. Combine water and cornstarch and add to apple juice. Bring to a boil and cook for 1 minute, stirring constantly. Remove from heat and add apple slices. Store in glass jar in refrigerator. Use as topping for pancakes, waffles, ice cream or as syrup substitute. Makes 2 cups.

Claudie Triche

COCOA BROWNIES

½ cup butter, softened
2 eggs
1 teaspoon vanilla
1 cup sugar
¾ cup all-purpose flour
¼ cup cocoa
¼ teaspoon salt
½ cup chopped pecans

Combine butter, eggs and vanilla, mixing well. Gradually add sugar, flour, cocoa and salt, blending thoroughly. Stir pecans into batter. Spread batter in greased and floured 8x8x2-inch baking pan. Bake at 350 degrees for 20 to 22 minutes; do not overbake. Score surface in 2-inch squares, then cool in pan before cutting. Serves: 16.

Sheila Savoy

JUDY'S CHOCOLATE CRINKLE COOKIES

½ cup vegetable oil
4 (1 ounce) squares
  unsweetened chocolate,
  melted
2 cups sugar
4 eggs
2 teaspoons vanilla
2 cups unsifted all-purpose
  flour
2 teaspoons baking powder
½ teaspoon salt
powdered sugar

Combine oil, melted chocolate and sugar, blending well. Add eggs, 1 at a time, beating well after each addition. Stir in vanilla. Combine flour, baking powder and salt. Add dry ingredients to chocolate mixture, mixing thoroughly. Chill dough overnight. Drop dough by teaspoonfuls into powdered sugar, pick up and drop into sugar again to coat well. Place on baking sheet. Bake at 350 degrees for 10 to 15 minutes. Makes 48.

Toni Gwinn

JIFFIES FROM VIRGIE MADRID

18 graham crackers, crumbled
1 (14 ounce) can sweetened
   condensed milk
1 (6 ounce) package semisweet
   chocolate chips
1 cup chopped pecans

Combine cracker crumbs, milk, chocolate and pecans, mixing well. Pour mixture into 8x8x2-inch baking pan. Bake at 350 degrees for 30 minutes. Cut into squares while warm and remove from pan. Serves: 16.

Lala Sylvester

MOM'S GINGER COOKIES

¾ cup vegetable shortening
1 cup sugar
1 egg, beaten
1 tablespoon plus 1 teaspoon
   molasses
2 cups all-purpose flour
2 teaspoons baking soda
1 teaspoon cinnamon
1 teaspoon ginger
½ teaspoon ground cloves
sugar

Cream shortening, sugar, egg and molasses together until smooth. Combine flour, baking soda, cinnamon, ginger and cloves. Add dry ingredients to creamed mixture, blending well. Roll dough into small balls, then roll in sugar and place on baking sheet. Bake at 350 degrees for 12 to 15 minutes. Recipe can be doubled. Makes 36.

Karen Kilpatrick

SWEET AND SIMPLE PEANUT BUTTER COOKIES

1 cup extra crunchy peanut
   butter
1 cup sugar
1 egg

Combine peanut butter, sugar and egg, mixing thoroughly. Shape dough into small balls, place on baking sheet and press with fork tines to flatten. Bake at 350 degrees for 10 minutes or until golden brown. Makes 24.

Carol Thomas

POTATO CHIP COOKIES

1 cup margarine, softened
¾ cup sugar
1 teaspoon vanilla
2 cups all-purpose flour
¾ cup crushed plain potato
  chips
½ cup chopped pecans

Cream margarine, sugar and vanilla together until smooth. Add flour, crushed chips and pecans, mixing lightly but thoroughly. Roll dough into balls, place on baking sheet and press with fork tines to flatten. Bake at 350 degrees for 10 to 15 minutes. Makes 24 to 30.

Sheila Cooper

DEE DEE'S SUGAR COOKIES

½ cup butter, softened
1 cup sugar
1 egg
1 teaspoon lemon extract
2 to 2¼ cups all-purpose flour
2 teaspoons baking powder
½ teaspoon salt

Cream butter and sugar together until smooth. Add egg and flavoring, blending well. Sift flour, baking powder and salt together. Add dry ingredients to creamed mixture; dough will be stiff. Roll dough on lightly floured surface, cut with cookie cutters and place on baking sheet. Bake at 375 degrees for 8 minutes; do not overbake. Makes 36.

Dee Dee Perot

GRANDMOTHER TOWNSEND'S TEA CAKES

½ cup butter, softened
1¼ cups sugar
2½ cups all-purpose flour
1½ teaspoons baking powder
2 eggs
2 tablespoons milk
1½ teaspoons vanilla

Cream butter and sugar together until smooth. Sift flour and baking powder together. Add dry ingredients, eggs, milk and vanilla to creamed mixture, mixing well. Place dough on lightly floured surface, roll out, cut with cookie cutters and place on baking sheet. Bake at 350 degrees until golden brown. Decorate with colored icing or sprinkles. Makes 48.

Kim Johnson

YOUNG'S TEA CAKES

1 cup margarine, softened
1½ cups sugar
2 eggs
1 tablespoon vanilla
3 cups all-purpose flour
1 teaspoon baking powder
½ teaspoon baking soda

Using electric mixer, cream margarine, sugar and eggs together until smooth. Stir in vanilla. Combine flour, baking powder and baking soda, blending well. Drop dough by teaspoonfuls on ungreased baking sheet. Bake at 350 degrees for 10 to 12 minutes. Makes 36.

Karen Kilpatrick

UNBELIEVABLE FUDGE

1 cup butter
1 (8 ounce) package pasteurized
  process cheese
2 (16 ounce) packages
  powdered sugar
½ cup cocoa
2 teaspoons vanilla
1 cup chopped pecans

Combine butter and cheese in saucepan. Heat over low heat until melted, stirring to blend. Add powdered sugar, cocoa, vanilla and pecans, mixing well. Spread in greased 13x9x2-inch baking pan. Allow to cool before cutting into squares. Makes 3½ pounds.

Twylla Seaman

MAMIE'S CHOCOLATE BALLS

2 (16 ounce) packages
  powdered sugar
1 (14 ounce) can sweetened
  condensed milk
½ cup butter, softened
3 cups finely chopped pecans
1 (12 ounce) package semisweet
  chocolate chips
¼ pound paraffin

Combine powdered sugar, milk, butter and pecans, mixing well. Chill for at least 1 hour or until cold. Shape dough into walnut-sized balls. Melt chocolate chips with paraffin in top of double boiler over hot water. Using toothpick, dip each pecan ball into chocolate mixture and place on wax paper to dry. Makes 24.

Melissa Aldredge

PEANUT BUTTER BON BONS

1 (6 ounce) package
  butterscotch chips
1 (6 ounce) package semisweet
  chocolate chips
½ block paraffin
1 (16 ounce) package powdered
  sugar
1 cup peanut butter
¾ cup butter, softened

Combine butterscotch chips, chocolate chips and paraffin in top of double boiler over hot water. Stir until melted, blending well. Combine powdered sugar, peanut butter and butter, mixing well. Shape dough into 1-inch balls, dip in chocolate mixture and place on wax paper to dry. Makes 48.

Kathryn Smith

PEANUT CLUSTER CANDY

1 (6 ounce) package semisweet
  chocolate chips
1 (6 ounce) package
  butterscotch chips
2 tablespoons peanut butter
2 cups Spanish peanuts

Melt chocolate chips, butterscotch chips and peanut butter together in saucepan over low heat, stirring to blend. Add peanuts. Drop mixture by teaspoonfuls on wax paper and let cool until firm. Serves: 20 to 25.

Terri Cunningham

PECAN PRALINES

2 cups sugar
1 cup firmly-packed brown
  sugar
¾ cup whipping cream
2 tablespoons butter
1 teaspoon vanilla
4 cups pecans

Combine sugar, brown sugar and cream in saucepan. Bring to a boil and cook for 3 minutes. Stir in butter, vanilla and pecans. Drop mixture by tablespoonful to form 1½-inch pralines on aluminum foil or wax paper sheet, adding cream if mixture thickens too quickly. Makes 18 to 24.

Rose Marie Salim

BUTTER PECAN THINS

1 cup butter
1 cup sugar
1 tablespoon light corn syrup
3 tablespoons water
1 (6 ounce) package semisweet chocolate chips
1 cup finely chopped pecans

Melt butter in saucepan. Add sugar, syrup and water. Cook, stirring often, to hard crack stage (a small amount dropped in water hardens immediately). Pour onto sheet of wax paper on work surface and use spatula to quickly spread paper thin. Cool for about 1 hour. Melt chocolate and use spatula to spread over candy. Sprinkle pecans on chocolate. Let dry for several hours, then break into pieces and store in air-tight container. Candy is best made on cold, dry winter days as it will require longer to dry in summer; never make on humid or rainy days. Makes 20 to 24 pieces.

Juanita Murphy

PLANTATION PECAN CRUNCH

2 cups butter
2 cups sugar
½ teaspoon salt
¼ cup water
2 tablespoons corn syrup
1 (6 ounce) package semisweet chocolate chips
2 cups finely chopped toasted pecans

Melt butter in heavy saucepan. Add sugar and cook, stirring constantly, until dissolved; do not burn. Add salt, water and syrup. Cook to brittle stage or to register 290 degrees on candy thermometer, stirring constantly. Remove from heat and pour into 2 shallow pans, spreading evenly to a thin layer. While candy cools, melt chocolate chips in top of double boiler over hot water. Spread chocolate on candy layer and sprinkle with pecans. Let stand to cool, then break into pieces like peanut brittle. Makes 25 to 30 pieces.

Sharon Gahagan

KENTUCKY COLONELS

70 to 80 pecan halves
½ cup bourbon
4 cups powdered sugar, divided
¾ cup butter, softened
6 (1 ounce) squares semisweet
  chocolate
1 square paraffin (about size of
  1 chocolate square)

Soak pecans in bourbon overnight. Drain pecans, reserving bourbon. Add bourbon to 2 cups powdered sugar, mixing well. Cream butter until smooth, add 2 cups powdered sugar and mix well. Combine bourbon mixture and creamed mixture. Shape dough around pecan halves, forming into balls. Chill until firm. Melt chocolate and paraffin together in top of double boiler over hot water, blending well. Using wooden pick, dip chilled candy balls into chocolate and place on wax paper to dry. Makes 70 to 80.

Elizabeth Post

MOM'S GLAZED PECANS

½ cup half and half
¼ cup water
2 cups sugar
1 teaspoon vanilla extract
4 cups pecan halves

Combine half and half, water, sugar and vanilla in saucepan. Cook over medium heat, stirring constantly, until sugar is dissolved and syrup registers 220 degrees on candy thermometer. Remove from heat, add pecans and stir until coated. Spread pecans on wax paper sheet. Makes 4 cups.

SuSu Burke

Restaurants

CRAB SOUP

½ cup chopped green onions
½ cup margarine
2 (10¾ ounce) cans cream of
  mushroom soup, undiluted
2 soup cans milk
1 pound white crabmeat
1 teaspoon liquid crab boil
2 cups half and half
salt and black pepper to taste

Sauté green onions in margarine in large saucepan until softened. Add soup, milk, crabmeat, crab boil, half and half, salt and black pepper. Bring to a boil, reduce heat and simmer for 20 minutes, stirring often. Serves: 8.

Rose and Johnny Wayne Cox
Merci Beaucoup

BLACKENED SNAPPER BOURBON STREET

8 (5 to 7 ounce) red snapper
  fillets
½ cup butter, melted
1 cup blackened seasoning mix
½ pound lump crabmeat
2 cups hollandaise sauce
  (homemade preferred)

Baste both sides of fillets with melted butter. Generously sprinkle blackened seasoning on both sides of fillets. Place in very hot iron skillet and cook for 2 minutes on each side. Transfer fillets to individual serving dishes. Sprinkle ¼ of crabmeat over each fillet and top with ½ cup hollandaise sauce. Serves: 4.

Joe Nichols
Mariner's Seafood and Steak House

GRESHAM'S GOLDEN FISH FRY

4 cups corn flour
4 cups cornmeal
½ cup seasoned salt
2 tablespoons black pepper
1 tablespoon paprika
2 tablespoons garlic powder
1½ teaspoons cayenne pepper

Combine flour, cornmeal, seasoned salt, black pepper, paprika, garlic powder and cayenne pepper, mixing well. Mixture can be used for fried catfish, shrimp, oysters or green tomatoes. To fry, dip ingredient in all-purpose flour, then in cool water and then in fish fry mixture. Deep-fry in oil heated to 350 degrees until golden brown. Makes 8 cups.

Kent Gresham
The Landing

SHRIMP FETTUCCINE

2 medium-sized onions,
  chopped
2 tablespoons 17-herb
  seasoning
1 teaspoon chicken base
  granules or 3 bouillon cubes
1 tablespoon Cajun seasoning
2 tablespoons margarine
5 pounds shrimp, peeled and
  deveined
3 cups whipping cream
¼ cup plus 1 tablespoon
  cornstarch
½ cup cold water
1½ (16 ounce) packages
  fettuccine

Sauté onion, herb seasoning, chicken base or bouillon and Cajun seasoning in margarine until onion is softened. Add shrimp and whipping cream. Simmer for 20 minutes, stirring occasionally. While shrimp cooks, prepare fettuccine according to package directions. Dissolve cornstarch in cold water. Add to shrimp and cook, stirring constantly to prevent sticking, until thickened. Serve sauce over hot, drained fettuccine. Serves: 12.

Corwyn Aldredge Jr.
The Press Box

LASYONE'S RED BEANS AND SAUSAGE

1 (16 ounce) package dry red
  kidney beans
½ cup vegetable oil or bacon
  drippings
½ teaspoon parsley flakes
10 cups water
2 teaspoons sugar
2 teaspoons salt
2 teaspoons seasoned salt
¼ teaspoon red pepper
1 teaspoon granulated garlic
1 medium-sized green bell
  pepper, chopped
1 medium-sized onion, chopped
2 stalks celery, chopped
1 cup chopped smoked sausage

Combine beans, oil or bacon drippings, parsley, water, sugar, salt, seasoned salt, red pepper, garlic, bell pepper, onion and celery in 4-quart stock pot. Cook, uncovered, over medium heat for 1½ hours. Add sausage and cook for an additional 30 minutes or until beans are tender, adding more water if needed. Serve with white rice. For additional sausage, cut smoked sausage into links, pan fry and place on red beans and rice to serve. Serves: 10 to 12.

JoAnn and James Lasyone
Lasyone's Meatpie Kitchen & Restaurant

RUSSELL'S POTATO CASSEROLE

4 or 5 large baking potatoes, cut
  in ¼-inch slices
1 (16 ounce) block sharp
  Cheddar cheese, cut in ¼-inch
  slices
1 (16 ounce) package smoked
  sausage, cut in ¼-inch slices
1 medium-sized onion, chopped
1 green bell pepper, chopped
1 clove garlic, minced
salt and black pepper to taste
2 (10¾ ounce) cans cream of
  mushroom soup, undiluted

In order listed, layer ½ of potatoes, cheese and sausage in 12x8x2-inch baking dish. Combine onion, bell pepper and garlic, mixing well. Sprinkle ½ of onion mixture on sausage layer. Repeat layers. Spread soup on layered ingredients. Bake at 350 degrees for 45 minutes. Casserole may be cooked in microwave oven; cook until potatoes are tender. Shrimp or crayfish can be substituted for or added to sausage. Serves: 8 to 12.

Russell Sisson
Alton's Kitchen

BEAN SURPRISE

½ cup tortilla chips
¼ cup cubed Monterey Jack
   cheese
1½ cups Spicy Veggie Beans
1 tablespoon chopped cilantro
1 tablespoon chopped jalapeño
   pepper (spicy) or red bell
   pepper (sweet)

Spicy Veggie Beans:
4 to 6 cups dried pinto beans
water
4 cloves garlic, chopped
1 tablespoon Cajun seasoning
1 tablespoon spicy spaghetti
   seasoning
salt to taste
2 tablespoons vegetable oil
   (optional)

Prepare Spicy Veggie Beans. Place beans in Dutch oven, cover with water and bring to a boil. Drain water. Cover beans with water again and bring to a boil. Drain water. Add water to measure 2 inches above beans and bring to a boil. Add garlic and cook for 1 hour. Stir in Cajun seasoning, spaghetti seasoning, salt and oil. Cook for 1 additional hour, adding water as needed to keep beans covered while cooking. Beans can be stored in refrigerator for up to 5 days. Serves: 12. For single serving, place chips and cheese in bottom of individual serving bowl. Add 1½ cups cooked beans with liquid. Sprinkle with cilantro and jalapeño or bell pepper.

Faye Gray
Alley Cafe

BRENDA'S CHOCOLATE CHIP PIE

¾ **cup plus 2 tablespoons margarine, melted**
½ **cup sugar**
½ **cup firmly-packed brown sugar**
½ **cup all-purpose flour**
2 eggs
1 cup chopped pecans
1 cup semisweet chocolate chips
1 unbaked 9-inch pastry shell

Combine margarine, sugar, brown sugar and flour, mixing well. Add eggs and beat well. Stir in pecans and chocolate. Pour filling into pastry shell. Bake at 325 degrees for 50 minutes. Serves: 8.

Brenda Nowlin
Just Friends

Glossary
of
Photographs

GLOSSARY OF PHOTOGRAPHS

Natchitoches, Louisiana, founded in 1714, is the oldest permanent settlement in the Louisiana Purchase. The U. S. Department of the Interior has designated thirty-three blocks of the downtown district as a "National Historic Landmark." The downtown district and an abundance of restored Creole-style plantation homes along Cane River Lake provide a wealth of photographic opportunities.

We are as proud of the historical structures in our city as we are of the recipes in our cookbook! This glossary will add history to your culinary "tour" of our city. Come visit us. Natchitoches is easily accessible from I-49, seventy miles south of Shreveport, Louisiana.

❀ Denotes those structures individually listed on the National Register of Historic Places by the U. S. Department of the Interior.

• Indicates those structures found in the National Historic Landmark District of Natchitoches.

❀ • **LEMEE HOUSE, 310 JEFFERSON STREET:** Renowned as the only house in Louisiana with a cradled roof, the Lemee House also is unique in Louisiana for its floored basement. Italian brick mason Joseph Soldini, partner in the firm of Trizzini and Soldini, built the house between 1843 and 1849. Originally, Trizzini and his family lived in the house. The Association for the Preservation of Historic Natchitoches utilizes the house as its headquarters.

• **IRON LACE SPIRAL STAIRCASE, 720 FRONT STREET (IN REAR):** Gabriel St. Ann Prudhomme designed and supervised the casting of the staircase and balustrades of iron lace which adorn the galleries of the Prudhomme Building. The staircase, c. 1853, is located at the rear entrance of the Carriage House Market which features fine gifts, a Clementine Hunter art gallery, and a showroom of E. B. Prudhomme originals. (318) 352-4578.

❀ **LECOMPTE COTTON PRESS, MAGNOLIA PLANTATION:** This twenty-five foot hand-hewn cypress wood press, probably turned by mule power, is the only type in the country still found in its original location. The press propelled a rectangular piston into a box forming cotton bales of four to five hundred pounds. The press, c. 1830, predates the modern day cotton gin and is located on Magnolia Plantation, which is also known for its significant complex of preserved plantation outbuildings.

LAMBRE-GWINN HOUSE, 1972 WILLIAMS AVENUE: This one hundred fifty year old cypress structure was originally the home of Odalie Prudhomme Lambre and was located on a farm in the Cane River, Shell Beach area. In April 1980, owners Ross and Toni Gwinn dismantled and rebuilt the c. 1850 the home overlooking the northern end of Cane River Lake. The Gwinn's currently operate their home as a bed and breakfast as well as a popular site for weddings, receptions, private parties, and group tours. For further information, or to make an appointment for a group tour, contact Ross or Toni Gwinn. (318) 352-4944.

MAGNOLIA PLANTATION, HWY. 119, CANE RIVER COUNTRY: Designated as a National Bicentennial Farm, Magnolia Plantation has remained in the original family since a French land grant was made to Jean Baptist LeCompte II in 1753. It is a working plantation devoted to the raising of cotton, soybeans, and cattle. The excellent complex of outbuildings at Magnolia include eight brick slave quarters, a blacksmith shop of early French post on-sill architecture, one of twenty-seven pigeonairres left in the state, the plantation store, a corn crib, a cotton gin with a massive hand-hewn cypress cotton press, and a large Acadian cottage style overseer's house.

Magnolia Plantation is open for tours daily from 1:00 p.m. to 4:00 p.m. or by appointment. Contact owner, Betty Hertzog at HC 66 Box 1040, Natchez, LA 71456. (318) 379-2221.

PORTRAIT OF JEAN PIERRE PRUDHOMME, 1673-1739: The portrait of Jean Pierre Prudhomme (an oil on canvas) by an unknown artist is held in a private collection. Prudhomme, original owner of Oakland Plantation, was the first man to successfully raise cotton west of the Mississippi River. Oakland Plantation, designated as a National Bicentennial Farm and listed on the National Register of Historic Places, is photographed in *Cane River Cuisine* cookbook.

• **METOYER-BROWN TOWN HOUSE, 366 JEFFERSON STREET:** The Metoyer-Brown home, the largest brick residence in Natchitoches, was the town house of the Creole planter Benjamin Metoyer and his descendants until 1920 when it was sold to Joseph Henry. Henry sold the house to the Natchitoches Parish Police Jury which converted it to the parish hospital. The present owners, Steve and Cynthia Brown, have restored the house to its c. 1850 appearance, a typical two-story late Greek Revival house with French influence.

• **TANTE HUPPÈ HOUSE, 424 JEFFERSON STREET:** Tante Huppè, c. 1827, is an excellent example of the Greek Revival style. The windows are fitted with six-over-six, double hung sashes, and are covered by the original shutter blinds. The interior millwork (some of which retains its painted graining) is original. A punkah, an overhead fly fan, is still intact over the dining table. Alterations to this house, owned by Robert Deblieux, have been minimal. The house, associated with numerous old Natchitoches Creole families, contains the most intact Creole family library in the state of Louisiana. The house is open to the public.

• **THE WILLIAM AND MARY ACKEL HOUSE, 146 JEFFERSON STREET:** This beautiful home was the first brick structure to be built in the city of Natchitoches. It was constructed c. 1820 by Benjamin F. Dranguet and is probably the only two-story house in the area where the outside brick extends to the roof line. The walls, constructed with bricks made on-site by slaves, are three bricks thick. Each room on the ground floor has an outside entrance. Once used as an apothecary and a store, it was acquired in 1964 by the William A. Ackel family and is named for their children, William and Mary. It is currently operated as a bed and breakfast. (318) 352-3748.

• **RUSCA-SALIM HOUSE, 332 JEFFERSON STREET:** This two-story frame residence with central hipped roof and projecting gables is one of the best examples of Queen Anne style architecture in Natchitoches. The original owner, J. D. Rusca, was a merchant who maintained a general store next to his home. Mr. and Mrs. Robert S. Salim restored the c. 1899 house in 1980.

✿ • **KAFFIE HOUSE, 448 JEFFERSON STREET:** This multi-colored Queen Anne style house was the residence of the Kaffie family. The original dark-stained millwork and paneling inside are retained. Since very few outbuildings remain in the historic district, the unusual shed-roof building located in the backyard is of special interest. It was a combination servant house, storage shed, and privy. The Kaffie House, c. 1890, is currently the law office of Luster, Conine and Brunson.

• **CLOUTIER TOWN HOUSE AT DUCOURNAU SQUARE, 744-748 FRONT STREET:** The carriageway of this Creole-style building leads to the only remaining courtyard of Creole origin outside the city of New Orleans. In 1820, Francois LaFonte purchased the property and built his town house and carriage house. The first floor of his town house served as his business and the second floor as his residence. He occupied the building until 1847. In 1881, J. A. Ducournau bought the town house and carriage house and identified the structures by placing two nameplates (from a building he sold in New Orleans) on the Front Street sidewalk. In 1977, the Cloutier family acquired and restored the structures. With its large collection of Natchitoches Creole furnishings and art and memorabilia, the Cloutier Town House serves today as a popular bed and breakfast and as a picturesque site for weddings and parties. Group tours may be arranged by appointment.

For more information contact Conna, Marcie, or Melissa Cloutier at (318) 352-5242 or 1-800-351-ROOM or write Ducournau Square/Front Street, Natchitoches, LA 71457.

NATCHITOCHES (CITY OF LIGHTS) CHRISTMAS FESTIVAL: The first Saturday in December annually marks this nationally recognized family weekend celebration. In 1927 Max Burgdorf, the superintendent of city-owned utilities, created the first lighted set piece located on the downtown riverbank. In 1936, Allan Cox and Sam West added fireworks to the lighting program. The Christmas Festival attracts over 100,000 spectators with its fun run, junior and main parades, barge/boat parades, food contests, food booths, local and regional crafts, and spectacular fireworks display. The fireworks show, produced by the renowned Zambelli Fireworks Company, leads to the grand finale, the illumination of the 170,000 multi-colored Christmas lights which reflect in Cane River Lake and illuminate the downtown Historic District.

The Christmas lights, which truly make Natchitoches the "City of Lights," can be viewed from the weekend following Thanksgiving through New Year's Day. For more information call the Chamber of Commerce at (318) 352-4411 or write the "City of Lights" Christmas Festival at 781 Front Street, Natchitoches, LA 71457.

✿ • **CHAPLIN HOUSE, 434 SECOND STREET:** Thomas P. Chaplin and his wife, Lisa Breazeale Chaplin, engaged a man known as Zeno to virtually singlehandedly build this Victorian house. This feat was achieved by Zeno without the benefit of architectural drawings or plans. Descendants of the original family occupied the c. 1890 house until 1978 when

Dr. Mildred Bailey acquired the property. The Chaplin House contains a large collection of the works of nationally-known artist, Clementine Hunter.

- **DUPLEIX-TAYLOR HOUSE, 320 JEFFERSON STREET:** Frenchman Louis Dupleix came to Natchitoches in 1848 and built his house fronting directly on the street so that the sidewalks passed under the columned portico. Around the turn of the century, Jack Bryan dismantled, moved, and rebuilt the house on its present site, set back from the street. The home is presently owned by Mr. and Mrs. Henry Cook Taylor. It served as a filming location for the movie *Steel Magnolias*.

KEEGAN HOUSE, 225 WILLIAMS AVENUE: Beautifully shaded and landscaped by pine trees, dogwoods, and azaleas and situated on a corner lot, the Keegan house is a one and one-half story frame Colonial Revival dwelling. A temple front facade of six Tuscan columns encloses the wide front gallery with tall six-over-six windows of original hand-blown glass panes. Architectural evidence suggests that the building was constructed during the 1850's.

TAUZIN-GAHAGAN PLANTATION HOME, 1950 WILLIAMS AVENUE: Centuries old oak trees, registered with the Louisiana Live Oak Society, surround the Tauzin Plantation Home. This three-story style structure was built between 1830 and 1840 by Marcellin Tauzin, a Frenchman whose family arrived in Natchitoches during the late 1700's. Hand-hewn and pegged cypress timbers taken from the original pre-1800 home on the site, form the framework for the second and third stories. Bricks made on the plantation were used in constructing the first floor pillars and exterior and interior walls. Descendants of Marcellin Tauzin owned the property until 1977 when it was purchased and restored by Mr. and Mrs. Henry Cole Gahagan, Jr. The home is decorated with period Louisiana plantation furnishings. This home was a site for the filming the movie *Steel Magnolias*.

CREPE MYRTLES: Planting of native Chinese crepe myrtles in Natchitoches precedes the Civil War. In 1952 the Natchitoches Women's Club, under the direction of Sudie Lawton, began the continuing movement to make Natchitoches the Crepe Myrtle City. These beautiful trees line Front Street and are part of the landscape of many businesses and beautiful homes.

- **ROSE LAWN, 905 WILLIAMS AVENUE:** Rose Lawn, one of the largest and most colorful of Louisiana's Victorian "painted ladies," was named after its once beautiful gardens. It is a tribute to the Queen Anne architectural style and was built in 1903 by Mr. James Henry Williams for his second bride, Miss Eliza Cornelia Payne. Miss Eliza approved the design for the home based on a magazine picture. Until 1991, her son, J. H. Williams, Jr. and his wife, Claudia Melle Scarborough Williams, lived in the house. It is currently owned by Mr. and Mrs. Ralph C. Ingram, Jr., the daughter and son-in-law of J. H. and Claudia Williams. Many of the original pieces of furniture are still in the home which is open for group tours. For more information, call (318) 352-6850.

ST. AUGUSTINE CHURCH, OFF HIGHWAY 119, ISLE BREVELLE, LA: The history of the church, originally constructed c. 1803, and the Isle Brevelle community are directly related to the Metoyer family. The church is named in memory of Augustine Metoyer, who donated the land. He was the eldest son of former slave, Marie Therese Coincoin and the French officer, Claude Thomas Pierre Metoyer. From the union of this couple nearly all the families of the Isle Brevelle community derive their unique origin. The original church can be seen in a portrait of Augustine Metoyer which hangs in the present church building, which was built in 1916. The church complex consists of a modern rectory and recreational hall as well as the historic graveyard where Augustine Metoyer, his wife, and numerous decendants are buried.

St. Augustine is the first and only church in the history of Catholicism in the United States which was built and founded by people-of-color. It has become a territorial church embracing all Catholics within its limits. A tradition of family and togetherness continues today in the Isle Brevelle community with its annual church fair held on Saturday and Sunday, the second weekend in October during the Fall Tour of Historic Homes. The fair features traditional foods, needle work, and family fun. For more information call (318) 379-2521 or write HC66 Box 915, Natchez, LA 71456.

MELROSE PLANTATION, HIGHWAY 119, CANE RIVER COUNTRY: The Melrose complex, consisting of eight structures, was originally begun by the Metoyer family, children of Marie Therese Coincoin. Born in 1742, Marie Therese was a slave who was sold to and later freed by Frenchman, Thomas Pierre Metoyer. Between 1794 and 1803, Marie Therese and her sons received the land which became Melrose Plantation, the first plantation in Natchitoches Parish. Melrose produced prosperous crops of indigo, tobacco, and cotton. According to the 1830 census, the Metoyers were the wealthiest slave-owning family of free people-of-color in the United States. In the 1840's the plantation, for the first time, passed to white ownership and in the 1880's was purchased by the Henry family. Miss Cammie Garrett Henry, who later became the mistress of Melrose, loved the arts and made it a cultural mecca frequented during the Great Depression era by writers, historians, artists, and artisans. Some of the writers whose talents graced Melrose include Lyle Saxon, Kate Chopin, and Francois Mignon.

The Big House was constructed around 1833 and is a Louisiana type plantation home. The lower floor is constructed of brick, and the upper story is of native wood. Other unique and historical buildings in the Melrose complex include the Yucca House and the famous African House. The African House, featured in *Cane River Cuisine*, was once used as a provisions house. This building resembles a native Congo architectural form and is said to be the only one of its kind on the North American continent. Today, the African House features plantation murals by the famous artist and long-time native of Melrose, Clementine Hunter. Hunter came to Melrose at the age of sixteen to work as a house cleaner and cook for the Henry family. Beginning around the age of sixty, she re-created in her paintings a vibrant visual history of Southern plantation life. Today her highly-valued art can be found in galleries all over the world.

Melrose is owned by the Association for the Preservation of Historic Natchitoches, P. O. Box 2248, Natchitoches, LA 71457, (318) 379-0055, and is open for tours on a daily basis. It is featured during the group's annual Tour of Historic Homes, the second weekend in October and during the Melrose Arts and Crafts Festival, the second weekend in June.

BRIARWOOD, CAROLINE DORMON NATURE PRESERVE, LA HWY 9: Caroline Dormon, botanist, teacher, forester, conservationist, and spokeswoman, made her home, Briarwood, a haven to propagate and hybridize Louisiana's native plants, especially the iris. The first woman employed in forestry by the United States government, Dormon, who lived from 1888 to 1971, helped establish the 600,000 acre Kisatchie National Forest which covers seven Louisiana parishes. Dormon's cabin and private quarters are part of this complete botanical and wildlife sanctuary. Experienced proteges of Dormon lead tours for the public every weekend in April, May, August, and November on Saturdays from 9:00 a.m. to 5:00 p.m. and on Sundays from 12:00 noon to 5:00 p.m. For further information, contact the Caroline Dormon Nature Preserve, Inc., P. O. Box 226, Natchitoches, LA 71457. (318) 576-3379.

BULLARD MANSION COLUMNS, NORTHWESTERN STATE UNIVERSITY CAMPUS: The columns that stand on the high ground east of the main gates of Northwestern State University were part of a Greek Revival mansion built in 1832 by Charles Adams Bullard and his wife, Julia Ann Bludworth Wiley Bullard. The structure faced eastward overlooking the Red River floodplain and principal channel, now Chaplin's Lake.

The Religious order of the Sacred Heart acquired the property in 1856 and operated Bullard Mansion as a female preparatory school. The school closed in 1875.

In 1884, the deteriorated property was chosen by the State Board of Education as the site of Louisiana State Normal, an institution for the preparation of teachers. Louisiana Normal became Louisiana State Normal College and in 1970 evolved as Northwestern State University. In 1913 the Bullard Mansion, the oldest structure on campus, was torn down; however, three stately white columns were preserved. Today these columns symbolize Northwestern State University.

Northwestern State University provides services for over 8,000 students at campuses in Natchitoches, Shreveport, Leesville, and Cenla offering many undergraduate and graduate programs. The Scholar's College (a division of the University) offers the only state-operated selective admissions program in arts and sciences in Louisiana. The University has expanded its technology base with the NASA program and a state-of-the-art communications learning satellite program. The University campus also provides facilities for the Department of the Interior's National Center for Historical Preservation Technology.

For admissions information contact the Office of Admissions and Recruiting, Northwestern State University, Natchitoches, LA 71497. (318) 357-4503.

For alumni information contact the Office of Alumni Affairs, Northwestern State University, Natchitoches, LA 71497. (318) 357-4414.

OLD METHODIST CHURCH/LOS ADAES FOUNDATION, LA HWY 6 WEST, ROBELINE, LA: The Los Adaes Foundation, headquartered at the Old Methodist Church, c. 1884, is an organization of men and women involved in efforts to preserve the historic site of the Methodist Church and to reconstruct Los Adaes, an original Spanish fort located on the El Camino Real. The quilting guild of the foundation preserves the traditions of the group's local ancestry and serves as a fundraising group for the church's restoration. The organization demonstrates quilting at the Robeline Heritage Festival and at the Natchitoches Folk Festival, which is held the third weekend in July at Prather Coliseum on the Northwestern State University campus. The foundation leads special group tours of the Old Methodist Church.

- **FORT ST. JEAN BAPTISTE STATE COMMEMORATIVE AREA, CORNER OF JEFFERSON STREET AND MILL STREET (EAST OF COLLEGE AVENUE):** An "outpost" to prevent the Spanish from moving into French Louisiana, Fort St. Jean Baptiste was built c. 1716 on the banks of the Red River (now Cane River Lake). Ignace Francois Broutin, a French architect-engineer, was sent to the fort in 1732 to make improvements. His original detailed drawing combined with the extensive research of Irma deBlieux Sompayrac Willard provided information necessary for the 1979 construction of a replica of the fort which is situated a few hundred yards south of the original site. A palisade of 2,000 treated pine posts surrounds the fort. A warehouse, powder magazine, guardhouse, commandant's house, kitchen, church, and barracks faithfully represent the original structures. Colonial times are recreated through scheduled live demonstrations. The Fort is open daily from 9:00 a.m. to 5:00 p.m. For further information contact P. O. Box 1127, Natchitoches, LA 71457 or call (318) 357-3101.

CANE RIVER LAKE: Originally known as "Riviere aux Cannes," Cane River was a part of the mighty Red River. In 1720, Louis Juchereau de St. Denis was commissioned by the India Company as Commandant of the Upper Cane River. Natchitoches became a busy port for goods shipped from New Orleans, and a prosperous mercantile trade developed along Front Street during the steamboat era. In 1832, when the Red River changed its course, Cane River became an oxbow lake, and trade was limited to the months of higher water. In 1915, both ends of Cane River were dammed and the narrow (250 foot average width), thirty-five mile long Cane River Lake was formed.

Today, beautiful Cane River Lake connects downtown Natchitoches to the Cane River Country plantations south of town and provides many opportunities for our community. Farmers utilize the rich soil and water from the lake for irrigation. Recreational uses include collegiate skulling races, fishing tournaments, waterskiing, jet skiing, paddle boating, and swimming. Nature lovers enjoy a variety of bird species including ducks, kingfishers, herons, egrets, and an occasional osprey. Paddleboat rides, daily tours on pontoon boats, or chartered evening cruises are all available for viewing the natural beauty of Cane River Lake. For more information, contact the Chamber of Commerce at (318) 352-4411.

Special Thanks

A & P Groceries
- Jackie Aaron
- Janette Aaron
- Kay Aaron
  Ackel Bros.
  Margaret Ackel
  Melba Ackel
- Pauline Ackel
- Margaret Adkins
- Sara Katherine
  Ahrens
- Missy Aldredge
  Lena Allbritton
  Mr. and Mrs. Darryl
  Andrews
- Bobbie Archibald
- Julie Archibald
- Elizabeth Arthur
  Association for
  Preservation of
  Historic
  Natchitoches
  St. Augustine
  Catholic Church
  Dr. Mildred Bailey
- Rosemary Baker
  Rienaldo Barnes
- Cindy Barnum
- Kathleen Batten
  Barbara Bayone
- Gayle Bernard
- Marion Bienvenu
  Oscar J. Bienvenu
  Patsy Hughes
  Blanchard
- Mary Ellen Boozman
- Lisa Bostick
- Jo Kay Boyle

- Sandra Bradley
  Josie Breazealle
- Phyllis Breedlove
- Rita Kaye Breedlove
- Ann W. Brittain
  Brookshires Groceries
  and Bakery
- Merita Brouillette
- Cynthia Brown
- Glenelle Brown
- Mary Frances Brown
- Sandra Brown
  Dr. Steve M. Brown III
  Mr. and Mrs. Bill
  Bryant
- Linda Burke
- Susu Burke
- Melody Busby
  Neil Cameron
- Stephanie Campbell
  Cane River Cruises
  Carriage House Market
- Lanell Causey
- Dawn Celles
  Choate's Interiors
- Conna Cloutier
  Marcia Cloutier
  Melissa Cloutier
- Rhetta Cloutier
  Susan Cloutier
- Lillian Cohen
- Virginia Cohen
- Molly Collins
- Frances Conine
- Tanya Conlay
- Cele Cook
- Sheila Cooper

- Karen Corkern
- Suzanne Crews
- Charlotte Cross
- Marva Cunningham
- Mary Ellen "Cissy"
  Cunningham
  Judge Peyton
  Cunningham
- Terri Cunningham
- Linnye Daily
  Shawn Daily
- Cecelia Dalme
- June Dalme
  Damar Farms
- Delores Deason
- Elouise DeBlieux
- Jane DeBlieux
- Pam DeBlieux
- Pat DeBlieux
  Robert "Bobby"
  DeBlieux
  Designers Market,
  Baton Rouge, LA
- Frances De Vargas
- Vennie Dobson
  Mary Doherty
  Carolyn Dorman
  Nature Preserve,
  Inc.
- Mary "Dolly"
  Dowden
- Mary Dranguet
  Mr. and Mrs. Tommy
  Dunagan
- Lola Dunahoe
  Marcus Dupont
  Vickie Dupont
- Mimi Dyess

• *League member*

Special Thanks

- Beth Edens
  Dorris Ellzey
- Chris Evans
  Mr. and Mrs. Leroy
    Eversull
- Suzette Fiallos
  Dovie Flores
- Jo Ann Ford
- Tammy Ford
  Fort St. John Baptiste
    State Commemorative
    Area
- Kay Foshee
  Mike Fraering
  Jan Frederick
  Luke Frederick
- Amanda Friedman
- Edwina Friedman
  Sam Friedman
- Mary Fulton
  Mike Gaffney
- Sharon Gahagan
  Henry Cole Gahagan
- Vicki Gahagan
  Mayo Gallien
  Annette Gandy
  Jim Garlington
- Ann Giering
- Beverly Giering
- Anne Gilmer
- Rhonda Guidroz
- Toni Gwinn
  Ross Gwinn
- Beverly Harrell
  Ruby Harrison
- Anna Harrington
- Carolyn Harrington
- Jan Harrington

Joyce Hayne
- Cheryl Hennigan
- Dana Henry
- Gayle Henry
- Juanita Henry
- Marteel Henry
  Ambrose Hertzog
  Betty Hertzog
- Pam Hetherwick
- Annette Hill
- Mary Lea Hoffpauir
- Beth Holland
- Melanie Howell
- Kathy Hudson
  Edmond Prudomme
    Hughes
- Lucille Ingram
  Ralph Ingram, Jr.
  Mr. and Mrs. Ralph
    Ingram, Sr.
- Anita James
  Jeanne's Country
    Garden
  Jefferson House Gifts
- Jane Johnson
- Kim Johnson
- Lou Johnson
- Lynne Johnson
- Marian Keator
- Pat Kelly
- Betty Key
- Mary and Paul Keyser
- Cammie Khoury
- Juanita Kilpatrick
- Karen Kilpatrick
  Young Kilpatrick
  Mr. and Mrs. Eugene
    Knecht

- Dodie Knight
- Becky Koll
  Krewe de St. Denis
- Martha Kyzar
  Debbie LaCaze
- Mary Lou Lacaze
- Mary Lee Lambre
  The Landing
    Restaurant
- Rebecca Lavespere
  Law Office of Luster,
    Conine, and
    Brunson
- Lydia Lee
- Marietta Lee
  Mr. and Mrs.
    Raymond E. Lee
  Lana Litton
- Pat Long
- Pauline Long
  Los Adaes
    Foundation
- Gwen Lott
  Louisiana State Park
    Services
- Cecilia Lucky
- Sarah Luster
  John W. Luster
- Rebecca A. Luster
- Elizabeth Madden
  Maggio's Liquor
  Linda Manning
  Kenny Mayeaux
  Tony Mayeux
  Christine Maynard
- Debbie Maynard
- Sheila Maynard
- Debbie McBride

• *League member*

294

- Mary Beth McCain
- Rosie McCoy
- Sandra McCullen
- Sarah McElwee
- Jeanne McGlathery
- Adrene McKnight
- Dootsie McNeely
- Brenda Melder
- Connie Melder
- Gay Melder
  Merci Beaucoup
- Vickie Methvin
  Miller Distributing
  Mary Margaret Miller
  Junior Moran
- Eve Morreale
- Vickie Murchison
- Cecile Murphy
- Juanita Murphy
  Mike I. Murphy
  Natchitoches City
    Police
  Natchitoches
    National Fish
    Hatchery
- Fay Norman
  Northwestern State
    University
- Martha DeBlieux
    Palmer
- Rachael Palmer
- Vickie Parrish
  Susie Parsons
  Delores Payne
- Dee Dee Perot
- Faye Phillips
- Dr. Cissy Picou
- Anita Pierce

- Ginger Pierson
- Lynn Pierson
- Margaret Pierson
- Pat Pierson
- William Pitts
- Evie Posey
  Mary Lee Posey
- Frances Pratt
  Mr. and Mrs. J.
    Alphonse
    Prudhomme
  James Prudhomme
- Sally Prudhomme
- Hope Pulley
  Dan Rachal
- Claudia Rees
  Dan Regard
  Luz Remos
- Vanessa Robertson
- Sarah Romine
  Ross Gwinn
    Landscaping
    and Nursery
- Carolyn Roy
- Joyce Ryder
- Rose Marie Salim
  Robert S. Salim
- Marion Salter
- Elaine Sandifer
- Betty Scott
- Lana Scott
- Shirley Scott
- Twylla Seaman
- Cathy Seymour
- Cate Simpson
- Jane Simpson
- Penny Simpson

- Ann Sklar
- Sue Sklar
- Shirley Smiley
- Cindy Smith
- Emily Smith
  Jo Smith
- Kathryn Smith
- Pam Smith
  Mr. and Mrs. Ronald
    H. Smith
  Maxine Southerland
- Allison Stamey
- Brenda Stamey
- Jo Stamey
- Carolyn Stothart
- Cathy Sutton
- Margaret Sutton
- Libby Swafford
- Lala Sylvester
- Evelyne Taylor
- Jokie Taylor
  Henry Cook Taylor
- Lillian Taylor
- Marilyn Taylor
- Diane Temple
- Mary Jean Thomas
  G. F. Thomas
- Gladys Thomas
  Maxwell Thomas
- Pat Thomas
- Tama Thomas
  Robert Thomas
  Sandra Thomas
- Flo Todd
- Madeline Todd
- Patricia Todd
- Barbara Townsend
- Dot Townsend

• *League member*

Special Thanks

- Karen Townsend
- Reneva Trahant
- Claudia Triche
- Jerri Turpin
- Faye Vandersypen
- Marti Vienne
- Lisa Wallace
- Gene Watson
- Claire Weaver
- Sue Wells Weaver

- Darla Webb
- Mary Linn Wernet
- Shelley West
- Margaret Wheat
- Martha Kay
   Whitehead
- Ronnell Whitehead
- Betsy Widhalm
- Mary Lu Wilkerson
- Carol Williams

- Claudia Williams
   J. H. Williams, Jr.
- Marilyn Williams
   R. B. Williams
- Sara Nell Williams
- Mazie Williamson
   Jackie Wilson
- Patti Wingo
- Aimee Wright
- Joanne Yankowski
- Thelma Young

INDEX

A

ALLIGATOR
David Daily's Alligator and Shrimp
Sauce 218
Almond Creme Parfait 266
Almond Tea 54
Amaretto Cake 244
Amaretto Peach and Pecan Spread 44

APPETIZERS
Amaretto Peach and Pecan Spread 44
Asparagus Canapés 45
Baked Brie 34
Barney's Crab Mousse 39
Bayou Brie with Pecan Topping 34
Blackeyed Pea Dip 37
Calico Marinated Veggies 51
Cheese and Strawberries 36
Cheesy Crab Dip 40
Cinnamon Fruit Dip 44
Cliff's Cocktail Chicken 49
Crab Canoe 40
Crab Mornay 41
Crawfish Mousse 41
Cucumber Party Sandwiches 47
Fee Fee's Chicken Mousse 42
Hot Chili Cheese Dip 35
Hot Seafood Dip 43
Italian Hearts of Palm Dip 38
Jalapeño Cheese Log 35
Jo Ann's Crustless Quiche 46
Marinated Cauliflower 51
Marinated Crab Fingers 47
Mexican Shrimp Dip 43
Mushroom Cups 46
Oriental Chicken Wings 49
Oysters en Brochette with Garlic Butter
Sauce 50
Pimiento Cheese 36
Raw Radish Dip 37
Salmon Pâté 42
Shrimp Butter 44
Spicy Spinach Squares 48
Spinach Vegetable Dip 39
Terry's Salsa Dip 38
Toasted Bread Squares 45
White Chocolate Party Mix 52
Zucchini Squares 48

APPLES
Applesauce-Bran Muffins 133

Cheddar-Apple Bread 125
Cranapple Compote 120
No Sugar Apple Topping 271

APRICOTS
Baked Apricots 107
Crispy Crêpes with Apricot Sauce 269

ARTICHOKES
Artichoke Chicken 228
Calico Marinated Veggies 51
Chilled Rice and Artichokes 160
Cream of Artichoke Soup 69
Hot Seafood Dip 43
Oyster and Artichoke Soup 65
Seafood Spectacular 186
Shrimp and Artichokes in Cheese Sauce 166
Spinach Artichoke Casserole 149

ASPARAGUS
Asparagus Canapés 45
Chicken and Asparagus 229
Dilly Shrimp with Asparagus 172
Aunt Paralee's Salad 106
Auntie's Nut Cake 250

AVOCADOS
Superb Hot Crabmeat-Avocado Salad 92

B

"B" and Madeline's Bubbly Punch 55
B&B Pudding and Sauce 265

BACON
Bacon Laced Chicken 213
Broccoli-Grape Salad 95
Broiled Tomato Slices 152
Cheese, Bacon and Tomato Pie 85
Potato Bacon Soup 80
Special Occasion Egg Casserole 86
Baked Apricots 107
Baked Brie 34
Baked Eggplant 142
Baked Onions 144

BANANAS
Banana Punch 55
Banana Split Pie 257
Barbecued Shrimp 173
Barney's Crab Mousse 39
Bayou Brie with Pecan Topping 34

BEANS
Bean Surprise 283
Black Bean Soup 70

Index

Cowpoke Beans 138
French Market Soup 71
Green Beans Piquant 139
Herbed Lima and Green Beans 138
Lasyone's Red Beans and Sausage 282
Lima and Ham Soup....................................... 70

BEEF
Busy Day Vegetable Soup 63
Celebration Steaks 196
Cornbread and Sausage Dressing 163
Cowpoke Beans 138
Down and Dirty Rice Dressing 161
Easy Mock Dirty Rice 161
Eggplant Casserole....................................... 227
Hearty Vegetable Soup 62
Homemade Chili 61
Margaret's Curry Pilaf 225
Mary's Hearty Beef Stew 60
Meat Pies.. 227
Mexican Steak 196
Mexican Tamale Squares 222
Mexican Tortilla Chip Soup 60
Natchitoches Meat Pies 226
Pepper Steak 197
Pizzeria Pizza 238
Rice Dressing with Spicy Tomatoes 160
Rolled Steak 220
Royal Hawaiian Steaks 197
Smothered Burritos 225
South of the Border Lasagna 224
Spicy Steak and Corn Soft Tacos 221
Beignets 125

BEVERAGES
Almond Tea 54
"B" and Madeline's Bubbly Punch 55
Banana Punch 55
Best Minted Iced Tea.................................... 54
Bloody Mary Mix 58
Champagne Rosé Punch 57
Coffee Punch for 100 56
Friendship Tea 55
Frozen Margaritas 58
Kay's Amaretto 57
Milk Punch 56
Mocha Punch 56
Bing Cherry-Port Wine Sauce 113

BISCUITS
Cheese Biscuits 130
Quick Biscuits 129
Black Bean Soup 70
Black Forest Cake 246
Blackened Snapper Bourbon Street 280
Blackeyed Pea Dip 37
Bloody Mary Mix 58

BLUEBERRIES
Blueberry Muffins 134
Cream Cheese Tarts 263
Bobby's Barbecue Sauce 110
Bordelaise Sauce 113
Bourbonnaise Sauce.. 116
Bran Muffins 133
Bread Makers' Honey Buttermilk Bread 122

BREADS
Bread Makers' Honey Buttermilk Bread 122
Cheddar-Apple Bread.................................... 125
Cranberry Bread.. 127
Mama's French Toast 129
Mr. G's Cinnamon-Swirl Bread.................... 126
Ranch Dressing Cheese Puffs 129
Sausage Bread 127
Strawberry Bread and Glaze 128
Zucchini Bread 128
Breakfast Fajitas 86
Breakfast Pastry 126
Breakfast Tortillas 84
Breast of Chicken with Capers 207
Brenda's Chocolate Chip Pie 284

BROCCOLI
Broccoli Cornbread....................................... 131
Broccoli Salad 95
Broccoli Soup 72
Broccoli-Grape Salad 95
Chicken Crescent Rolls 228
Crab and Broccoli Soup 64
Crabmeat and Broccoli Casserole 176
Cream of Broccoli Soup 73
Broiled Tomato Slices...................................... 152
Busy Day Vegetable Soup 63
Butter Cake 243
Butter Pecan Thins... 277
Buttermilk Hush Puppies 130
Buttermilk Pie 258
Buttermilk Rolls 122
Butterscotch Pie 259

C

CABBAGE
24 Hour Slaw 96
King Cabbage Casserole................................ 139
Nutty Cole Slaw... 96
Cajun Fried Chicken 209

CAKES
Amaretto Cake 244
Auntie's Nut Cake 250
Black Forest Cake 246
Butter Cake 243
Chocolate Pound Cake 247

Crème de Menthe Cake 252
Death by Chocolate 263
Easter Bunny Carrot Cake 245
Fudge Cake with Frosting 248
Joan's Mounds Cake 244
Lillian Giering's Nut Cake 250
Louise's Pound Cake 251
Marshmallow and Chocolate Chip Cake 249
Nut Cake 249
Pineapple Coconut Cake 253
Pistachio Nut Swirl Cake 251
Pound Cake 252
St. Denis King's Cake 242
White Fruit Cake 253
Calico Marinated Veggies 51

CANDIES
Butter Pecan Thins 277
Kentucky Colonels 278
Mamie's Chocolate Balls 275
Mom's Glazed Pecans 278
Peanut Butter Bon Bons 276
Peanut Cluster Candy 276
Pecan Pralines 276
Plantation Pecan Crunch 277
Unbelievable Fudge 275
Cane River Corn Soup 76
Cane River Crabmeat Casserole 179
Carlisle Corn Muffins 132

CARROTS
Carrot Bisque 74
Carrot Soufflé 140
Carrots Marsala 140
Easter Bunny Carrot Cake 245
Cashew Chicken Salad 91

CASSEROLES
Baked Apricots 107
Baked Eggplant 142
Cane River Crabmeat Casserole 179
Cheesy Hash Brown Casserole 146
Chicken and Asparagus 229
Chicken and Squash Casserole 233
Chile Relleno 239
Company Breakfast Casserole 85
Cornbread and Sausage Dressing 163
Cornbread Dressing 162
Cowpoke Beans 138
Crab and Shrimp Almondine 169
Crabmeat and Broccoli Casserole 176
Crabmeat and Shrimp Casserole 176
Crabmeat Delight 178
Crawfish Fettuccine 183
Creole Crawfish Casserole 182
Deviled Crab 180

Easy Macaroni and Swiss Cheese 157
Eggplant Casserole 142, 227
Fresh Tomato Cheesy Rice Casserole 159
Green Chili Cheese Rice 159
King Cabbage Casserole 139
Lael's Potatoes 145
Mexican Chicken Lasagna 232
Mexican Tamale Squares 222
Mushroom Casserole 143
Nakatosh Rice Casserole 158
Onion Surprise Casserole 144
Quick and Easy Barbecue Shrimp 173
Red Neck Potatoes 147
Russell's Potato Casserole 282
Sausage and Egg Casserole 84
Scalloped Mushroom Almondine 143
Scallops au Gratin 188
Seafood Jamboree 185
Shrimp Delight 168
Southwest Cornbread Dressing 162
Special Occasion Egg Casserole 86
Spinach Artichoke Casserole 149
Spinach with Sour Cream and Feta
  Cheese 148
Sweet Potato Casserole 151
Zucchini Casserole 149
Zucchini Noodle Bake 157

CATFISH
Catfish Evangeline 191
Catfish Marguery 190
Oven-Blackened Catfish 189
Stuffed Baked Catfish 192

CAULIFLOWER
Cauliflower Italiana 140
Cauliflower with Red Pepper Sauce 141
Marinated Cauliflower 51
Marinated Shrimp and Vegetables 94
Celebration Steaks 196
Champagne Rosé Punch 57

CHEESE
Amaretto Peach and Pecan Spread 44
Asparagus Canapés 45
Bacon Laced Chicken 213
Baked Brie 34
Bayou Brie with Pecan Topping 34
Blackeyed Pea Dip 37
Breakfast Fajitas 86
Breakfast Pastry 126
Breakfast Tortillas 84
Broiled Tomato Slices 152
Buttermilk Hush Puppies 130
Cheddar-Apple Bread 125
Cheese and Strawberries 36
Cheese, Bacon and Tomato Pie 85

Index

Cheese Biscuits 130
Cheese Chicken 203
Cheese Soup with Garlic Croutons 75
Cheesy Crab Dip 40
Cheesy Hash Brown Casserole 146
Cheesy Potato Soup 79
Cheesy Vegetable Soup 82
Chicken Croissants 229
Chile Relleno 239
Chocolate Raspberry Truffle Cheesecake 256
Chocolate Sandwich Cookie Cheesecake 254
Cinnamon Fruit Dip 44
Company Breakfast Casserole 85
Company Caesar Salad 100
Crab Canoe 40
Crab Mornay 41
Crab Quiche 87
Crawfish Quiche 87
Cream Cheese Tarts 263
Cucumber Party Sandwiches 47
Easy Macaroni and Swiss Cheese 157
Fresh Tomato Cheesy Rice Casserole 159
Green Chili Cheese Rice 159
Hot Chili Cheese Dip 35
Italian Hearts of Palm Dip 38
Jack's Cheesecake 255
Jalapeño Cheese Log 35
Jalapeño Cheese Muffins 134
Jalapeño Cornbread 132
Jo Ann's Crustless Quiche 46
Jo's Mushroom Soufflé 85
Lena Leigh's Chili Corn 141
Les Amies 25th Anniversary Seafood
    Quiche 88
Marjorie's Cheesecake 255
Mexican Chicken Lasagna 232
Mushroom and Spinach Manicotti 237
Onion Surprise Casserole 144
Pimiento Cheese 36
Pizzeria Pizza 238
Ranch Dressing Cheese Puffs 129
Raw Radish Dip 37
Red Neck Potatoes 147
Salmon Pâté 42
Sausage and Egg Casserole 84
Sausage Bread 127
Scallops au Gratin 188
Seafood Spectacular 186
Shrimp and Artichokes in Cheese Sauce 166
Shrimp Butter 44
Smothered Burritos 225
South of the Border Lasagna 224
Special Occasion Egg Casserole 86
Spinach Quiche 88

Unbelievable Fudge 275
Veal Cordon Bleu 198
Zucchini Noodle Bake 157

CHEESECAKES
Chocolate Raspberry Truffle Cheesecake 256
Chocolate Sandwich Cookie Cheesecake 254
Jack's Cheesecake 255
Marjorie's Cheesecake 255

CHERRIES
Black Forest Cake 246
Cream Cheese Tarts 263

CHICKEN
Artichoke Chicken 228
Bacon Laced Chicken 213
Breast of Chicken with Capers 207
Cajun Fried Chicken 209
Cashew Chicken Salad 91
Cheese Chicken 203
Chicken and Asparagus 229
Chicken and Sausage Gumbo with Okra 69
Chicken and Squash Casserole 233
Chicken Beer Bake 208
Chicken Crescent Rolls 228
Chicken Croissants 229
Chicken Epicurean 230
Chicken Florentine 211
Chicken Imperial 235
Chicken in Patty Shells 203
Chicken Loaf 230
Chicken Marsala 207
Chicken with Squash 231
Cliff's Cocktail Chicken 49
Country-Style Chicken Kiev with Sauce 210
Crawfish Stuffed Chicken Breast 206
Crawfish-Stuffed Chicken Breast with
    Garlic Sauce 205
Creole Gumbo 68
Crispy Walnut Chicken 231
Easy Chicken Marsala 206
Eve's Asian Chicken 211
Fee Fee's Chicken Mousse 42
French Market Soup 71
Hawaiian Chicken Salad 91
Home Style Chicken and Dumplings 212
Leek-Stuffed Chicken Breasts with
    Walnut Cream Sauce 234
Light Grilled Chicken Breasts 209
Mexican Chicken Lasagna 232
Orange Chicken 208
Oriental Chicken Wings 49
Savory Crescent Chicken 210
Stove Top Chicken 204
Sunday Chicken 204

Chile Relleno 239
Chilled Rice and Artichokes 160

CHOCOLATE
Black Forest Cake 246
Brenda's Chocolate Chip Pie 284
Butter Pecan Thins 277
Chocolate Chip Pie 260
Chocolate Pecan Pie 261
Chocolate Pound Cake 247
Chocolate Raspberry Truffle Cheesecake 256
Chocolate Sandwich Cookie Cheesecake 254
Cocoa Brownies 272
Death by Chocolate 263
Fudge Cake with Frosting 248
Jiffies from Virgie Madrid 273
Joan's Mounds Cake 244
Judy's Chocolate Crinkle Cookies 272
Kentucky Colonels 278
Lydia's Frozen Chocolate Pie 258
Mamie's Chocolate Balls 275
Marshmallow and Chocolate Chip Cake 249
Mocha Mousse Cups 264
Plantation Pecan Crunch 277
Unbelievable Fudge 275
White Chocolate Party Mix 52
Cinnamon Cucumber Pickles 118
Cinnamon Fruit Dip 44
Citrus Green 104
Coffee Punch for 100 56
Cold Lemon Soufflé with Raspberry Sauce 267
Company Breakfast Casserole 85
Company Caesar Salad 100
Company Cornish Hens 213

CONDIMENTS
Cranapple Compote 120
Fresh Herb Flavored Butter 117
Green Pepper Jelly 120
Tomato Salsa 117

COOKIES AND BARS
Cocoa Brownies 272
Dee Dee's Sugar Cookies 274
Grandmother Townsend's Tea Cakes 274
Jiffies from Virgie Madrid 273
Judy's Chocolate Crinkle Cookies 272
Mom's Ginger Cookies 273
Potato Chip Cookies 274
Sweet and Simple Peanut Butter Cookies ... 273
Young's Tea Cakes 275

CORN
Cane River Corn Soup 76
Creamy Corn Soup 77
English Pea Salad 97
Lena Leigh's Chili Corn 141

New England Corn Chowder 77
Spicy Shrimp and Corn Chowder 66
Spicy Steak and Corn Soft Tacos 221
Velvet Corn Soup 76

CORNBREAD
Broccoli Cornbread 131
Buttermilk Hush Puppies 130
Carlisle Corn Muffins 132
Cornbread and Sausage Dressing 163
Cornbread Dressing 162
Down South Hush Puppies 131
Jalapeño Cornbread 132
Southwest Cornbread Dressing 162

CORNISH HENS
Company Cornish Hens 213
Cornish Hens with Herbed Butter and
    Mandarin Rice 214
Country-Style Chicken Kiev with Sauce 210
Cowpoke Beans 138

CRAB
Barney's Crab Mousse 39
Cane River Crabmeat Casserole 179
Catfish Marguery 190
Cheesy Crab Dip 40
Crab and Broccoli Soup 64
Crab and Shrimp Almondine 169
Crab Canoe 40
Crab Mornay 41
Crab Quiche 87
Crab Soup 280
Crabmeat and Broccoli Casserole 176
Crabmeat and Shrimp Casserole 176
Crabmeat Delight 178
Crabmeat Imperial 236
Cream of Crab Soup 63
Creole Gumbo 68
Deviled Crab 180
Gulf Bounty Soup 67
Hot Seafood Dip 43
Les Amies 25th Anniversary Seafood
    Quiche 88
Louisiana Crab Bisque 64
Marinated Crab Fingers 47
Pasta, Shrimp and Crabmeat 177
Scallops au Gratin 188
Seafood Jamboree 185
Seafood Spectacular 186
Seafood Stuffed Pork Chops 202
Superb Hot Crabmeat-Avocado Salad 92

CRANBERRIES
Cranapple Compote 120
Cranberry Bread 127

CRAWFISH
Catfish Evangeline 191
Crawfish Boil for a Dozen 181
Crawfish Fettuccine 183
Crawfish Mousse 41
Crawfish Pies 184
Crawfish Quiche 87
Crawfish Stuffed Chicken Breast 206
Crawfish-Stuffed Chicken Breast with
    Garlic Sauce 205
Creole Crawfish Casserole 182
Fried Crawfish Tails 182
Roy's Crawfish Pie 183
Shrimp or Crawfish Enchilada 175
Shrimp or Crawfish Fettuccine 170
Cream Cheese Tarts 263
Cream of Artichoke Soup 69
Cream of Broccoli Soup 73
Cream of Crab Soup 63
Creamed Spinach Gourmet 148
Creamy Corn Soup 77
Creamy Orange Fruit Sauce 116
Crème de Menthe Cake 252
Creole Crawfish Casserole 182
Creole Gumbo 68
Crispy Crêpes with Apricot Sauce 269
Crispy Walnut Chicken 231

CUCUMBERS
Cinnamon Cucumber Pickles 118
Cucumber Party Sandwiches 47

D

David Dailey's Alligator and Shrimp Sauce ... 218
Dee Dee's Sugar Cookies 274
Delightful White Rémoulade Sauce 114

DESSERTS
Almond Creme Parfait 266
Beignets 125
Cold Lemon Soufflé with Raspberry
    Sauce 267
Cranapple Compote 120
Crispy Crêpes with Apricot Sauce 269
Death by Chocolate 263
Fruit Trifle 266
Strawberries Over Snow 268
Strawberry Chiffon Squares 267
Strawberry Mousse 268
Stuffed Oranges 107
Toffee Torte à la Betsy 270
Deviled Crab 180
Dijon Shrimp 174
Dilled Zucchini Soup 81
Dilly Shrimp with Asparagus 172

DOUGHNUTS
Beignets 125
Down South Hush Puppies 131

DRESSINGS
Cornbread and Sausage Dressing 163
Cornbread Dressing 162
Down and Dirty Rice Dressing 161
Rice Dressing with Spicy Tomatoes 160
Southwest Cornbread Dressing 162

DUCK
Helen's Baked Wild Duck 217
Holiday Roast Duckling with Almond
    Apricot Sauce 215
Prairie Lake Ducks 216
Roast Wild Duck 216

E

Easter Bunny Carrot Cake 245
Easy Béarnaise Sauce 111
Easy Chicken Marsala 206
Easy Macaroni and Swiss Cheese 157
Easy Mock Dirty Rice 161

EGGPLANT
Baked Eggplant 142
Eggplant Casserole 142, 227
Ratatouille 153

EGGS
Breakfast Fajitas 86
Breakfast Tortillas 84
Company Breakfast Casserole 85
Crab Quiche 87
Crawfish Quiche 87
Jo's Mushroom Soufflé 85
Pickled Boiled Eggs 119
Sausage and Egg Casserole 84
Special Occasion Egg Casserole 86
Spinach Quiche 88
English Pea Salad 97
Eve's Asian Chicken 211

F

Fee Fee's Chicken Mousse 42
Fettuccine à la Stephen 156

FISH
Blackened Snapper Bourbon Street 280
Catfish Evangeline 191
Catfish Marguery 190
Gresham's Golden Fish Fry 281
Gulf Bounty Soup 67
Oven-Blackened Catfish 189
Ray's Fish Francaisse 192
Seafood Jamboree 185

Index

Stuffed Baked Catfish 192
French Fried Shrimp 169
French Market Soup 71
Fresh Herb Flavored Butter 117
Fresh Tomato Cheesy Rice Casserole 159
Fried Crawfish Tails 182
Friendship Tea 55

FROG LEGS
Frog Legs with Tomato Sauce 189

FROZEN DESSERTS
Frozen Strawberry Fluff 271
Lemon-Lime Sherbet 270
Lydia's Frozen Chocolate Pie 258
Non-fat Berry Freeze 270
Sally's Peanut Ice Cream Pie 257
Frozen Margaritas 58
Frozen Strawberry Fluff 271

FRUIT *(see also individual listings)*
Aunt Paralee's Salad 106
Fruit Trifle 266
Fruit with Sweet and Sour Dressing 104
Lemon-Lime Sherbet 270
Lillian Giering's Nut Cake 250
Spicy Melon Boat 105
White Fruit Cake 253
Fudge Cake with Frosting 248

G

Gary's Pasta Salad 90
Gazpacho 80
Grandmother Townsend's Tea Cakes 274

GRAPES
Broccoli-Grape Salad 95

GRAVIES
Giblet Gravy 111
Green and Gold Squash Pie 150
Green Beans Piquant 139
Green Chili Cheese Rice 159
Green Pepper Jelly 120
Gresham's Golden Fish Fry 281
Gulf Bounty Soup 67

H

HAM
Company Breakfast Casserole 85
Fettuccine à la Stephen 156
Lima and Ham Soup..................................... 70
Veal Cordon Bleu 198
Hawaiian Chicken Salad 91
Hazel's Shrimp Jambalaya 172

HEARTS OF PALM
Italian Hearts of Palm Dip 38

Hearty Vegetable Soup 62
Helen's Baked Wild Duck 217
Helley Hot 153
Herbed Lima and Green Beans 138
Holiday Roast Duckling with Almond
    Apricot Sauce 215
Home Style Chicken and Dumplings 212
Homemade Chili 61
Hot Chili Cheese Dip 35
Hot Seafood Dip 43
Hot Tamales 223

HUSH PUPPIES
Buttermilk Hush Puppies 130
Down South Hush Puppies 131

I

Italian Hearts of Palm Dip 38

J

Jack's Cheesecake 255
Jalapeño Cheese Log 35
Jalapeño Cheese Muffins 134
Jalapeño Cornbread 132
Jiffies from Virgie Madrid 273
Jo Ann's Crustless Quiche 46
Joan's Mounds Cake 244
Jo's Mushroom Soufflé 85
Judy's Chocolate Crinkle Cookies 272

K

Kay's Amaretto 57
Kentucky Colonels 278
King Cabbage Casserole 139

L

Lael's Potatoes 145
Lasyone's Red Beans and Sausage 282
Laura's Meat Marinade 114
Leek-Stuffed Chicken Breasts with
    Walnut Cream Sauce 234
Lemon-Chablis Fish Sauce 114
Lemon-Lime Sherbet..................................... 270
Lena Leigh's Chili Corn 141
Les Amies 25th Anniversary Seafood Quiche .. 88
Light and Easy Tomato Aspic 98
Light Grilled Chicken Breasts 209
Lillian Giering's Nut Cake 250
Lima and Ham Soup 70
Linguine and Vegetable Supreme 156
Louise's Pound Cake 251
Louisiana Crab Bisque 64
Lydia's Frozen Chocolate Pie 258

M

Mama's French Toast 129
Mamie's Chocolate Balls............................... 275
Mandarin-Walnut Salad 101
Margaret's Curry Pilaf.................................. 225
MARINADES
   Laura's Meat Marinade.............................. 114
Marinated Cauliflower................................... 51
Marinated Crab Fingers 47
Marinated Shrimp and Vegetables 94
Marinated Shrimp Kabobs 171
Marinated Tomatoes 97
Marjorie's Cheesecake.................................. 255
Marshmallow and Chocolate Chip Cake 249
Mary's Hearty Beef Stew 60
Maxwell's Caesar Salad 99
Meat Pies 227
Melt-in-Your-Mouth Pecan Pie 261
Mexican Chicken Lasagna 232
Mexican Shrimp Dip...................................... 43
Mexican Steak 196
Mexican Tamale Squares 222
Mexican Tortilla Chip Soup 60
Mile-High Lemonade Pie 260
Milk Punch 56
Mint Fruit Dressing For Melons 105
Mocha Mousse Cups 264
Mocha Punch 56
Mom's Ginger Cookies 273
Mom's Glazed Pecans 278
Mr. G's Cinnamon-Swirl Bread 126
Mrs. Williams' Rolls 124
MUFFINS
   Applesauce-Bran Muffins 133
   Blueberry Muffins 134
   Bran Muffins 133
   Carlisle Corn Muffins 132
   Jalapeño Cheese Muffins 134
   Oat Muffins 135
   Strawberry Muffins with Orange Butter
    Glaze 135
MUSHROOMS
   Jo's Mushroom Soufflé 85
   Marinated Shrimp and Vegetables 94
   Mushroom and Spinach Manicotti 237
   Mushroom Casserole 143
   Mushroom Cups 46
   Mushroom Sauce for Bill 115
   Scalloped Mushroom Almondine 143

N

Nakatosh Rice Casserole 158

Nanny's Pickled Okra 117
Natchitoches Meat Pies................................. 226
New England Corn Chowder 77
No Sugar Apple Topping 271
Non-fat Berry Freeze 270
Nut Cake 249
Nutty Cole Slaw 96

O

Oat Muffins 135
OKRA
   Chicken and Sausage Gumbo with Okra 69
   Creole Gumbo 68
   Nanny's Pickled Okra................................ 117
   Sensational Shrimp and Okra 171
Old Fashioned Rice Pudding.......................... 265
ONIONS
   Baked Onions 144
   Onion Surprise Casserole.......................... 144
   Onion-Tomato-Rice Soup 79
   Spicy Onion Soup 78
ORANGES
   Creamy Orange Fruit Sauce 116
   Orange Chicken 208
   Orange Raisin Sauce................................. 112
   Stuffed Oranges 107
Oriental Chicken Wings................................. 49
Our Favorite Barbecue Sauce 110
Oven-Blackened Catfish 189
OYSTERS
   Oyster and Artichoke Soup......................... 65
   Oyster and Spinach Soup 65
   Oyster Loaf... 187
   Oysters en Brochette with Garlic Butter
    Sauce 50
   Plantation Oysters 187

P

PASTA
   Chicken Marsala 207
   Crawfish Fettuccine 183
   Easy Macaroni and Swiss Cheese 157
   Fettuccine à la Stephen 156
   Gary's Pasta Salad 90
   Linguine and Vegetable Supreme 156
   Mushroom and Spinach Manicotti 237
   Pasta, Shrimp and Crabmeat 177
   Seafood Spectacular 186
   Shrimp and Pasta Salad 93
   Shrimp Fettuccine 281
   Shrimp Linguine 168
   Shrimp or Crawfish Fettuccine................... 170

Shrimp St. Denis 167
Smoked Salmon Pasta with Caviar 194
Zucchini Noodle Bake 157

PASTRIES
Beignets 125
Breakfast Pastry 126
Peanut Butter Bon Bons 276
Peanut Cluster Candy 276

PEAS
Blackeyed Pea Dip 37
English Pea Salad 97
Pecan Pralines 276
Pepper Steak 197

PICKLES AND PRESERVES
Cinnamon Cucumber Pickles 118
Green Pepper Jelly 120
Nanny's Pickled Okra 117
Pickled Boiled Eggs 119
Squash Pickles 119

PIES
Banana Split Pie 257
Brenda's Chocolate Chip Pie 284
Buttermilk Pie 258
Butterscotch Pie 259
Chocolate Chip Pie 260
Chocolate Pecan Pie 261
Cream Cheese Tarts 263
Lydia's Frozen Chocolate Pie 258
Melt-in-Your-Mouth Pecan Pie 261
Mile-High Lemonade Pie 260
Plantation Pie 262
Rum Pie 262
Sally's Peanut Ice Cream Pie 257
Pimiento Cheese 36

PINEAPPLE
Banana Split Pie 257
Pineapple Coconut Cake 253
Pineapple Fruit Dressing 106
Pistachio Nut Swirl Cake 251
Pizzeria Pizza 238
Plantation Oysters 187
Plantation Pecan Crunch 277

PORK
Hot Tamales 223
Meat Pies 227
Natchitoches Meat Pies 226
Polynesian Pork Chops 201
Pork Chops and Southern Style Gravy 201
Pork Roast with Stuffing 200
Seafood Stuffed Pork Chops 202
Stuffed Pork Chops 199
Potato Chip Cookies 274

POTATOES
Cheesy Hash Brown Casserole 146
Cheesy Potato Soup 79
Lael's Potatoes 145
New England Corn Chowder 77
Potato Bacon Soup 80
Potato Croquettes 146
Potato Dijon 145
Potato Refrigerator Rolls 123
Red Neck Potatoes 147
Russell's Potato Casserole 282
Pound Cake 252
Prairie Lake Ducks 216

PUDDINGS
B&B Pudding and Sauce 265
Mocha Mousse Cups 264
Old Fashioned Rice Pudding 265

Q

Quick and Easy Barbecue Shrimp 173
Quick Biscuits 129

R

Ranch Dressing Cheese Puffs 129

RASPBERRIES
Cold Lemon Soufflé with Raspberry
   Sauce 267
Non-fat Berry Freeze 270
Ratatouille 153
Raw Radish Dip 37
Ray's Fish Francaisse 192
Red Neck Potatoes 147

RESTAURANTS
Bean Surprise 283
Blackened Snapper Bourbon Street 280
Brenda's Chocolate Chip Pie 284
Crab Soup 280
Gresham's Golden Fish Fry 281
Lasyone's Red Beans and Sausage 282
Russell's Potato Casserole 282
Shrimp Fettuccine 281

RICE
Chilled Rice and Artichokes 160
Cornish Hens with Herbed Butter and
   Mandarin Rice 214
Crabmeat and Broccoli Casserole 176
Crabmeat and Shrimp Casserole 176
David Dailey's Alligator and Shrimp
   Sauce 218
Down and Dirty Rice Dressing 161
Easy Mock Dirty Rice 161
Fresh Tomato Cheesy Rice Casserole 159

Green Chili Cheese Rice 159
Hazel's Shrimp Jambalaya 172
Margaret's Curry Pilaf 225
Nakatosh Rice Casserole 158
Old Fashioned Rice Pudding 265
Onion-Tomato-Rice Soup 79
Rice Dressing with Spicy Tomatoes 160
Sebastian Rice 158
Shrimp Delight 168
Roast Wild Duck 216
Rolled Steak 220

ROLLS
Buttermilk Rolls 122
Mrs. Williams' Rolls 124
Potato Refrigerator Rolls 123
Savory Pull-Apart Rolls 123
Whole Wheat Rolls 124
Royal Hawaiian Steaks 197
Roy's Crawfish Pie 183
Rum Pie 262
Russell's Potato Casserole 282

RUTABAGAS
Savory Rutabagas 147

S

SALAD DRESSINGS
Citrus Green 104
Mint Fruit Dressing For Melons 105
Pineapple Fruit Dressing............................ 106
Salad Dressing Parmesan 103
Spinach Salad Dressing.............................. 102
Sunflower Dressing 103

SALADS
24 Hour Slaw 96
Aunt Paralee's Salad 106
Baked Apricots 107
Broccoli Salad.. 95
Broccoli-Grape Salad................................. 95
Cashew Chicken Salad 91
Company Caesar Salad 100
English Pea Salad 97
Fruit with Sweet and Sour Dressing........... 104
Gary's Pasta Salad 90
Hawaiian Chicken Salad 91
Light and Easy Tomato Aspic 98
Mandarin-Walnut Salad 101
Marinated Shrimp and Vegetables 94
Marinated Tomatoes................................... 97
Maxwell's Caesar Salad.............................. 99
Nutty Cole Slaw... 96
Shrimp and Pasta Salad 93
Shrimp Salad 92
Spicy Melon Boat 105

Spinach Salad 102
Stuffed Oranges 107
Summer Marinated Tomatoes..................... 98
Superb Hot Crabmeat-Avocado Salad 92
Sally's Peanut Ice Cream Pie 257

SALMON
Salmon Pâté 42
Smoked Salmon Pasta with Caviar 194

SAUCES
Bing Cherry-Port Wine Sauce 113
Bobby's Barbecue Sauce............................ 110
Bordelaise Sauce 113
Bourbonnaise Sauce 116
Creamy Orange Fruit Sauce 116
Delightful White Rémoulade Sauce............ 114
Easy Béarnaise Sauce 111
Lemon-Chablis Fish Sauce......................... 114
Mushroom Sauce for Bill 115
No Sugar Apple Topping 271
Orange Raisin Sauce.................................. 112
Our Favorite Barbecue Sauce..................... 110
Snappy Horseradish Sauce 112
Sour Cream Hollandaise Sauce................... 115

SAUSAGE
Breakfast Fajitas.. 86
Cane River Corn Soup 76
Chicken and Sausage Gumbo with Okra 69
Cornbread and Sausage Dressing 163
Creole Gumbo 68
French Market Soup 71
Lasyone's Red Beans and Sausage 282
Pizzeria Pizza 238
Sausage and Egg Casserole 84
Sausage Bread 127
Smothered Burritos 225
Savory Crescent Chicken 210
Savory Pull-Apart Rolls 123
Savory Rutabagas 147
Scalloped Mushroom Almondine 143

SCALLOPS
Gulf Bounty Soup 67
Scallops au Gratin 188
Seafood Jamboree 185
Sebastian Rice 158

SHRIMP
Barbecued Shrimp 173
Cane River Corn Soup 76
Catfish Marguery 190
Crab and Shrimp Almondine...................... 169
Crabmeat and Shrimp Casserole 176
Creole Gumbo 68
David Daily's Alligator and Shrimp
Sauce 218

Dijon Shrimp 174
Dilly Shrimp with Asparagus 172
French Fried Shrimp 169
Gulf Bounty Soup 67
Hazel's Shrimp Jambalaya 172
Hot Seafood Dip 43
Les Amies 25th Anniversary Seafood
     Quiche 88
Marinated Shrimp and Vegetables 94
Marinated Shrimp Kabobs 171
Mexican Shrimp Dip 43
Pasta, Shrimp and Crabmeat 177
Quick and Easy Barbecue Shrimp 173
Scallops au Gratin 188
Seafood Jamboree 185
Seafood Spectacular 186
Seafood Stuffed Pork Chops 202
Sensational Shrimp and Okra 171
Shrimp and Artichokes in Cheese Sauce 166
Shrimp and Pasta Salad 93
Shrimp Butter 44
Shrimp Creole 167
Shrimp Delight 168
Shrimp Fettuccine 281
Shrimp Linguine 168
Shrimp or Crawfish Enchilada 175
Shrimp or Crawfish Fettuccine 170
Shrimp Salad 92
Shrimp Scampi 170, 174
Shrimp St. Denis 167
Spicy Shrimp and Corn Chowder 66
Terry's Broiled Shrimp 166
Smoked Salmon Pasta with Caviar 194
Smothered Burritos 225
Snappy Horseradish Sauce 112

SOUPS
Black Bean Soup 70
Broccoli Soup 72
Busy Day Vegetable Soup 63
Cane River Corn Soup 76
Carrot Bisque 74
Cheese Soup with Garlic Croutons 75
Cheesy Potato Soup 79
Cheesy Vegetable Soup 82
Chicken and Sausage Gumbo with Okra 69
Crab and Broccoli Soup 64
Crab Soup 280
Cream of Artichoke Soup 69
Cream of Broccoli Soup 73
Cream of Crab Soup 63
Creamy Corn Soup 77
Creole Gumbo 68
Dilled Zucchini Soup 81
French Market Soup 71

Gazpacho 80
Gulf Bounty Soup 67
Hearty Vegetable Soup 62
Homemade Chili 61
Lima and Ham Soup 70
Louisiana Crab Bisque 64
Mary's Hearty Beef Stew 60
Mexican Tortilla Chip Soup 60
New England Corn Chowder 77
Onion-Tomato-Rice Soup 79
Oyster and Artichoke Soup 65
Oyster and Spinach Soup 65
Potato Bacon Soup 80
Spicy Onion Soup 78
Spicy Shrimp and Corn Chowder 66
Velvet Corn Soup 76
Zucchini Soup 81
Sour Cream Hollandaise Sauce 115
South of the Border Lasagna 224
Southwest Cornbread Dressing 162
Special Occasion Egg Casserole 86
Spicy Melon Boat 105
Spicy Steak and Corn Soft Tacos 221

SPINACH
Chicken Florentine 211
Creamed Spinach Gourmet 148
Mushroom and Spinach Manicotti 237
Oyster and Spinach Soup 65
Spicy Spinach Squares 48
Spinach Artichoke Casserole 149
Spinach Quiche 88
Spinach Salad 102
Spinach Salad Dressing 102
Spinach Vegetable Dip 39
Spinach with Sour Cream and Feta
     Cheese 148

SQUASH
Chicken and Squash Casserole 233
Chicken with Squash 231
Green and Gold Squash Pie 150
Ratatouille 153
Squash Pickles 119
Stuffed Squash 150
St. Denis King's Cake 242
Stove Top Chicken 204

STRAWBERRIES
Banana Split Pie 257
Frozen Strawberry Fluff 271
Non-fat Berry Freeze 270
Strawberries Over Snow 268
Strawberry Bread and Glaze 128
Strawberry Chiffon Squares 267
Strawberry Mousse 268

Strawberry Muffins with Orange Butter
Glaze 135
Stuffed Baked Catfish 192
Stuffed Oranges 107
Stuffed Pork Chops 199
Stuffed Squash 150
Summer Marinated Tomatoes 98
Sunday Chicken 204
Sunflower Dressing 103
Superb Hot Crabmeat-Avocado Salad 92
Sweet and Simple Peanut Butter Cookies 273

SWEET POTATOES
Plantation Pie 262
Sweet Potato Casserole 151
Sweet Potatoes with Orange Slices 151

T

24 Hour Slaw 96
Terry's Broiled Shrimp 166
Terry's Salsa Dip 38
Toasted Bread Squares 45
Toffee Torte à la Betsy 270

TOMATOES
Broiled Tomato Slices 152
Cheese, Bacon and Tomato Pie 85
Fresh Tomato Cheesy Rice Casserole 159
Gazpacho 80
Helley Hot 153
Light and Easy Tomato Aspic 98
Marinated Tomatoes 97
Onion-Tomato-Rice Soup 79
Ratatouille 153
Rice Dressing with Spicy Tomatoes 160
Summer Marinated Tomatoes 98
Terry's Salsa Dip 38
Tomato Pie 152
Tomato Salsa 117

TURKEY
Cornbread and Sausage Dressing 163

U

Unbelievable Fudge 275

V

VEAL
Veal Cordon Bleu 198
Veal Piccata 198
Veal Vermouth 199

VEGETABLES *(see also individual listings)*
Busy Day Vegetable Soup 63
Calico Marinated Veggies 51
Cheesy Vegetable Soup 82
Fettuccine à la Stephen 156
French Market Soup 71
Gary's Pasta Salad 90
Hearty Vegetable Soup 62
Helley Hot 153
Linguine and Vegetable Supreme 156
Mandarin-Walnut Salad 101
Mary's Hearty Beef Stew 60
Ratatouille 153
Savory Rutabagas 147
Shrimp and Pasta Salad 93
Velvet Corn Soup 76

W

WATERMELON
Spicy Melon Boat 105
White Chocolate Party Mix 52
White Fruit Cake 253
Whole Wheat Rolls 124

Y

Young's Tea Cakes 275

Z

ZUCCHINI
Chicken with Squash 231
Dilled Zucchini Soup 81
Zucchini Bread 128
Zucchini Casserole 149
Zucchini Noodle Bake 157
Zucchini Soup 81
Zucchini Squares 48

Notes

Notes